A HOUSE DIVIDED

- A story of survival -

Katherine Rose Kreher

Published by
The Communications Exchange, LLC

Published by
The Communications Exchange, LLC
P.O. Box 64
Wauconda, IL 60084-3703
www.commexchange.net

Printed in the United States of America
First Printing: January 2008

ISBN # - 978-0-9793224-0-2
Library of Congress Control Number -2007931034

Printed by Evangel Press
P.O. Box 189
Nappanee, IN 46550-0189
www.EvangelPress.com

Cover design by Kevyn Uhlmeyer, Best Line Designs

August 10, 2009

To Courtney —
     May all your
choices bring you
the happiness you
deserve.

               Katherine
               Kreher

Acknowledgements

I tend to be a linear thinker. Life works best for me when there is a logical order to my routine. I also have an overdeveloped sense of fairness, which permeates every facet of my life. Given this information, it is not surprising that I struggled with the sequence in which I should thank my family and friends for their support.

A House Divided – A Story of Survival is written from the heart. It seems to make sense, then, to write this tribute from the heart without having to adhere to an artificial sequence. So here it is—straight from the heart with love.

Thanks to my maternal grandmother for showing me the importance of family, for modeling a highly developed work ethic, and for living a principled life.

Thanks to my mother and father for believing in me when I didn't have the courage to believe in myself and for blessing me with unconditional love all the days of their lives.

Thanks to my four children (Craig, Mike, Tom, and Emily) for transforming me into a decent human being and loving me in spite of my many flaws. I am honored to be their mother. Each reacted differently to the book. Craig had difficulty reading it, saying he was very busy with work and family responsibilities. Mike carefully annotated each page with suggestions for improvement and words of encouragement; he read both the first and second drafts. Tom read the last draft of the book and added several important vignettes. Emily, like Mike, read the book twice. The first time, she had little to say; the second time, however, she viewed the book from the eyes of a would-be author.

Thanks to my two nieces, Beth Carlson and Karin Steinbach, for their continued encouragement throughout this long process. These young women received a copy of the second draft of my manuscript through the mail on the same day. Each stayed up all night to read the entire manuscript without knowing her sister had done the same thing.

Thanks to my friends who gave of their time to read my manuscript (all 306 typewritten pages) for no monetary reward. I am especially grateful to Gail Hoban, Diane Goodman, Kathy Fillmore, and Lorraine Donohue for their editorial comments. They challenged me to rethink critical passages, suggested needed rewrites, and corrected a variety of mechanical errors. (Even though I didn't think there would be any mistakes. After all, I *do* have a degree in English!)

Thanks to Marshall Cook, a writing instructor at the University of Wisconsin, Madison, who has been a continual source of inspiration and knowledge. Marshall teaches creative writing at the university and has written dozens of books, yet he still finds time to mentor first-time authors. Lucky me.

Thanks to Kevyn Uhlmeyer, a business colleague and friend, whose creativity and suggestions have been invaluable. Her cover design captures the divisive nature of our family.

Thanks to three colleagues and friends who agreed to write a testimonial for the back cover: Bruce Engle, Director of the LOSS program at Catholic Charities in Chicago, Illinois; Allan Byrne, a retired pastor of the Whitewater United Methodist Church in Whitewater, Wisconsin; and Ed Kulowitch, a Stephen Ministry Leader at Messiah Lutheran Church in Wauconda, Illinois.

And, finally, my deepest thanks to my husband Steve. Without his encouragement and patience, this book would not be a book. I can't recall exactly how many times we read the manuscript aloud looking for that perfect word or phrase, reworking passages that could potentially confuse the reader, and searching for errors one of us might have missed.

While Steve's editing skills were invaluable, his quick wit and sense of humor shored me up when I desperately needed shoring up. His steadfast love and devotion helped assuage the pain of my first marriage, which I relived each time I rewrote a chapter. We all deserve a champion—someone who believes, wholeheartedly, in our ability to succeed. Steve is my champion; he believes in me and truly wants me to achieve success.

When a book *project* becomes a finished *book*, it is not solely through the efforts of the author. An author, especially a first-time author, needs encouragement, feedback, and a safe space in which to grow. The people mentioned on these pages were my support network. They were my mentors. They are my heroes.

Disclaimer

This book is a memoir. All names have been changed to protect the identity of the persons in the story. As with all memoirs, Katherine tells her story from the only perspective she has—her own.

Says Katherine,

> "This story is the truth as I lived it. Over the years I carefully recounted each event, each detail, in a journal. I also saved the letters I wrote to Karl and the letters Karl wrote to me. When I completed the first draft, I realized this story was more than a vehicle of healing for me and more than a historical account of our lives for my children. It is a story I hope others can relate to and benefit from. It is a story of life after a failed relationship and forgiveness after the suicide of a loved one."

Table of Contents

Acknowledgements v

Disclaimer ix

Chapter 1: The Morgue 1

Chapter 2: The Memorial Service .5

Chapter 3: A Pastoral Visit 9

Chapter 4: A Lincoln Farewell 11

Chapter 5: A Child Named Karl .13

Chapter 6: A Child Named Katherine 17

Chapter 7: Karl: The Young Man 21

Chapter 8: Katherine: The Young Woman 25

Chapter 9: Breaking With Tradition 33

Chapter 10: An Unsteady Courtship 37

Chapter 11: The Hopeful Years 43

Chapter 12: Craig Karl 49

Chapter 13: Michael Adam and Thomas Joseph 53

Chapter 14: Emily Rose 57

Chapter 15: The Childhood Years 61

Chapter 16: Karl: The Middle School Years 65

Chapter 17: A Family Sport 77

Chapter 18: Band for Two 83

Chapter 19: Family Celebrations .85

Chapter 20: Issues of Fairness 93

Chapter 21: Germany 99

Chapter 22: Katherine's Career .105

Chapter 23: Under the Influence 111

Chapter 24: The Trip to Milwaukee 115

Chapter 25: The Decision 117

Chapter 26: It's Over 119

Chapter 27: The Separation 121

Chapter 28: The First Few Months 127

Chapter 29: Papers and Presentations 131

Chapter 30: The Lenten Service .135

Chapter 31: The Divorce 143

Chapter 32: Health Challenges for Grandma Rose 149

Chapter 33: The Letter Years 157

Chapter 34: Who's in Charge Here, Anyway? 163

Chapter 35: No Take Backs 177

Chapter 36: Ron 181

Chapter 37: Yet Another Divine Intervention 187

Chapter 38: No Roses for My Funeral 191

Chapter 39: Challenges to the Divorce Decree 197

Chapter 40: Mary: Wife #2 203

Chapter 41: A Chance for Reconciliation 207

Chapter 42: Pension versus House 211

Chapter 43: A 3:00 a.m. Phone Call 215

Chapter 44: Brenda: Wife #3 217

Chapter 45: Craig and Tracey's Wedding 221

Chapter 46: The Depression Deepens 225

Chapter 47: Resolution of Money Issues 235

Chapter 48: Steve 239

Chapter 49: A Beginning and an Ending 247

Chapter 50: Karl's Final Days 253

Chapter 51: A Legal Nightmare 267

Chapter 52: The Aftermath 271

Chapter 53: Saying Goodbye to Bear 279

Chapter 54: Jack and Emily's Wedding 285

Chapter 55: Christmas Day 291

Chapter 56: Epilogue 295

CHAPTER 1

The Morgue

I cannot remember the color of the walls. They might have been beige. They might have been light grey. But I remember the cold. I remember the stark emptiness of the room save for the motionless form stretched out on the metal gurney, covered only by a white, cotton blanket. The impersonal surroundings contrasted sharply with the vividly defined, real life drama about to unfold.

The woman at the County Coroner's Office waited quietly at the side of the steel bed as we huddled close to the cart. Speaking softly, she told us that his face and neck were badly bruised. Even so, we were not prepared for what we saw. As she slowly folded down the thin covering and tucked it around his upper chest, we saw his gaunt Germanic profile, the beak-like nose more pronounced than when he was alive. Purple-black bruises ringed his neck, the indentations from the rope clearly visible.

Our emotions erupted simultaneously: Craig, in a strangled voice, tears streaming down his face, repeated the words, "Dad, I could have helped you. I could have helped you if you had only let me. What will I tell the boys, Dad? What will I tell the boys?"

Mike, randomly thrashing the air with his arms, screamed, "How could you do this to us? How could you do this to us? You taught us never to quit, Dad. You taught us never to quit."

Tom, leaning against the cart, his eyes riveted to his father's face, sobbed quietly.

Emily, burying her face in her hands, chanted over and over again, "I kept telling him how much I loved him and that we could help him if he would only let us."

Joey, a family friend and "adopted father" to Mike, followed Mike around the barren room, trying to still his young friend's rage.

I felt a hatred foreign to me, contempt so intense it frightened me. Those muffled, whimpering sounds surely weren't mine. Someone must have turned down the thermostat—I rubbed the frozen tips of my fingers against my damp palms. Mentally I cursed this man I had chosen for my husband a lifetime ago. I must have loved him once, wanted him to be the father of my children. But on this day I cannot recognize love; I can only recognize anger and bitterness. How dare he do this to my children and to me?

The man was dead, yet I wanted to hurt him. For being weak. For being stupid. For being selfish. For bringing so much pain to all of us.

I can't recall how many minutes passed before Mike's aimless gesturing subsided. With effort, he straightened his body, turned away from the wall, and, for the first time, looked around the barren room. Seeing Tom hunched over the foot of the gurney, he crossed the room and gave his twin brother a body hug. Keeping one arm wrapped around his brother's neck, he pulled Tom over to where Craig was standing. The three boys embraced. Emily left my side to join the circle. In a choked voice, tears still flowing freely, Mike said, "Don't ever do this to me, you hear? Don't you ever do this to me. Promise me. Say it. Say you'll never do this to me."

His siblings mumbled inaudible words of assurance. Joey and I stood in the background, holding hands, watching, excluded from this fleeting moment of family intimacy.

My oldest son Craig, a trauma nurse in Las Vegas, insisted on seeing pictures of the suicide scene. At first the woman hesitated, then relented. The pictures, grim, macabre, showed a troubled and desperate man. Clad in blue jeans, a white V-neck tee shirt, and paint-spattered tennis shoes, he had tied a length of white nylon rope around a ceiling beam and fashioned a noose out of the other end. When the police arrived, they had cut the rope and lowered the body. The photos showed Karl lying next to a swivel chair knocked over on its side.

The ride home from the morgue was alternately filled with conversation and devoid of words.

We replayed the horrific events of the last twenty-four hours. Brenda had phoned each of the children Saturday morning to tell them their father had committed suicide. When Craig received the call, he immediately dialed Mike's number and then Tom's. Neither brother was available: Mike had stayed at a friend's house the night before, and Tom was working.

When Mike replayed his messages later in the day, he heard the news from Craig before he heard Brenda's message. As soon as Mike learned his father was dead, he called me, his voice tight, his words unevenly spaced. "I can't believe it, Mom. Why did he do it? I wanted to help him."

Tom could not be reached by telephone because the office switchboard was closed on Saturdays. I drove over to the warehouse and told his supervisor first, then Tom, that his father was dead. Emily was participating in an out-of-town volleyball tournament that weekend; she didn't know until Saturday evening that her father had killed himself.

I had felt numb when I heard the news. Yet here it was: the end of a life—he had chosen to quit. The end of hope—he had failed to make peace with himself, his children, and me. The end of an era—both of his parents dead, and now him.

The children and I wondered how the events had really played out that Saturday morning. Brenda told the children

Karl was still in bed when she left the house to run errands. When she returned, the basement door was closed, a farewell note on the table. She phoned her pastor first, then later the police.

We talked about the bitter exchange of words just before entering the morgue. The children, Joey, and I arrived in the parking lot the same time as Brenda and her family. Brenda, dark glasses covering most of her pale face, walked over to us, flanked on each side by a daughter. Elke, Karl's sister, trailed behind. One daughter stepped forward, looked directly at me and said, "You have no right to be here. Haven't you caused enough trouble?"

Mike, nerves raw from tension and lack of sleep, bristled, snapped back. "Who are you to tell my mom what to do? She'll do whatever she damn pleases!"

I met the daughter's gaze steadily and said, "I am here for my children. Mike is right. No one tells me what to do."

They elected to let us view the body first, disappearing into a side door of the colorless brick and stucco building. We didn't see or talk to them again until the memorial service three days later.

CHAPTER 2

The Memorial Service

The memorial service resembled a wedding, meticulously choreographed by Brenda. As family members, friends, and coworkers filed into the large, yet austere, sanctuary, the ushers asked if they wanted to sit on Brenda's side or the children's side. Brenda's family and friends sat on the "bride's side" of the church. Our family and friends sat on the "groom's side." The four children lined the front pew; Mike sat closest to the inside aisle, then Emily, Jack (Emily's fiancé), Tom, Connor (Craig's older son), and Craig. Steve and I elected to sit in the second pew behind Mike. To our right were Tracey (Craig's wife), Brett (Craig's younger son), and Joey.

I remember not being able to control the trembling of my body and feeling Steve's arm around my shoulder, his strong hand pulling me tightly towards him. But I couldn't accept his physical reassurances that everything would be okay. Things would never be okay again. I was at once very angry and very sad. I was angry with this man who had committed so selfish and violent an act. I was sad because the events of the past twenty years could have been so different, so much better, had Karl and I made different, and better, choices.

The organ began to play the first few bars of "Rock of Ages." As I stood up, I glanced behind me. Fellow teachers and administrators, students, family members, neighbors, and friends packed the pews and filled the aisles of the community church. Hundreds of onlookers stood shoulder to shoulder, waiting patiently for the ushers to bring more folding chairs.

The pastor, presiding behind the pulpit on the bride's side of the sanctuary, spoke glowingly of Karl. He told us this fine man had attended church services regularly, served as a deacon in the church, and affected the lives of countless students in many positive ways both in the classroom and on the tennis courts. All this in sharp contrast to the way he had treated our children over the last two decades.

Then it was Mike's turn to speak. Ignoring the pastor's signal to use the pulpit that he had just vacated, Mike walked up the altar steps to the pulpit on the groom's side of the church. Face distorted with emotion, fighting back tears that would come later, he spoke the words of the 23rd Psalm haltingly, yet eloquently.

> The Lord is my Shepherd, I shall not want.
> He makes me lie down in green pastures;
> He leads me beside still waters; he restores my soul.
> He leads me in right paths for his name's sake.
> Even though I walk through the darkest valley,
> I fear no evil;
> For you are with me;
> Your rod and your staff—they comfort me.
> You prepare a table before me in the presence of my enemies;
> You anoint my head with oil; my cup overflows.
> Surely goodness and mercy shall follow me all the days of my life,
> And I shall dwell in the house of the Lord my whole life long.

If my body trembled before, it shook visibly now. I knew again the rage I had felt at the county morgue. The hate I felt for this man was palpable; it consumed me. No child, stricken with shock and grief at his father's death, should have to stand in front of throngs of people and share words of comfort with family, friends, and strangers. Who was comforting Mike at this moment? Were the Lord's rod and staff comforting Mike as he spoke this prayer? There stood my middle son, his face rigid with pain, willing himself to stay in control of his emotions.

"On behalf of my brothers and sister, I ask God to forgive my dad for what he did. And I hope that someday we can forgive him for what he did." A plea for his father's salvation. Concern for his father's afterlife. Every few words of his message punctuated by his fist hitting the pulpit. Will his father dwell in the House of the Lord forever? How I loved this child for his courage and determination, qualities clearly lacking in his father.

If the division of the sanctuary was apparent *before* and *during* the service, it became more apparent *after* the service. Brenda and her family camped on one side of the all-purpose room, and the children formed a receiving line on the other side. Most visitors went through both lines. Steve and I stood in a small outdoor courtyard across the hall from the kitchen where several women had begun setting up a refreshment table. A few high school faculty members who had known both Karl and me during the early years of our marriage greeted me warmly and offered their sympathies. Others shook my hand politely, averting their eyes, clearly blaming me for this tragedy. They might have been remembering the stories Karl circulated after we separated: I no longer loved him; I hadn't appreciated the long hours he worked; I was having an affair with another man. None of which was true.

Suddenly one of the pastors Steve and I had not met approached us. Working hard not to betray confidences, yet wanting to help me through this ordeal, Reverend Stillwell shared small bits of information about what the days must have been like for Karl just before the suicide. He had been deeply troubled by so many recent life changes: the deterioration of his third marriage, the realization that he had failed his children in so many ways, and the knowledge that he could no longer continue teaching because of his poor physical and mental health. All of these circumstances underscored Karl's belief that he was, in the end, a loser. He had, in fact, lost control of almost every aspect of his life. For Karl, being a loser was intolerable, shameful.

As the afternoon drew to a close and we walked across the empty parking lot to our cars, I wondered how long the grieving process would last for my children and how different this journey would be for each of them. I focused on the children's trauma; it helped me avoid acknowledging my own sense of loss.

Our neighbors provided a wonderful support system for us. On hearing the news of Karl's death, they delivered platters full of assorted sandwiches, cheeses, relishes, salads, and desserts. There were cards with handwritten notes and phone calls expressing sympathy and offering help. Beneath all the good intentions of our friends, however, was the desire to know why Karl had killed himself. The explanations the children and I gave were speculative, tainted by our history with the man and by the emotions of the moment. Only Karl knew why.

CHAPTER 3

A Pastoral Visit

I call myself a Christian. I believe in God and, most days, can feel Him working in my life, nudging me here, chiding me there. But I am human. Sometimes I question the power of the Scriptures to heal my hurts. Sometimes I lose patience when I think my prayers have not been heard. Sometimes I allow despair to overpower hope.

The head pastor from our church paid us a visit a few days after the memorial service. Moved by the children's grief, he prayed with us, read several passages from the Bible, and tried to explain the unexplainable. Patiently, he listened to what my children had to say. Uncomfortable with what he was hearing, however, he clung to timeworn platitudes—expressions of compassion that might have been relevant in grief situations where death resulted from natural causes. His words of sympathy, though genuine, sounded hollow. He was unable to penetrate the depth of the children's grief. Clearly, he wasn't used to dealing with this kind of horror.

The children were seated in a semi-circle on the worn-out living room couch and love seat, legs and arms sprawled out in various directions. Steve and I sat behind them on straight-back dining room chairs. Steve, a part of our family for only six months, asked if his contributions to the discussion would be welcome. Everyone nodded agreement. My heart ached for these children—and also for me. How great a part had I played in Karl's demise? It had been more than ten years since our divorce, yet I knew, even at the end of his life, that he still cared for me. To what extent had our divorce accelerated the downward slide that began in childhood?

Emily was conspicuously silent throughout much of the pastor's visit. Tom arrived fifteen minutes late and talked about how he had been reading the Bible a lot lately and hoped it would help him get through these difficult days. Mike asked, "How will my father be judged? Will I ever see my father again?" And Craig angrily described his father's refusal to reach out for help.

They told the pastor about the "moment of silence" in honor of their father planned for half time during the high school football game the following evening. One of the school counselors, whom they had all known during their years at Lincoln, had personally invited them to attend. The children described in detail where they would be standing during the ceremony and voiced their concerns about what people might say to them afterwards and how they would react.

After a final prayer, the pastor excused himself, offering the option of future meetings, yet visibly relieved this emotional meeting was about to conclude.

The children hugged one another tight as they said their good-byes, each grappling with their own private guilt and remorse.

CHAPTER 4

A Lincoln Farewell

Evening temperatures hovered in the 80's for Lincoln's final home football game. Two of the four children wore cut-offs; all wore short-sleeved tee shirts. They were apprehensive about the unusual half-time activities planned for the varsity football game, knowing the entire student body would pay tribute to their father.

Pat Whitman, a former student of Karl's, had prepared a statement on Karl's behalf. Before he began to read his speech, he asked the crowd to stand for a moment of silence. Color Guard members lowered the United States flag to half-staff and draped the school spirit flag on the fifty-yard line. Then Pat began to speak:

> Karl Kreher gave thirty years of his life to educating students; twenty-six of those years were here at Lincoln High School. He showed a genuine concern for students that went beyond that of most teachers. Whether it was teaching math or coaching soccer, basketball, or tennis, Mr. Kreher instilled desire, determination, and character in his students and players. He taught us to love the battle, but to be humble in victory and positive in defeat.
>
> More importantly, he taught us life skills. He did this with such vigor and passion that he was recognized by his peers with his induction into the Illinois Tennis Coaches Association Hall of Fame, one of only five coaches from Lincoln ever to receive Hall of Fame status. Mr. Kreher was a teacher who made

a difference and touched thousands of lives. Tonight we honor him and thank him for all that he has given us.

The words stunned my children. This was not the Karl Kreher they knew. The Karl Kreher they knew had a volatile personality, his anger surfacing at unexpected moments. Yes, he taught his students and his children to love the battle because beating someone else, whether on a tennis or basketball court, shored up his sagging self-esteem, if only for a moment. No, he was seldom humble in victory; in fact, a victory of any kind put him in a short-lived euphoric stupor. Inevitably, though, the nagging self-doubts reappeared.

The Karl Kreher my children knew saw every life event in terms of winning and losing. And you had better not lose because losing was a sign of weakness

Yes, I believe he made a positive difference in the lives of thousands of students. And in many important ways he made a positive difference in the lives of our four children. Yet there was a dark side to this man that negated the positives; only those closest to him knew this dual personality existed.

The moment of silence at Abraham Lincoln High School that Friday evening marked the passing of a teacher who had dedicated countless hours of his time to the math department and to the sports program. How sad that he had treated his colleagues and his students far better than he had treated his family.

CHAPTER 5

A Child Named Karl

Karl was born in September of 1940 in a tiny town that later became part of West Germany. He was the firstborn son of a newly married farm couple, Hans and Lena. As was the custom of the day, the marriage of his parents had been prearranged. Lena, the oldest of four sisters, had reached the appropriate marrying age, and her parents had chosen Hans as the desirable partner.

At the innocent age of seventeen, however, Lena endured a personal loss so great she was unable to recover from the tragedy. Less than a year before meeting Hans, Lena had been engaged to a young man she had loved. Her fiancé, however, had been killed in a freakish farming accident. At eighteen, he was too young to die.

Overcome with grief, Lena turned inward, refusing to allow herself even a moment of happiness. The prospect of marrying a man she did not love intensified her loneliness, dignified her pain. Affection and joy were not a part of the marriage contract, she reasoned; she would be loyal to Hans and work hard in the fields—that was the agreement. In return for her labors, she would be spared the stigma of spinsterhood and bear her husband's children. Over time, Lena became her mother, a long-suffering Deutsche Frau.

Karl was less than a year old when Lena gave birth to Otto. By Christmas of 1941, Hans had been summoned to serve in the German Army, leaving behind a sad, yet attractive, young woman to work the family farm and tend to two small infants, creations of a loveless union.

Hans, like many enlisted young men in Hitler's service, did not embrace Hitler's views—did not believe all of Europe must be under Nazi control. Nor did he share Hitler's hatred of the Jews. But when Hans was called to serve under the Fuhrer, he donned his country's uniform, slung a rifle over his shoulder, and fell in step with his maniacal leader.

During 1944 and 1945, German, English, and American soldiers infiltrated the rural town of Baumheim, an unobtrusive dot on the map. Toddlers watched, wide-eyed and frightened, as men in uniform raped and pummeled their mothers. Homes and fields were indiscriminately pillaged and set on fire. The Kreher household was spared total destruction, but Lena was threatened at gunpoint more than once.

How much does a young child remember of his childhood? Did Karl have any recollection of soldiers begging for food, threatening to break down a bolted door? Did he remember the long, hard trek through the countryside in the middle of a cool, mist-filled night to catch a boat that would take him to a foreign land? What childhood fears lay buried in his subconscious?

Karl's earliest memories were of his brother and him playing in the barn and working in the fields alongside his mother. He remembered being shaken awake just before dawn when his father returned from the war, the heavy smell of whiskey and body odor replacing the pungent aroma of newly cut hay. He remembered the occasional buggy ride to a neighbor's for an exchange of vegetables and fruits. And he remembered the screams of his mother when she gave birth to his sister Elke.

In 1952, when Karl was twelve, the Kreher family left Germany in the middle of the night; the German government had confiscated their land. They layered their clothing and carried only their most treasured possessions. Karl and Otto hid their toy soldiers, crudely carved out of wood by their father, under their shirts. Elke clutched her tiny rag doll in both hands. They almost missed the boat that would take them to America, Lena's pace slowed by the weight of a six-year-old in her arms.

The displaced family landed in New York on a grey and chilly November morning, along with hundreds of fellow German refugees, all fatigued, foul smelling, and frightened. None of the emigrants spoke English. With heads bowed, struggling to maintain their outward composure, the men shook hands with one another while the women patted one another's shoulders in a sad farewell.

The Kreher family traveled southwest to Missouri to try their hand at farming once again; this time, however, they farmed the fields of strangers. Eventually they settled on the south side of Chicago. Hans found work as a janitor at an auto plant while Lena fed cylinders to an ever-hungry machine for eight hours a day at a nearby plastics factory. She had two complaints: all of her coworkers were fat and, by the end of the day, her feet hurt.

After years of austere living—eating day-old pastries and one-pot meals, frequenting second-hand clothing shops, and watching television as their sole source of entertainment—they purchased a huge two-story brownstone that had the potential for rental income. At about the same time, Germany began making reparations to farmers who had lost their land. Hans and Lena began to build a miniature financial empire, but, sadly, they knew little about enjoying their children and their time together. As the years passed, Hans and Lena came to be strangers.

No one remembers just when her hot flashes and cold sweats began. At night Lena would lie awake listening to Hans breathe in and breathe out in a measured rhythm while a shapeless assortment of shadowy phantoms danced before her eyes along the moonlit walls. No one remembers just when Lena first began swallowing pills to still the recurring panic attacks. She shared this part of her world with no one. She would suffer in silence. This was her lot in life.

CHAPTER 6

A Child Named Katherine

Iwas born on a hot summer's day in June of 1943; for six glorious years, I was the baby in our extended family. My brother William was three years old when I came along, and my cousin Frankie wasn't born until I was in first grade.

The 1940's, like previous decades, offered a multitude of opportunities for men and boys, but limited opportunities for women and girls. Yet the male-dominated decade couldn't suppress my mother's independent spirit. She dropped out of school at age fourteen to help support her family, which made her very sad—she was one of the smartest students in her class. Determined to contribute to the war effort (and earn money for food), Mom worked in a factory making tags for goods shipped overseas long before it was fashionable for women to work outside the home.

Dad was a mechanic at a factory on the south side of Chicago that made airplane parts. Although he lacked formal schooling, his work ethic was exemplary. Dad was always willing to learn new skills, eager to work overtime, and had an extraordinary ability to see good in everyone—even when he lost his thumb and the two adjoining fingers on his left hand due to equipment malfunction.

In addition to his enviable work ethic, I will always remember my father as a patient, gentle man—save for one incident. A stretch of Gulf and Western train tracks lay directly across the street. My brother and I always knew when the boxcar brigade was due; we would sit on our front steps and wave to the conductor leaning out of the window. One time I ran across the street to play on the railroad tracks with a friend. When Dad came home from work, he called me to dinner. I didn't respond. He found me picking a bouquet of wild flowers on the far side of the tracks. I was so busy playing I didn't hear his whistle. It was the only time I remember being spanked.

My mom, dad, brother, and I lived in the middle flat of a three-story, white frame house. Uncle Frank, who was married to one of my mom's sisters, Aunt Winnie, owned the building. A childhood bout with polio had left him with a deformed leg; his lopsided gait and gruff rebukes when William and I ran over his newly planted zinnias frightened us. Uncle Frank and Aunt Winnie, along with another of mom's sisters, Aunt Sophie, lived upstairs.

My uncle's half-brother, who was mentally challenged, lived in the basement. You could access the basement one of three ways: through the trap door in the tiny walkway off the dining room and from the front or back entrances to the house. No one knew much about mental illness in those days; even fewer people talked about it. "He's not mean," my Aunt Sophie would say. "We just don't know what he might do." He lurked in the shadows and corners of the darkened basement, avoiding contact with any of us. Years later, my mom told me the family kept a close watch on me while he was alive.

My maternal grandmother lived with us, too, which created a space problem—mostly a sleeping problem because the middle flat had only two tiny bedrooms. William and I shared an 8' by 10' bedroom until we were twelve and nine. A kitchen chair separated twin beds. Since there was no closet, our clothing was stored in the dining room dresser along with our Sunday dishes, flatware, and bath towels. My parents' bedroom was only slightly larger. One double bed and two dressers filled the room. Grandma slept on the dark green horsehair sofa in the living room. The straight-back couch was scratchy and hard, yet she never complained. In fact, I don't remember ever seeing my Grandma sleep—until the end, when she got sick.

Grandma spent long hours every day at a nearby bakery scrubbing cookie pans; then she would come home and cook for all of us. One of my fondest childhood memories is the smell of her cream of potato soup. She made the base with bacon grease and flour; big chunks of potatoes and onions floated in the shiny, pepper-speckled sauce. Sometimes I helped her crimp pirogies filled with a mixture of riced potatoes, ricotta cheese, onions, salt and pepper or stuff cabbage rolls with cooked rice and lightly fried bacon. But the best meal of all was Grandma's chicken noodle soup with homemade noodles and lots of fresh vegetables. She didn't use vegetables because they were good for us; she used vegetables because we couldn't afford to buy meat.

Despite her heavy workload, she took time to attend church every morning—I mean *every* morning, not just every *Sunday* morning. Her long, thick hair, piled high on her head and firmly secured with three long hairpins, shone white even in the darkest night. During the week, colorless aprons hung unevenly on her shapeless, fragile frame. On Sundays, though, she wore a fitted navy blue dress to church and smelled like lilies of the valley.

I loved my grandma, but I never had a chance to really know her. She died in her sleep in 1950. I was seven; she was seventy-six. She was buried in a soft, lavender dress, a favorite silver-plated broach at her neck. From that day on, my mom hated lavender. I have Grandma's last pair of black, lace-up shoes. They cost $8 at Goldblatt's—the sticker price is still stuck to the sole of her right shoe. I also have her wire-framed reading glasses, four of her Bibles, and her wedding band. Sadly, I have no letters, no love notes, no record of her thoughts and feelings.

Up until Grandma's death, life on Beecher Street had been predictable, uncomplicated, serene. After Grandma died, though, I could feel more tension in our house. My cousin Frankie needed his own place to sleep, but the upstairs flat had only one bedroom. Uncle Frank raised the rent, hoping my parents would move out. Mom and Dad took on extra jobs. At the end of two years, they had saved $1300; they applied the entire sum to the down payment on a modest, brick ranch in a western suburb of Chicago. Mom and Dad continued to live carefully, paying off the balance of their $15,000 mortgage in five years. They used cash to pay for clothing, furniture, cemetery plots, and a new Chrysler every two years for Dad to drive.

The move to the suburbs did more than improve our financial status—it also improved the relationship between Dad and Uncle Frank. My father always thought the rent he had to pay to Uncle Frank was outrageously high, and Uncle Frank, a talented mechanic, tailor, and all-around handyman, didn't share my father's overzealous work ethic. The time was right for both families to have their own space.

Although I came from simple, Austrian peasant stock, my childhood years were blessed with abundance. I had the love and encouragement of two parents, good food, warm clothing, and adequate shelter—everything a child needs to flourish.

CHAPTER 7

Karl: The Young Man

Du/uring our three-year college courtship, Karl spoke only occasionally about his family. Although he was interested in hearing stories about my childhood, he was reluctant to relive his past. What follows is the information Karl chose to share with me.

Hans Kreher, a short, stocky man who spoke little English, made all the decisions in the family. Even though he and Lena both worked, Hans decided how much money went into the bank, how much money was spent on food, how much money was spent on clothing. Most of the two-family income was stashed away in savings accounts. One-pot meals (beef, carrots, and potatoes) with hearty homemade rye bread were normal fare. Each Saturday morning, Lena made a double recipe of streusel kaffeekuchen. By the following Wednesday the dessert was stale, but leftover portions were carefully meted out. Hans was served the choice pieces; the children came next, followed by Lena.

Each child had two changes of clothing (except for underwear and socks), one pair of shoes, and one jacket. Clothes were laundered only once each week to save on soap and water. The children were sent to bed when twilight fell to save on electricity.

Far worse than this meager existence, however, were the silence and physical isolation that crushed the children's youthful spirits and stripped them of their self-worth. There was minimal conversation between Hans and Lena and even less interaction between Hans and his children. Hans' occasional grunts and monosyllabic replies made sustained conversation difficult, if not impossible.

Karl and his brother worked hard to earn the respect and affection of their parents. Eagle Scout awards, honor roll accolades, basketball team trophies—none of these accomplishments drew praise from their parents. The boys were expected to do well in school. Although both Karl and Otto excelled in sports, their father chided them for wasting their time on frivolous athletic activities. Shooting hoops, running track, perfecting your backhand—all were useless skills unless they helped you to earn money.

During those early years in America, German was the only language spoken at home. Since neither parent was equipped to help the boys with schoolwork, Karl and Otto had to pay close attention in the classroom and learn English from their American friends. Elke fared better in grade school, benefiting from the extra tutoring by her two older brothers.

Because the age difference between the two boys was less than a year, they jockeyed for the dominant sibling position in the family. Karl, the taller, more aggressive son, excelled in academics and sports. Outwardly he prided himself on his ability to put himself through a state college, yet he was hurt when his mother later helped his brother with tuition at a private university. Otto, the younger son, was a shy, soft-spoken young man, reluctant to draw too much attention to himself. Each thought the other was the favorite son.

Neither Hans nor Lena took the time to attend their children's grade school or high school functions—not even student-teacher conferences. Lena did, however, attend the children's high school graduation ceremonies. Hans, who worked second shift and seldom occupied the house at the same time as the children, had to work on these special occasions. Had he asked for a vacation day and been denied?

Had he tried to swap shifts with a coworker? Karl didn't know the answers to these questions; he only remembered his father wasn't there.

Despite the emigration to America, these were German-bred children. And German children were taught to honor and respect their parents. When Karl would talk about his high school years, he would make excuses for his father, saying he was always busy working. When he spoke of his mother, however, his tone would soften. He told me she often bought the children socks with leftover food money and smuggled candy bars and gumdrops into the house for them when Hans was at work. She was the only mother figure he knew, and she was a good mother—a victim of her heritage, to be sure, but a good mother.

CHAPTER 8

Katherine: The Young Woman

My grandma was married twice. She had eleven children with her first husband (seven girls and four boys), but only nine reached adulthood. Elizabeth died at the age of seven from polio, and Catherine died at birth. Mom was the baby of the family. Her oldest sister, my Aunt Margaret, was twenty-five when she was born. Aunt Margaret was already married and had children of her own when Grandma gave birth to my mom. Mom was fondest of Aunt Winnie and Aunt Sophie, age and gender fostering this closeness. Their love for one another and their shared responsibility for my grandma after the death of her second husband explain why all three sisters chose to live together on Beecher Street after they had married.

They continued to live together even after Grandma died. Because the three sisters were so close to one another, our move from Chicago to the western suburbs was a stressful experience for them. The twenty-two miles of separation seemed an enormous distance. Middle-of-the-week phone calls became the norm as well as Sunday treks to our house for family dinners. Roast pork loin with sauerkraut, baked chicken, corn on the cob, creamed string beans, and mashed potatoes were my favorites. My mom was a good cook and, at the age of nine, I was eager to duplicate her culinary achievements.

We moved in July of 1952; by August, my mom was working at a company that made wheel covers four blocks from our house. Dad continued to work his 4:00 p.m. to midnight shift, accepting overtime whenever possible. William was in junior high and busy with after-school sports. Since I was usually the first one home in the afternoon, I cleaned the vegetables, peeled the potatoes, prepared the meat for the oven, and set the table for dinner. Although it would be a few years before Mom let me use the stove without her being there to supervise, these tasks made me feel important.

The move to the suburbs also marked a change in William's and my relationship. When I was a toddler, my brother was very protective of me. No one could recollect any sinister events that required his protection, but all my aunts and uncles told me he adored me and watched over me. I loved my oversized baby dolls who wore a size one in toddler's clothing, and I proudly displayed my collection of storybook dolls. Secretly, though, I coveted my brother's Lionel trains, erector set, racecars, and the oversized, maroon three-wheeler with the footrests in the back for me to stand on. William sometimes took me for rides up and down our street; the faster he pedaled, the more I shrieked with delight. The more I giggled and screamed, the faster he pedaled. I loved spending time with William. I would have savored these brother-sister moments even more had I known this closeness would not last.

By the time William turned thirteen, his opinion of me had taken a 180-degree turn. I was no longer someone to watch over; instead, I was someone to snitch on. I was no longer a ready substitute for kick-the-can; instead, I was the kid on the block whom my brother wished would disappear—forever. I became invisible to William. I was no longer a part of his life. I had lost a brother and a friend, and I was very sad.

My dad tried to explain that this was just a phase William was going through, and I wanted with all my heart to believe him. But as my brother and I grew older, his teasing and insults wore me down. William didn't like me. I began to feel like I was second-rate. An incident at one of my dad's poker parties confirmed my thinking.

Playing poker and fishing were my dad's favorite pastimes. Our new house had a full, though unfinished, basement, which Dad used for his poker parties. In preparation for these get-togethers, Mom would slow-cook several rump roasts, slice the meat wafer thin, sauté mounds of green peppers and onions, and serve roast beef sandwiches on French bread to fifteen or more cigarette-smoking, beer-drinking, foul-mouthed cronies of my dad. My brother and I loved these Friday evening gatherings; we stayed up later than usual, watching wrestling and the roller derbies on TV while our dad won or lost his $50. That was his limit—$50. If he lost all his money during the first two hours of play, he was finished gambling for the evening, spending the rest of the night cheering on friends and family members.

I remember one such party in great detail. It was a typical summer evening in the Midwest—the air was thick with heat and humidity. Dad's poker buddies seemed especially loud. I was sitting on the steps of the front porch with my mom watching the sun disappear when I heard Uncle Al's voice get louder as he climbed the basement stairs to use our only bathroom. "Yeah, Adam, girls are nice, but there's nothing like a son. In a few years you'll have William sitting at your poker table, and he'll be looking forward to those fishing trips, same as you."

I didn't move, pretending not to hear the hurtful words. For a moment, I forgot to breathe. Then my mom shifted her weight, put her arm around my shoulders, and drew me close. "It's okay, Honey. No harm meant. Your daddy loves you."

Mom didn't have to tell me that Dad loved me—I *knew* he loved me. But the incident started me thinking about the father/son, mother/daughter connections. Did my brother really love to fish? Or did he love fishing because our Dad loved fishing and he wanted the closeness the sport created?

Did I really love to cook? Or did I love to cook because it gave Mom and me a chance to be alone together in the kitchen?

I hated cigarette smoke, thought playing cards for money was stupid, and disliked fishing because I always ended up with a bad sunburn. So if I had to do those boring boy things with my dad to earn his love, I would fail. He would have to love me even though I was a girl.

I don't know if Mom ever told Dad about my overhearing Uncle Al's remark. I didn't talk about it with my dad until many years later. It was a Saturday morning, and Dad and I were in the car on our weekly errand run: currency exchange, post office, cleaners, and groceries. Mom was home cleaning house, and William was at football practice. I asked him if he had ever been disappointed that I was born a girl. He didn't look surprised by the question. Dad pulled into a nearby parking lot and turned off the ignition. Taking my hands in both of his, he told me he was the luckiest man in the world to have had the best of both worlds: he was proud to be the father of a boy *and* a girl. Somehow, I knew what his answer would be before he spoke the words.

In high school, my brother and I grew further apart. He was a major player in the "macho" crowd, and I wasn't one of his fans. I saw him as self-centered and arrogant. He bullied me to do his household jobs, press the creases in his wash pants, and wait on him. I hated him for testing my mom and dad's patience. He never came home by curfew, challenged my mom's every directive, and continually wheedled my dad out of money.

My brother's disdain for me taught me some early assertiveness skills, which, at times, bordered on aggression. I used the bathroom in our house as a haven from William's temper tantrums; it was the only room in the house with a door that locked. Of course, I instigated much of the anger that was directed at me. I did the ironing for everyone else in the family, but not for him. When he hadn't dried the dishes or fed the dog, I let my folks know about it. And I flaunted my *A's* and *B's* mercilessly.

On occasion, though, William's softer side would surface and he would invite me to play ping-pong or canasta with him. William also loved to laugh. Sometimes he would tell me a joke or funny story he had heard from one of his friends and then break into hysterical laugher. I always laughed along with him even though I didn't always know why I was laughing.

I was much more of an introvert than William. I was a good student and an avid reader. We took a summer vacation to northern Wisconsin every year. The day before we left, I would check out a dozen novels and short story collections from our town library. I spent the week reading, helping Mom cook, and looking forward to occasional visits to town for desserts and souvenirs. Dad and William fished from early in the morning until the mosquitoes came out at dusk. Sometimes Dad and Mom went out in the boat together while William and I played along the shore with the children whose parents owned the cabin we rented.

In high school, I was part of the college prep group. I joined choir and student council and made the honor roll every semester. I was a typical overachiever, the college-bound child of parents who never finished high school. Since Mom didn't know how to drive and Dad worked second shift, I missed most of my high school sporting events and dances. But whenever I was in a choral concert or play, my parents were in the audience. To attend these events, Dad had to trade shifts with one of his coworkers, yet he never complained about the inconvenience.

When I was a freshman, William was a senior. My first class in the afternoon was Beginning German, taught by a white-haired instructor who rode her bicycle to school every morning and spoke very little English. Room 101 was located directly across from the cafeteria. My brother and several of his friends had the last lunch period of the day; they would form a semi-circle in front of the cafeteria doors and gesture and laugh at me as I stood in line outside my classroom, waiting for my turn to recite the quote of the day "auf Deutsch." A perfectly turned phrase would enable me to move past the stone-faced Fraulein Schroeder. "Eins mehr!" she would say if my tone were too timid or my accent not quite right. The embarrassment I felt from Fraulein Schroeder's stern reprimands has faded over the years, but sometimes I still hear the jeers and laughter of my brother and his friends. I so wanted to be accepted by William.

In the fall of his senior year, William bought a car. Every morning he would leave me standing on the bus corner while he drove to a neighboring suburb to pick up his girl friend for school. He didn't feel sorry for me even when the weather was bad. During the worst winter storms I stood on that corner, bundled from chin to ankle in my grey, full-length, fake-fur coat, while the wind and snowflakes swirled around me.

Sometime during the '60's, my brother and I made peace. The Marine Corps may have made a difference in his attitude toward family. And I became more forgiving of my brother's need for approval by his peers. Later when William and I would talk about our childhood, we were amazed at how each of us had such different memories. Although we never shared the closeness I had hoped for in a sibling, we were able to move past the hurts of our growing-up years. The truce, however, came too late for me—I had lived the life of an only child.

My two closest girl friends filled the void. One attended all of my college prep classes with me and the other sang alto with me in the choir. I loved high school. The years were filled with laughter and tears, joy and disappointment, success and failure. But, mostly, they were filled with fun. A new high school had just been built on the west side of town. Because the school board had approved a phased-in approach, only freshmen and sophomores were able to attend the first year it opened. I was a sophomore that year, which meant that I was an upperclassman for three straight years.

During this same time, I became very involved in the youth group at our church. My parents were not churchgoers, but I remember my grandma going to church every morning, her German Bible tucked in the crook of her left arm, the handle of her black plastic purse gripped firmly in her right hand. Back straight, confident in the power of the Scriptures, Grandma walked the four blocks to St. Paul's Lutheran Church regardless of the weather.

The Protestant faith confused me. I was told that you had to *believe* in order to have everlasting life. But what about all the people in my family who didn't believe in a higher power? How could the nonbelievers be relegated to hell just because they didn't believe in God? Many of them were good people who had helped others all of their lives—like my Dad. Dad seldom went to church, yet he was one of the most caring men I had ever met. I struggled with who would be saved and who would be damned.

I have always believed in the power of prayer. I believe that someone greater than me is at work in the universe, someone who shores me up when the daily burden of living becomes too great. I believe that God has given me wisdom and the ability to make good choices, but the rest is up to me. I am accountable for my actions. I have learned to pray for patience and wisdom rather than specific outcomes because I am confident patience and wisdom will lead me to right outcomes.

I learned early on that going to church opens up countless opportunities for volunteering: serving food in soup kitchens, canvassing the neighborhood for used coats for children, reading to the elderly, and visiting shut-ins. I also learned that a church is made up of people just like me—people who strive to be good but don't always achieve their desired level of goodness. I can look past the frailties of a congregation because getting involved in church activities helps satisfy my need to be needed.

When I look back on these growing-up years, I remember both the good times and the sad times. I remember the Sunday afternoon family gatherings and the home-cooked meals. I remember how hard Dad and Mom worked so my brother and I could have more than they did as children. I remember the lives of loved ones who have since passed away. And I remember my personal struggle to find my place in our family.

CHAPTER 9

Breaking with Tradition

Going away to college was at once exciting and frightening; I longed for the adventure, yet feared the unknown.

It marked an historic moment for our family because I was the first person to attend college. Although my decision set a precedent, not everyone shared my enthusiasm. My dad was skeptical about my actually *using* a teaching degree. He insisted I would get married and have children, thereby wasting *my* time and *his* money on higher education. My brother thought I was a snob, insisting that all schooling, college or otherwise, was pointless.

A comment by Aunt Winnie hurt me the most. After one of our Sunday afternoon extended-family dinners, with me out of earshot, Aunt Winnie chided Mom for supporting my college plans. She told Mom I would become a tramp and disgrace the family name. When Mom and I were alone in the kitchen that evening, Mom told me about Aunt Winnie's remark. I felt as though someone had just slapped my cheek hard. When I was able to speak, I asked Mom what she had said to Aunt Winnie. Mom looked away and said, "I wanted to avoid a family fight, so I told her you had set some very high standards for yourself and that you have wanted to become a teacher since you were in junior high school." This was one of the few times I was disappointed in my mother. Even though Aunt Winnie was six years older than her, Mom should have challenged Aunt Winnie's comments about my becoming a tramp and disgracing the family name.

During the next few days, I replayed the unheard conversation in my head and became increasingly angry with Aunt Winnie. I didn't deserve a remark like that and Mom should not have had to defend my decision to go to college. I let another week go by, and then I could be silent no longer. I called Aunt Winnie with the intent of telling her how disappointed I was at hearing her hurtful comments. I thought I had rehearsed my lines enough times to remain composed, but within minutes I became self-righteous and accusing. I told her she had no right to upset my mom, and if she ever had more comments to make about me, my behavior, or my future plans, she should talk to me directly. My final words were, "I love you, Aunt Winnie, but I am really angry with you."

The Aunt Winnie incident occurred in early June of '61. July passed by and there were still strained feelings between Aunt Winnie and me. Maybe Mom had handled the situation correctly after all.

Making endless to-do lists, cleaning closets, and shopping for clothes consumed my waking hours during my last weeks at home. Mom and I shopped for skirts, matching sweaters, shoes, underwear, and toiletries. My parents funded part of the cost; the remainder of the money came from my allowance and the earnings from my part-time job as a file clerk in Mom's office.

Suddenly it was August; within weeks, I would be leaving home. I knew that college would change me. Life could never be the same again. I was saying good-bye to my parents and the security of my childhood to embrace a future filled with uncertainties.

The trip downstate was exhilarating; I wanted every precious moment of anticipation to last forever. My parents and I chatted about school, family members, and friends whose lives they were involved with through work. We stopped for lunch before arriving at the dorm during the appointed drop-off hours. I was on the seventh floor of

Holden Hall and very grateful the elevators were working. My roommate wasn't scheduled to arrive until the next day, so I chose a bed and closet and began to unpack. Suddenly it was time for Mom and Dad to leave. After final hugs and kisses, I stood in front of my new ten-story home and waved good-bye until their burgundy station wagon disappeared from view.

I loved the independence and freedom of college. Except for keeping the dorm curfew, I was able to come and go as I pleased. College, like high school, gave me another chance to prove my self-worth through academic success. I stayed up late studying, took Saturday morning walks through quiet neighborhoods to clear my head, and wrote letter after letter to my parents and high school friends.

I tried to convince myself that marriage was not important. After all, I hadn't dated much in high school and never considered myself to be especially attractive. Plus, at 5'10" I had towered over most of the boys. What chance did I have of finding a suitable partner? I decided to concentrate on my studies and set a goal to make the Dean's List every semester.

Although Dad may have doubted the usefulness of a bachelor's degree for a young woman, he didn't have to worry about whether or not I would reach my goal. I was on a mission—to become the first person in our family to graduate from college.

CHAPTER 10

An Unsteady Courtship

My primary objective for going to college was to earn a teaching degree, but secretly I also hoped to find Mr. Right, someone whose goals and values mirrored mine. Dad was correct in his thinking that marriage often derailed a woman's career. In the mid 1960's, most women continued to put their lives on hold while they raised their children. But my desire to teach and make a difference in people's lives was strong. I truly believed I could combine the responsibilities of motherhood and the demands of a teaching career. I loved the challenge of the endless reading, writing reports, and giving presentations, yet I desperately wanted to recreate the safety and stability of my childhood for my own children.

I knew my chances of finding a husband at school were slim because the student population had a ratio of 4:1—four girls to one boy, not unlike other teaching colleges in Illinois. This statistic didn't prevent me from looking—and hoping.

After just one week of classes, I had identified two prospects, both members of my German II class. Nick was a few years older than the rest of us; he lived at home with his parents and worked part-time at a major insurance company in a nearby town. He was smooth and direct and invited me to a movie the following Saturday evening. I accepted. Karl, born and raised in the Harz Mountains, spoke fluent German. He was tall, handsome, and somewhat shy. Karl lived on campus in Walter Hall, one of the largest men's dorms on campus. Since our dorms were in the same general direction,

Karl began waiting for me after class so we could walk across campus together.

Nick was definitely more skilled in the ways of women than Karl and, intellectually, he was very stimulating. But I hated the taste of cigarettes on his breath, and I refused to be pushed into sexual encounters this early in the courtship. I really wanted a teaching degree, and nothing was going to get in my way. Not even Nick.

Nick and Karl knew I was interested in both of them. Nick didn't seem to mind that Karl walked me home after class. Within a few months, however, Karl asked me how serious I was about Nick. I told him Nick was a friend and that occasionally we went to a movie together or out for a hamburger. Karl still hadn't asked me for a date, but his question told me he liked me.

At the beginning of every school year, the dorms had floor parties. One Friday evening the men on the third floor of Walter Hall invited all the women on the seventh floor of Holden to join them for a get-acquainted mixer. Karl knew I lived on the seventh floor of Holden and had offered to walk over and pick me up for the party. I agreed even though I knew the date image would prevent me from meeting other men.

I spent too much time on my hair and makeup, all the while imagining conversations we might have later that evening. I thought I looked terrific in new hunter green and camel brown plaid slacks and a matching hunter green sweater. Somewhere, on an unrelated shopping spree, I had found two-tone green and camel brown flats. Even my roommate teased me about how much time I had spent getting ready for this date.

Karl was five minutes early. As we walked out of the dorm, heads turned. We were both tall, his short, dark, curly hair a marked contrast to my fawn-colored, pageboy cut.

We talked of German class assignments and other school-related projects. Eventually the conversation shifted to family.

He glossed over the painful details of parents who lived together without talking to one another. Intuitively I knew to tone down the love and laughter that had been a part of my heritage. I discovered he was a year ahead of me in school and three years my senior. He had lost a few years of education when his family came to the States from Germany in 1952.

When we arrived at the recreation center, we noticed singles picking at high-calorie snacks and couples swooping and swaying to Elvis singing "Blue Moon" and the Righteous Brothers harmonizing in "Unchained Melody." Newly-formed foursomes congregated around a Ping-Pong table. Karl told me he wasn't much of a dancer, but he was very good at Ping-Pong. I told him I could hold my own and often beat my brother at the game. We began playing other couples and invariably ended up as the winning team.

Then we decided to play singles. He beat me three games to two; I could tell he was upset that he had lost those two games. On subsequent weekends we often played best of five; each time he seemed challenged, yet intimidated, by my skill level. The stage had been set for a highly competitive relationship. Although we didn't know it then, the concept of winning and losing would factor into every decision we made together.

The evening ended amicably. As Karl and I neared the front entrance to my dorm, we were both surprised and embarrassed to see the number of couples kissing and hugging one another. Didn't they care if anyone was watching? Abruptly, Karl thrust his right hand in front of me. "Thanks for a very nice evening."

I shook his outstretched hand. "You're welcome. I enjoyed our time together, too." He turned and left, leaving me to navigate around the groping couples. I wished we had been one of them.

In late November Karl gave me an ultimatum: "It's either Nick or me. I don't want to be just one of your boyfriends. I want to be the only man in your life." Flattered by his possessiveness, I agreed to stop seeing Nick. I told Nick I thought he was far more serious about our relationship than I was. "You're looking for a wife, Nick, not a girlfriend. I'm only eighteen; I'm not ready to make a long-term commitment to anyone."

Soon after telling Nick I wasn't ready to make a long-term commitment, I made a decision that provided the foundation for a long-term commitment to Karl. Before completing my first semester classes, I signed up for summer school. My plan was to finish college in three years so I could graduate with Karl. By Christmas break of my freshman year, Karl and I had talked about getting married when we graduated.

Our three-year courtship was full of joy, long talks, and sadness. We attended most of the campus activities, studied together in the library, and began to get a clearer picture of one another's family life. My parents had heard me talk of Karl's loveless childhood and were concerned about our tentative plans to marry. They also knew how difficult it was for Karl to part with his money. My dad said, "Honey, if you marry Karl, you'll have trouble in two areas. He will never share your views on raising children, and the two of you will argue about how to spend your money. Think through this decision very carefully."

I don't know if Karl's parents ever shared their opinion of me with him, but I interpreted their coolness as disapproval. They disliked me for the very qualities that made me *me*: my independence, candor, drive, and unabashed passion for helping others. They wanted their son to marry a quiet, subservient German woman who would bow to his every desire, just as Lena had done for Hans.

We dated one another almost exclusively the first year we were together, we were "pinned" my second year of college, and we became engaged my third and final year. Twice I returned Karl's pin and once I returned my engagement ring. Much later, I realized that we were both having second thoughts about getting married.

Our arguments had familiar themes; unlike me, he had trouble expressing his feelings. Whenever I said, "I love you," he would pat me on the back or squeeze my hand. When I asked, "Do you love me?" he would reluctantly nod his head. He could not bring himself to say those three very important words: *I love you.*

We faced other challenges. We were both fierce competitors. Karl competed in sports and in the classroom. I competed in the classroom only. He coveted status and money. I longed for the ability to influence, to control outcomes.

If Karl didn't see himself as a winner, he became frustrated or angry. When he beat an opponent in tennis, he was not just the better *player*—he was the better *person*. If I ended up with a higher semester grade point average (which I generally did), he would spend weeks brooding over his perceived defeat. If I didn't reach an academic goal, I cried myself to sleep and in the morning created another plan of action. Because I only competed against myself, I just kept going until I succeeded.

Karl had difficulty spending money on himself—although he took careful stock of what other people had in terms of money, cars, clothing, and housing. Every accomplishment was measured against what the other person owned or had achieved. While he admired how his friends dressed, he denied himself the pleasure of nice clothes. When we first met, he prided himself on being able to make do with three shirts and two pair of slacks. His wardrobe could hardly be called a wardrobe. Although he liked the compliments I received when we went out, he scoffed at how freely I spent money on coordinated clothing.

Karl was also somewhat daunted by my obvious desire to excel at academics. We were both good students because we knew how to study. He had the upper hand in math and science, his major and minor, but I had the ability to assimilate information and turn it into a well-crafted written document. My brainpower both intrigued and irritated him; he was especially frustrated by my verbal skills. Years of reading novels, working crossword puzzles, and playing Scrabble had helped build an impressive vocabulary. In addition, classes I had taken to complete my speech minor had given me the confidence to debate issues with the best minds on campus.

Despite the differences in the way we were raised, I saw in Karl the potential to become a great teacher, a good husband, and a compassionate father. He and I shared a similar work ethic, and, because of his strong faith beliefs, I knew he would be loyal to me. With considerable love and wifely nurturing, I was certain I could help him become a happier person. Little did I know that my definition of "help" meant "change." I didn't want to accept that what I had read in my psychology texts was true. That by the time a person is in his twenties, he probably doesn't want to change. And even if he *wants* to change, he may not be *able* to change.

Although we truly cared for one another, Karl's fear of being alone and my fear of becoming an old maid propelled us towards a union that should never have taken place. We married in early June of 1964.

The late afternoon, candlelight wedding was a beautiful, but simple, affair held in my hometown Presbyterian church. Hans and Lena may have been the only guests present who were disappointed that we didn't get married in a Lutheran church. My best friend was the vocalist; I cried during her rendition of "Oh, Perfect Love." The reception was a catered buffet at our local VFW hall. Surrounded by a hundred friends and family members, I naively thought Karl and I had, indeed, created a perfect love.

CHAPTER 11

The Hopeful Years

In the ten days between the end of the regular semester and the beginning of summer school, Karl and I had just enough time to get married, pack up our collective belongings, and make the trip back to campus where our first apartment awaited us.

Still a student, I had to attend one more session of summer school. Completing my degree in three years and three summers had been mentally and physically taxing. The unrelenting pressure of papers, exams, presentations followed by more papers, exams, and presentations made me silently promise my unborn children they would *not* be three-year college graduates.

Karl was the sole bread-winner. Our live-on funds were meager; money received as wedding gifts and Karl's part-time earnings as a sales clerk at the nearby Sears paid for our food, utilities, and three months' rent.

Home was a furnished apartment above the local theater. After climbing twenty-four near-vertical steps, it was a relief to turn the oversized key in the tarnished lock, push open the solid oak door, and sink into the prickly horsehair loveseat. The chocolate brown two-seater, an undersized Formica table and two aluminum chairs covered with gray marbled plastic filled the 14' x 16' space. Just to the right next to a pair of etched-glass windows, a 1950's refrigerator, stove, and sink stood at attention beneath four water-stained, wooden cabinets. The only floor covering was a 4' x 6' tan and avocado paisley carpet remnant discreetly positioned to hide the scuffed and sun-bleached flooring between the loveseat and the kitchen table.

The tiny bathroom, located in the far corner of the bedroom, presented its own challenge. You had to be fully inside the bathroom facing the flush box when you closed the door, so it would clear the toilet seat cover. A full-size bed, covered with a faded blue-flowered spread pulled carelessly over a bumpy mattress and flattened pillows, was wedged in the corner of the 10' x 10' bedroom. The closet door only opened half-way, making it difficult for us to hang our clothing in the doll-size space.

But this was home, and we felt lucky to be together. After a roller-coaster engagement, studying for semester exams, and the stress of planning a wedding, our next challenge was finding that first teaching assignment. Math opportunities were plentiful—Karl had signed a teaching contract in a western suburb of Chicago the first week in May. Unfortunately, there were fewer opportunities for high school English and speech teachers. What complicated my circumstances is that I would not finish up my course work until mid-August, just one week prior to the scheduled opening of most secondary school districts.

I hadn't expected the summer of 1964 to go by so slowly. Karl spent the mornings fine-tuning his serve and backhand for weekend tennis tournaments, played nine holes of golf every afternoon, and sold hardware for four hours each evening. I wrote lengthy, puffed-up papers on Chaucer and Milton and agonized over weekly presentations for my final speech class. I resumed my early evening walks; the solitary forty-five minute diversion always cleared my head and improved my attitude. Finally, summer school ended.

Graduation day was anticlimactic. Since we were married on what would have been Karl's graduation day, he decided to join me in the August ceremonies. "Katherine Rose Kreher (nee Krause)" bellowed the chancellor to polite applause. "Karl

Joseph Kreher." More scattered applause. My dad and mom were there to witness our success and take us out to dinner. Karl's mom was also present. At first Lena told Karl she couldn't take time off work to attend his graduation, but when my parents called to invite her and Hans to ride with them downstate, Lena agreed to go. Hans chose to stay behind.

This was the first time I had seen Lena since our wedding. She was just as sullen and uncommunicative as she had been on our wedding day. When she and Hans had walked into my parents' living room the day we were married, my mom had looked closely at Lena and asked, "Is something wrong? Are you ill?"

Lena, unwilling to meet Mom's eyes, had replied, "What's to be happy about?" Her feelings towards me never wavered in the 20 years we were married. I was forever the outsider, a brash American woman who hadn't had the good fortune to be born on German soil.

After graduating from summer school, Karl and I packed up our belongings and moved in with my parents for six weeks. Our newly built apartment in one of the northwest suburbs of Chicago had not been completed as scheduled. We needed some short-term housing, and, as always, Mom and Dad were there to help. Two generations (including a new husband) living together in a one-bathroom, three-bedroom brick bungalow wasn't easy. In addition to the bathroom being in constant use, my parents may have struggled with our sleeping together—even though we were now married. The workmen couldn't move fast enough to suit us.

Our brand-new apartment was six miles from my high school (I had signed a contract the weekend before graduation) and sixteen miles from Karl's. My full-size bedroom set became "our" bedroom set. We purchased an Early American couch, chair, and rocker, a braided throw rug, two inexpensive coffee tables, and a maple kitchen set with four chairs from Sears, taking advantage of Karl's discount.

By the end of September we had settled into our separate teaching routines. His was a world of equations and story problems; mine was a world of teen-age relationships and self-discovery. Karl soon began reprimanding me for becoming too close to the students. I began reminding him that the world was not built upon right or wrong answers; shades of gray were everywhere.

Karl was a strict disciplinarian—he played by the rules and didn't allow the personal lives of his students to muddy his judgment. If a student were late three times, it counted as an absence. The *reason* for the tardy didn't matter. One second after the bell was one second after the bell. If you weren't in your seat when the buzz ended, you were late. Late was late.

I didn't share Karl's rigidity. Student *effort* was as important as student *results*. *Why* a student didn't turn in a written assignment may have been more important than the assignment itself. I wanted my students to know I was there to help them. I refused to feel confined by the boundaries of writing assignments and literary discussions. My job was to help these young adults sort out the complexities of life. The venue I used just happened to be writing assignments and literary discussions.

We both loved our chosen profession and we both spent long hours preparing for our classes. Each of us seemed driven to recreate our past experiences: Karl's had been a world of right and wrong, mine had been a world of possibilities and choices.

In addition to our disparate teaching styles, other differences quickly surfaced. We argued over the style of home we would eventually purchase. I wanted a two-story home because I grew up in a compact, one-story bungalow. Karl wanted a ranch style home because it was less expensive to maintain. Finances ultimately resolved the issue. We purchased a three-bedroom ranch with a full, unfinished basement. It was supposed to be our "starter" home but ended up being the only home we ever owned together.

Our very different childhood experiences greatly impacted our family planning decisions. I grew up alone and lonely. My older brother by three years minimized my presence. He rejected my awkward attempts at friendship—an offer to pitch balls so he could improve his batting average, a desire to round out his team for a game of Red Light Green Light, and a willingness to fetch ice cream cones from the corner grocery store where I didn't need to cross a busy street. Determined to create a family structure that had eluded me in childhood, I decided four was the magic number. I must have read too many novels because I determined we would have one child born in each season fifteen months apart. That was my plan.

Karl, on the other hand, coming from a family of scarce resources, wanted to minimize our financial obligations. Two children were preferred, three tolerated, and four deemed unacceptable. Since Karl and his brother were less than a year apart, he was amenable to having children fairly close together in age. He was more concerned with *how many* rather than *how soon.*

Genetics lent an urgency to our family planning. My mother had experienced a very short fertility period. By the time Mom was twenty-seven, she had stopped ovulating, which mystified her doctors. No pains, no hot flashes, no warning. I was convinced this unusual phenomenon would be my curse as well.

I became pregnant with our first child in early 1966, about the same time we purchased our home. I loved teaching sophomore English and speech, but by the end of my second year, I was ready to swap career for motherhood. At the close of the second semester in June, my students planned a baby shower for me. Parents and administrators supported their efforts. Cake, punch, diapers, toys, baby outfits, balloons, and fond wishes marked my final day of teaching. I was excited about the baby growing inside me, yet sad about leaving my young adults/friends behind. I had been a teacher for only two years, yet I knew this was my calling. I was able to reach even the most difficult teenagers because they knew I cared about them. Had I known this was the first and last full-time teaching assignment I would ever have, the sadness would have been unbearable.

That summer Karl enrolled in a master's degree program that required him to be onsite for two months. The campus was 130 miles away, which meant he was gone from early Monday morning until Friday evening. Karl spent most of his weekends playing tennis in local tournaments, so our time together was limited. What I remember most about the summer of 1966 was sitting on metal bleachers in 95 degree heat, waiting for interminable rain delays and dragged-out three-setters to end.

Karl had an insatiable need for recognition through winning, which came in the form of trophies and local newspaper write-ups, testimonies of his greatness. He gloated over his victories and agonized over his defeats. For a short time in college, Karl had considered the professional tennis circuit. By his own admission, fear of failure on a grand scale had destroyed this transitory dream.

I, too, had a need for recognition. Early on, however, I knew that sports would not be a platform for my skills. A creative play on words, a quick retort, an unexpected turn of a phrase—these were my strengths; they served me well in virtually every facet of my life.

The cooling breezes of September marked the end of summer. I savored the joy of prebirth anticipation, yet, underneath, I was restless. Was this uneasiness due to the birth of our first child or the loss of a much-loved profession? As Karl made plans to return to the classroom for his third year of teaching, I felt pangs of envy. My short-lived career had ended, as had the opportunity for me to go back to school. I wanted it all: children, teaching, and a chance to grow. But the year was 1966, and I couldn't have it all.

CHAPTER 12

Craig Karl

For most people, October 10, 1966, was an ordinary day. For me, the day was anything but ordinary. Our firstborn, Craig Karl, was born on October 10—my father's fifty-second birthday. Craig was the second grandchild, but first grandson, in the family. Karl had been hoping our first child would be born on his birthday in late September, but his birth date had come and gone with no contractions and no labor pains.

I was 9+ months pregnant, and normal breathing was hard for me. The baby was lengthwise in my uterus, and the pressure against my breastbone was constant. After Karl left for school, I took a long shower, thinking what a great birthday gift a new grandchild would be for my dad. I dressed slowly, omitting shoes and socks because it was difficult to bend over. Forcing still-damp feet into a pair of ragged, open-toed, white scuffs, I waddled down the short hallway until I faced the oversized living room windows. The blades of grass, newly cut and moist from the morning dew, sparkled like glitter on a Christmas ornament.

With tennis season over, Karl and I had spent the last few weekends on house projects. In addition to lawn detail, we had swept and dusted the garage, pitching the last of the dented, blacktop sealer cans. We painted the nursery walls tangerine and off-white; fluorescent orange, deep blue and sunshine yellow clowns somersaulted along an eight-inch paper border just below the ceiling. We retiled the hall bathroom floor with pinkish-gray marble tiles to match the pale pink fixtures and reorganized the contents of the entire basement: household paraphernalia, file cabinets, toys, and clothing.

Looking out the window, I remembered the only project left undone was the washing and ironing of the living room curtains. I decided I was up to the task. My first project, though, was to make rouladen and an apple pie, two of Dad's favorite dishes; Mom and Dad were driving out tomorrow to celebrate his birthday. I spent the morning trimming, tenderizing, rolling, and tying thin slices of round steak filled with chopped onions and raw bacon. These gourmet delicacies would then be browned and simmered over a low flame until tender. Then on to the apple pie: wafer-thin slices of Granny Smith apples sprinkled with cinnamon and dots of butter baked between two Crisco crusts with fluted edges.

By early afternoon, I had finished preparing the birthday meal. If I hurried, I could have the living room curtains washed and ironed by the time Karl got home from school. As the ivory panels swished and swirled in our new Sears washing machine, I cleaned the window panes and wiped the grime off the sills. By 5:00 Karl and I had rehung the living room sheers and ordered pizza for dinner. Still no sign of baby.

At 7:00 the phone rang; it was Mom and Dad checking in. "I'm feeling great," I lied, my belly distended and my ankles engorged. "Too bad. It doesn't look like today is the day." I didn't want to get my dad's hopes up that this baby might share his birth date.

A few minutes after I hung up the phone, my water bag broke. I changed my drenched underwear as Karl backed our white, two-door Chevy Impala out of the garage. Within four hours we were parents. Karl was so excited to have a son he actually lit up a cigar and pretended to smoke it. What a strange sight! He had always hated cigars because his father had been a heavy cigar smoker.

I bonded with this child immediately, knew instinctively how to hold him, vowed to protect him from all harm. I loved the smell of him and the way he curled up on my chest to sleep. We called my parents at 11:30 p.m. to tell them we would be celebrating two birthdays on October 10 from now on. The rouladen and apple pie found a temporary home in our freezer.

Craig was sleeping through the night within two weeks—partly as a result of weighing in at just under nine pounds at birth. When he fussed, the reason was generally obvious: wet, hungry, cold, hot. Karl welcomed holding Craig when he was happy, but he became visibly nervous and irritable when the baby was restless. As Craig demanded more of my time and energy, Karl became more engrossed in news shows and frequently retreated to his basement study to work on various house projects or grade papers in solitude. I saw this self-imposed isolation as a coping mechanism, a normal reaction to a change in our life style. Although Karl's behavior had always been marked by mood swings, I fully expected these periods of withdrawal to pass.

An incident I can still remember occurred at the home of some friends of ours when Craig was about six months old. We were invited for dinner, so I had given Craig his bottle just before the four of us sat down to eat, hoping to enjoy a meal prepared by someone else. I had propped Craig in his infant seat and placed the seat next to my chair so he could see me. Within five minutes he began to cry. I picked him up, put him over my shoulder, and began to rub his back. The wailing became more insistent. Karl tried walking back and forth with Craig, but motion and cooing failed to quiet him. I rocked him, changing positions frequently, but the screaming continued.

Since Craig was not given to taking naps, I decided he must be tired, especially because he was rubbing his eyes with his little fists. Karl and I eased him into his travel seat, gave him his pacifier, and put him in a dimly-lit bedroom just off the dining room—out of sight, but not out of earshot. Five minutes, we thought—that should do it. By this time, the beef roast and mashed potatoes were cold. I could tell Karl was frustrated. Our host and hostess, who had no children of their own, were clearly distracted by our unhappy child.

At the five-minute mark, Karl jumped up and headed toward the bedroom. Suddenly the crying increased in volume and I heard Karl say, "What is wrong with you? Mommy and Daddy need to eat their dinner. Stop crying."

Seeing how distraught Karl was, I had followed him into the bedroom. I was horrified to see him pick Craig up and begin shaking him; he was trying to deal with an infant by using logic and force. I pulled Craig from his grasp and in a lowered voice said, "Don't shake him—you could hurt him. You're making matters worse—you're scaring him."

Karl, unused to a public reprimand from me, became defensive. "I'm not doing anything to hurt him. He's a tough little kid—a little shaking is nothing. He needs to learn he can't do this during dinner."

I was both frightened by the way Karl was handling our child and embarrassed that our friends had witnessed this incident.

Two weeks later I discovered I was pregnant again.

CHAPTER 13

Michael Adam and
Thomas Joseph

Iwas not surprised to learn I was pregnant again. Karl and I had agreed the children should be close in age so they could enjoy one another's company. I was certain Karl would change his mind about wanting only two children when he saw how much fun raising a family could be. Craig had been born in the fall; this child would be a winter baby. My plan was working.

By the time I was seven months pregnant, I was huge. My gynecologist chided me for overeating, refusing to believe I was counting my daily intake of calories. During a routine checkup, he thought he detected two heartbeats and ordered an x-ray—we were years away from the safety of ultrasounds. The film confirmed his hunch: I was carrying twins. I remember walking out of the medical building that day fighting back tears of joy and wondering if I would get home before the first bout of diarrhea hit.

No one in either of our families had had twins before, so this was very big news. Karl reacted to the announcement with an air of disbelief, excitement, and a heightened concern about our financial situation. He worried that additional baby expenses might prevent us from sending in our mortgage payments on time each month. Karl hadn't completed all of the courses required for his master's degree, which would move him to the next step on the salary schedule. Since our annual income at that point was approximately $7,000 a year, finances were a real concern.

Craig was fifteen months old when Michael Adam and Thomas Joseph were born. Unlike Craig, they were morning babies. We drove through the familiar, snow-packed, deserted streets of town in the early hours of January 6, 1968. Mike clocked in at 3:30 with his brother right behind him at 3:34. They were big babies for twins, weighing in at seven and six pounds.

Physical differences surfaced immediately. Mike had dark hair and blue eyes; Tom had blonde hair and green eyes. Mike had a better tolerance for formula, whereas Tom battled colic until we switched him to regular milk.

Distinct personality differences surfaced within a few months. Mike enjoyed being held and played with; family members and neighbors delighted in tickling him and telling him how cute he was. Tom liked to be held by Mom and Grandma only; everyone else was supposed to intuitively abide by his "hands off" policy. Even Dad was not one of the chosen few.

Another major difference was a mark on Tom's forehead that became more noticeable within the first few weeks. At first the discoloration looked like a bruise from the birth canal. Then it took on the appearance of a faint red rash. By the end of three months, we knew Tom had a birthmark (strawberry hemangioma); it spanned the width of his forehead and extended from his hairline to within an inch of the tip of his nose. It was at its worst at seven months. Uneven bulges of red blood vessels measured a half inch above the flat surface of his normal facial skin. A series of dry ice treatments did little to camouflage the bright pink patches of skin.

Karl and I reacted to this turn of events very differently. He was quick to assign blame. My Aunt Sophie had been born with an extensive portwine birthmark on the left side of her neck and shoulders, so Karl was convinced this anomaly had come from my side of the family. Incredibly saddened that Tom's forehead was imperfect, I shouldered the additional burden of undeserved guilt.

The first six months after the birth of the twins was an emotional roller coaster for me. I was grateful that Craig and Mike were healthy babies, but I was also angry that Tom would have to go through life with a blemish on his face. Karl and I both feared the birthmark spreading across Tom's forehead might also be causing internal damage. Would Tom's brain be affected? Was a malignant tumor festering beneath the surface? Beaten down emotionally from Karl's accusations and physically exhausted from caring for three babies, I began to agree with Karl's logic. Tom's birthmark must have been my fault after all. In retrospect, Tom's birthmark not only shaped his individual personality, it also affected the dynamics of our entire family.

For months, as I changed diaper after diaper, prepared bottles of formula, and played games with Craig, I fought down the urge to curse my lot in life. Other women had children with perfect skin—why wasn't Tom's forehead perfect, too? My anger gave way to long periods of crying and despondency. Well-meaning friends encouraged me to join a Mothers of Twins club, but I wasn't interested in socializing. I tried to avoid looking at other babies. Yet, as a magnet drawn to metal, when I was out running errands, my eyes sought the clear, smooth foreheads of infants in strollers.

Even my plan for bearing four children fifteen months apart had gone awry. If I conceived again when Mike and Tom were six months old, which would support my fifteen-month time frame, it was possible I might have twins again. Physically and financially, how would we manage? So we waited. And waited. Karl was content with three children, but I still wanted four. You have your sons, I reasoned. I should have one more chance for a daughter.

CHAPTER 14

Emily Rose

When Craig was three and Mike and Tom were two, I became pregnant again. Despite Karl's earlier resistance to having more children, he was excited about having another child. He looked forward to evenings and weekends with his sons, encouraging me to bring them to high school sporting events when he assumed the role of coach or referee. He had completed the requirements for his master's degree, which had moved him further along on the salary schedule, so his initial fears over finances had subsided.

I loved being home with the children. We scheduled play time with other young moms and spent hours building real and imaginary objects with Lincoln Logs and Legos. Every day included reading time and story telling. Each child had a library card; six books, tapes, or puzzles could be checked out on each card. We visited the library at least twice a week. The night before, the children would gather up their library items and put them in their brightly colored cloth library bags. The sacks were then lined up in the front hallway for safe keeping—no last-minute, frantic searching for misplaced items in *this* household!

The children's activities kept me physically and mentally engaged, but keeping my emotions in check was another matter. Our pediatrician had assured me that Tom's birthmark had not affected his brain and that the probability of having another child with a birthmark was extremely low. Yet nothing prepared me for the mental turmoil of my third pregnancy.

At the six-month point I began waking in the middle of the night. In my dreams the shadowy shapes of disfigured and blemished children moved in slow motion around the room; one must surely be mine. At the slightest urging, I might have gone for counseling, but ours was a family who didn't seek outside help. We kept our problems to ourselves, muddling through life the best we could. After all, our ancestry was German and Austrian—two proud and independent ethnic groups.

Karl, wanting to make sure this was our last child, had scheduled an appointment for a vasectomy at 3:00 p.m. on March 14. My due date was March 12, but Emily Rose chose to arrive on March 14 at 2:00 p.m. Karl dropped me off at the hospital and drove across town for his appointment. He returned to the hospital after the surgery, his gait slow and deliberate.

By the time Karl arrived, our daughter had already been born. She was beautiful—ivory skin, grey-green eyes, a tangle of dark hair—and a smooth, clear forehead. I felt incredibly blessed, spared. Emily Rose was almost as big as her older brother Craig, weighing in at eight and a half pounds. Because of her size, sleeping through the night came easy for her. This was an unexpected gift because, by this time, the boys were no longer taking naps. I knew if I could count on four hours of sleep a night, I would survive.

From the very beginning, Emily resembled her older brother Mike. Both Mike and Emily had their dad's dark hair and hazel eyes, but they had inherited the smaller Krause nose. It was soon apparent that Emily favored her left hand, just like her brother Mike. And her coordination was much more advanced than other babies her age; like Mike, she would probably be a good athlete.

There were definite similarities between Craig and Tom as well. Thick, curly blonde hair, long faces, gray eyes—these traits came from the Krause lineage. In time, though, their tiny, upturned noses would replicate their father's Germanic profile. They were both right-handed and content to be engaged in sedentary activities for longer periods of time than Mike and Emily.

We made use of every inch of our tiny house. With Emily's arrival, the dining room became the nursery. Stacks of cloth diapers, plastic bibs, and terry sleepers arranged in neat rows covered one end of the massive oak table. Tubes of ointment, containers of powder, rolls of paper towels, and an assortment of pacifiers stored in plastic Rubbermaid organizers took up even more space. There was just enough room at one end of the table to serve tea and cookies to our friends and neighbors when they came to visit.

The living room became the boys' play area. Three wooden toy boxes stood end-to-end next to the couch. The long coffee table and two accent tables became platforms and garages for their trucks and Matchbox cars. Favorite stuffed animals slept on the couch at night, their soft bodies wrapped lovingly in baby blankets.

Tending to the needs of these young people day after day required limitless patience and energy. "Please, Lord," I prayed, "give me enough strength to meet their daily demands."

CHAPTER 15

The Childhood Years

One of the best things I ever did as a young mom (although I didn't know it at the time) was to begin a tradition of holding family meetings on a regular basis. Several times each week Karl, the children, and I would huddle together on one of the children's beds. The boys always remembered whose turn it was because the person whose bed we were sitting on would choose the first discussion topic for that evening. I encouraged the children to think back over their day and tell about the happiest, saddest, or scariest event that had happened to them. One would start and then the others added the details of what had really happened.

After twenty or thirty minutes of end-of-day chatter, I would read several bedtime stories. The person whose bed we were sitting on would choose the books to be read and sit on my lap during story time. Karl disliked this ritual because it required so much of his time. He often fell asleep on the bed or turned up the volume on the TV so he wouldn't miss a movie dialogue or a sporting event score. Sometimes he chose not to join us.

Even now, years later, I can remember the excitement of those very ordinary, yet very special, moments. Who would be the first one to jump up on the bed and steal some precious one-on-one time with Mom before the others arrived? Who would try to influence the opening topic for the night by whispering loudly in his brother's or sister's ear? "Tell about what John's dad said to you today." These were the good times.

Karl had difficulty being gentle with the children; he was comfortable with physical contact only when he was roughhousing with them. During dinner, he expected the children to be mini-adults. An overturned glass of apple juice, a comment expressing displeasure at the menu, a reluctance to finish all the food on one's plate—all warranted stern admonitions. "Don't be so clumsy" or "Be grateful that you have food to eat" or "You can't leave the table until you finish everything on your plate."

Unfortunately, there were more incidents of Karl shaking the children when they misbehaved. One day I read an article in *Good Housekeeping* that described the dangers of shaking children. I showed the piece to Karl, but he refused to take it seriously. Since the article appeared in a woman's magazine, he reasoned, it didn't have much merit.

The next day I called our pediatrician to verify what I had read. He confirmed every statement in the article. After dinner that evening, I confronted Karl with this newfound information. He just laughed and said, "If you have time during the day to read stupid women's magazines, you should get a job."

Turning from the kitchen sink to give him my full attention, in a voice just above a whisper, I said, "If you ever shake another child for any reason, I will call Dr. Crane and report you for abuse. It will be the end of your teaching career."

Karl stared back at me for a long time and then left the room. The shaking incidents stopped, but a heightened tension between us was born that day. No longer could I rely on Karl's judgment. If he thought it safe to shake our children, what else did he consider safe?

On several occasions my dad tried to talk to Karl about his rough treatment of the boys. In addition to the shaking, Karl would often slap the children for very little provocation. Then he would rub the part of their body where he had slapped them and say, "Oh, I didn't hurt you. You're okay." It's what I later named the "slap and kiss" approach to parenting, except there was no kiss after the slap. He would hurt them and then pretend that what he had done had not caused them pain.

When my dad suggested alternative ways to deal with the boys, Karl typically became quiet; he began avoiding opportunities to be alone with Dad. Dad was very careful not to push Karl too much—he didn't want to put any additional strain on our relationship. Looking back, I wish he had been more vocal in his feelings about how Karl handled our children. Looking back, I wish *I* had been more vocal about how Karl handled our children.

Although Karl's parenting skills needed improvement, his work ethic was beyond reproach. When Emily Rose came along, we needed more room. Excluding the basement, we had a total of 1200 square feet of living space. Karl decided to turn the attached two-and-a-half-car garage into a bedroom for the three boys and build a new two-car garage in our oversized back yard. This arrangement gave Emily her own bedroom; the small bedroom between Emily's room and ours became another play area for the children.

The following year Karl finished our basement. Dark wood-grained paneling lined the walls, ordinary fluorescent lights hung from white-on-white patterned ceiling tiles, and gray-brown-black multicolor indoor-outdoor carpeting covered the frigid cement floor. Next, he built a huge sandbox in the shape of a rowboat in the backyard. Each child had his/her own seat. He completed one task after another, all the while remaining distant from the children and me.

Once these all-consuming house projects had been completed, Karl's priorities shifted to activities *outside* the family while my priorities *remained* the family. We continued to disagree on parenting issues. During those rare times when we would agree on how to handle a situation, Karl would conveniently forget that we had come to a mutual resolution. In the end, he did whatever he wanted to do.

Another incident that compromised the safety of our children occurred when Craig was seven, Mike and Tom were six, and Emily was three. My mom and I had gone to a nearby shopping mall to buy school clothes for the boys. Karl had agreed to watch the children, but he had also planned to make some repairs to the stockade fence in the backyard and mow the grass while we were gone. When we returned from our shopping trip, all three of the boys were on the roof with Karl. Emily was sitting on the top rung of a ten-foot ladder playing with one of her dolls. He had completed the fence repairs and lawn work and decided to replace several roofing tiles that had come loose during a recent thunderstorm.

I helped the children down to the ground, sent them inside with Grandma, and cornered Karl in the garage. It was the first time I had ever totally unleashed my rage at him. I swore at him, called him some very nasty names, and told him he didn't deserve such good kids. I accused him of being a stubborn, unfeeling, unthinking German and threatened to leave him if he ever did such a stupid thing again. He accused me of babying the children and wanting the boys to be forever tied to my apron strings.

"What do you know about raising men?" he asked. "You're a wimp of a woman—you don't even have enough upper arm strength to do five pull-ups."

I had spent my entire life honing my communication skills, but right now I was struggling to communicate with the man I married. He didn't understand the fear behind my anger and I couldn't understand his desire to walk away from conflict. I tried to broach the roof incident three times during the next few weeks. Each time, Karl found a lame excuse to leave the room.

Neither of us respected the communication style of the other person. Nor did we respect the parenting style of the other person. We had four children needing constant love, nurturing and guidance, yet here we were doing battle with one another. In most battles, someone has to win and someone has to lose. In our house, though, there were no winners—everyone was a loser, especially the children.

CHAPTER 16

The Middle School Years

The children continued the childhood rotation of beds during family meetings. As preschoolers, they had snuggled close to one another for the nighttime reading of *Old Black Witch* or *Rumplestiltskin*. With everyone now in school, family meetings were loosely scheduled for Tuesday, Thursday, and Saturday evenings. Any one of us, however, could call a meeting if we had a topic we wanted to talk about. Sometimes the meetings were serious and sometimes we giggled uncontrollably.

Overall, these meetings strengthened our family unit. Looking back, however, one of the most destructive traditions Karl and I established was holding family meetings on teacher-parent conference (TPC) evenings. Our intentions were good—to hold each child accountable for his/her behavior and to reward effort. Unfortunately, the results of these meetings may have further divided our children into winners and losers. On these evenings Karl and I would come home armed with classroom behavior reports, graded homework that had not been returned to the children during class, and occasional lists of missing assignments.

As we congregated around the dining room table, the children decided who would go first. Karl and I would tell each child what he/she had done well in each subject followed by what needed to be improved. For the child who had done exceptionally well that grading period, this was his/her chance to shine in front of his/her siblings. For the child who had done poorly, however, these sessions must have been hell. The children received two grades each reporting period; one was the actual grade and the other represented effort. We rewarded effort by giving each child $5 for doing his/her best in a particular subject.

Unfortunately, feedback from TPC meetings seldom ended with the family meeting the night of the conference. For weeks afterwards—at meal times, after school, and before bed—we talked about appropriate social behavior in school, the importance of studying, and how to treat family members and classmates with respect.

Each of our children struggled with different issues during middle school. Craig worked hard to retain the legacy of the first born; Mike lusted after the title of first born; Tom battled a constant self-esteem problem; and Emily, since so much attention was focused on her brothers, wondered where she fit into the family.

Craig

Craig's teachers and coaches, knowing his dad was a teacher at the local high school and a respected athlete in the community, expected so much more of him than he was capable of giving. He would get headaches or stomachaches when he couldn't solve the extra credit story problems in math or didn't qualify for the starting lineup on the soccer team. "If you only had that killer instinct," his father would say with raised fist and clenched teeth. Craig was, after all, Karl's son, and must measure up to the expectations set by his father, teachers, and coaches.

The emotional side of Craig added to Karl's disappointment in his oldest son. Like mine, Craig's emotions were quick to surface. Sometimes he would burst into tears when teased by his brothers about his ears being too big or sulk if he lost a game of Sorry. When I tried to explain that Craig was very much like me with his emotions, Karl accused him of being a "girl" and a "Mama's boy."

Yet Craig had so many endearing qualities that his father neglected to acknowledge. He was very intuitive for his young age. He understood the subtleties of our adult child-rearing conversations and sensed the conflict between his father and me even though many of our frustrations with one another went unspoken. Craig knew when I was sad; oftentimes, when his father wasn't watching, he would sidle up next to me, wrap his skinny arms around my hips, and say, "Mom, are you okay? I love you, Mom." I wanted so much to pull him close to me, bury my face in his curly, golden hair, and let the tears come. But I couldn't implicate a ten-year-old in my personal sadness; it wasn't Craig's place to know how unhappy I was.

Unlike Tom, Craig didn't have a twin brother he was continually compared to, but he did have a neighborhood friend who excelled in math and science. It was an embarrassment for Karl that his oldest son wasn't a whiz in the two disciplines he taught. If Craig would just spend more time studying or listen more closely in class or stay after school for extra help, his report card would surely reflect higher test scores than Donny's. Not that Craig's grades were shabby—he earned *A's* and *B's* throughout grade school—they simply weren't the highest in the class. Craig occupied the most difficult position in our family: oldest son of a proud German-born father and overachiever American-born mother who demanded excellence of their children.

Craig was the first child to have music lessons. To balance Karl's zest for sports and competition, I decided music should have equal time. Each child would play an instrument of his/her choice for two years during the fourth and fifth grades. At the end of fifth grade, if the child chose not to continue, I promised to support the child's decision. Craig thoroughly enjoyed his tenor saxophone; he took lessons and played in the band throughout junior high and high school. His love of music and commitment to daily practice sessions and weekly lessons made it easier for his brothers and sister to accept music as a way of life in the Kreher household.

Mike

Mike, the older twin, had his father's dark hair, restlessness, and drive. Mike thrived on attention; he coveted the position of "first born," which, in his mind, may have been synonymous with "favorite." By the time he was two, Mike could throw a softball farther, swing a golf club harder, and run faster than his two brothers. Karl gloried in these early triumphs. Mike was a gifted athlete, his agility and gracefulness augmented by an uncanny ability to concentrate on a single goal. His ability to persevere and focus on the task at hand spilled over into the classroom; you could count on Mike's name to be among the honor students semester after semester.

For Mike, there was nothing as addictive as success. As soon as Mike had broken one record, he made plans to break the next. Basketball, soccer, cross-country–the sport itself didn't seem to matter. Unlike his father, Mike had the advantages of doting coaches, organized practices, first class sports facilities, and new athletic shoes every two to three months. Despite his many accomplishments, Mike's desire for attention seemed insatiable. I often thought his choice of drums as an instrument may have been driven by the noise factor that enabled him to hold sway over an audience. Despite his continuing love affair with sports, Mike played the drums–and took lessons–from the fourth to the eighth grade.

My sense of fairness may well have caused me to deny Mike some of the attention he craved. We had four children, all of whom required, and deserved, daily recognition. Because of his outgoing personality, the conversation during a typical dinner hour often centered on Mike's daily activities, Mike's successes, and Mike's funny stories. Just as I meted out my time holding the children when they were infants to ensure each of them had equal time, I often interrupted Mike's string of tales to allow the others a chance to talk.

"Craig, I noticed you scored a 95 on your book report," inviting him to elaborate on his success. "Tom, what happened in band today?" knowing full well he had just been moved up to first chair. "Emily, what did you and Kristy do in Brownies today?" It would have been easy to allow Mike to preside over every dinner conversation. Karl encouraged his tales by reminiscing about similar accomplishments he had achieved when he was young. But I refused to allow our dinner hour to be a one-child show.

Years later I wondered if Mike thought I loved the others more than I loved him because I never asked leading questions of him. Instead, I was the one taking the focus *away* from him. Not for a moment did I love him less, but I will admit that because Karl's favored treatment of Mike was so blatant, the anger I often felt towards Karl spilled over onto Mike. The only way Karl knew how to lift someone up was to put someone else down. So whenever Karl praised Mike, he would belittle Craig or Tom. I continued to be surprised by how little Karl knew about parenting. More importantly, I was appalled by his unwillingness to learn.

Understandably, Mike took on some of his father's characteristics; for too many years, he treated Tom as poorly as his father did. Karl was Mike's hero, so whatever Karl did, Mike did. I have forgiven Mike for how he treated his brother during their middle school years, but I don't think I can ever forgive Karl. Karl was the adult—he should have known better. Nor will I ever forgive myself for allowing this nonsense to continue for so many years. I prided myself on my intelligence, yet I allowed the desire to maintain a stable family environment and the hope for a better tomorrow to dull my judgment.

By the 1970's *counseling* had become a household word in the Kreher family. When Mike was in third grade, he began fighting with his classmates on the playground and acting out in class. His grades took a nosedive, and he was argumentative and disrespectful at home. We took Mike to our pediatrician who diagnosed him as hyperactive. Dr. Crane gave us three alternatives: counseling, a preservative-free diet, or Ritalin, a little-known drug. We eliminated Ritalin immediately because the long-term effects of the drug were unknown. It might stunt his growth, we were told. Changing the children's diet was a safe option although it increased our already staggering weekly food bills by about 20%. I considered taking Mike for counseling. He was taking on too many characteristics of his father, and I was worried about his increasingly surly behavior.

Karl categorically refused to be a part of any counseling sessions, insisting we could handle this problem ourselves without the intervention of an outsider. "This is stupid! Why are we paying someone to tell us something we already know?" After another conversation with our pediatrician, however, I agreed to meet with a child psychologist he had recommended. I liked Brian Wesley immediately; he had a way of making a person feel comfortable. It was here, with the help of Dr. Wesley, that I learned to be more of a mother and less of a teacher to our children. Years later when Dr. Wesley and I would talk about that first visit, he would tell me he knew from the start that our marriage was troubled and that Mike's behavior was partially a manifestation of our marital struggles.

Karl and I didn't know how to be perfect parents. No couple does. Yet some people are more willing to learn than others. Our church regularly offered parenting programs based on the James Dobson films, but I always went alone. Not once during our marriage did Karl ever read a book or an article on parenting to hear other people's views on the subject. After all, he grew up "just fine" and so would his children.

Tom

Growing up was a challenge for Tom; he was, after all, the youngest of three sons. In his earlier years, he had tried hard to please his father. But like Craig before him, nothing Tom did was good enough for Karl. Tom lacked the physical coordination and the mental tenacity of his twin brother and was continually reminded of his shortcomings. "Tom, you're just not quick enough—move your *feet—run..., run..., run!* Tom, you've got to study harder—go back to your room and check your answers—why can't you be like your brother Mike?" Ironically, Tom was the child who would figure out the correct answers to the extra credit story problems in math class. His grades seldom reflected his innate intelligence because he often forgot to turn in his day-to-day homework assignments.

Karl and I talked about the importance of not comparing the children with one another. We made a pact to help each child reach his/her potential, whatever that may be. During competitive activities, however, Karl was unable to maintain his composure and objectivity. After years of being told he didn't measure up to his two older brothers, Tom shut down. His birthmark and naturally reserved disposition had defined his personality and rendered him helpless to cope with the favoritism shown to his twin brother Mike.

The trite saying "The strong get stronger and the weak get weaker" applied to our family. After dinner, weather permitting, Karl would take the boys out to the backyard and play a game or two of Horse. The game could be played individually or in teams of two. The goal of the game was to make a basket every time you had control of the ball. If you made the basket, you continued to play; if you missed the basket, you were awarded a letter: H, then O, then R, S, and finally E. The first player to be awarded all five letters was out of the game. Tom was generally the first one sitting on the back stoop playing with the dog while his brothers and father continued to enjoy the game. Karl didn't share my sense of fairness; he didn't seem to care that Tom got much less playing time than his brothers.

Tom learned to swallow his tears when sitting on the sidelines because he hated being called "Crybaby" and "Sissy" by his father and brothers. His belief in himself appeared to evaporate in fifth grade; he refused to compete with his siblings on any level. One day Tom's teacher called to tell me not to be upset by Tom's score on the standardized Stanford-Binet achievement tests the students had just completed. It seems Tom had finished the test in less than 20 minutes; most of the other students, however, had taken the full two hours to complete the exam. Tom had filled in the circles on the answer sheet with a #2 pencil without reading any of the questions.

Fortunately, Tom, his brothers, and his father were away on a scouting trip the day the mailman delivered the results of the test. On prior tests, Tom had consistently scored in the 89th and 90th percentiles. This year Tom's overall score was a 16! This meant that 84% of all students his age had scored higher than he had. I was furious! Even though his teacher had warned me of this possibility and even though the incident was representative of where Tom was emotionally, I was angry. I was angry with Tom, with Karl, with the school system, with the world in general. After fixing myself a cup of tea and commiserating with my mother on the phone, I calmed down. Why was I angry at Tom's random test markings? He was, after all, a child whose best was never good enough.

Tom busied himself with solitary tasks. He loved to tinker. Unfortunately, he was more adept at taking things apart than he was at putting them together. Household casualties included a humidifier, my dad's boyhood radio, and a bicycle.

Tom was sensitive, thoughtful, quiet, and gentle—qualities not especially admired by his father. Tom enjoyed band more than any other subject and took his music lessons very seriously. He spent hours practicing his trombone only to be reminded by his father that the cost of music lessons had just been increased by fifty cents. "What's the point of music lessons?" his father asked. "It's never going to get you anywhere."

Tom's sixth grade music teacher suggested he take voice lessons along with his trombone lessons. Karl chided the teacher for suggesting any of his sons take "girlie" singing lessons. That evening, when Tom and I were alone, I told him I would pay for voice lessons out of my part-time teaching money. I suggested we keep it a secret between the two of us. Tom declined my offer, afraid one of his brothers would find out and tell his dad.

In seventh grade Tom won a band scholarship that enabled him to spend a week at a state university noted for its excellence in music. Tom, along with four other deserving students, attended specialized workshops during a particularly hot and humid stretch in July and participated in a university concert extravaganza at the end of the week. The college made a recording of the event and sent one to each of the students; Tom proudly displayed this record on a shelf in his bedroom. Like Craig, Tom continued to take music lessons throughout junior high and high school.

Emily

Compared to her brothers, Emily was an easy child to raise. However, I was also a different mother by the time Emily came along. I was more assertive, much less willing to play a subordinate role to Karl. When the children were babies, I knew how to avoid confrontations with Karl: simply agree with all of his decisions. My rationale was simple. If I made life too difficult for him, he might leave me. If he left me, how could I support our four children on my income? Who would take care of the children during the day while I worked? No, playing the role of the mediator, apologizing to the children for their father's unexpected outbursts, and making excuses for his behavior was the better way.

Besides, I still loved him; he worked hard for our family and occasionally spent time with the children—even though I didn't always agree with what he did while he was with them. And I continued to feel sorry for him; he just didn't seem to know how to get close to anyone. Maybe he would change after we were together longer. I tried to model good parenting practices; surely he and the children would learn from my example. "Don't be so hard on your father," I would say. "That's not what he really meant to say. Your father loves you. He had a long week and he's very tired. His childhood was very different than yours." On and on it went—I always had an excuse for him.

It might appear that Emily was far removed from the competitive arena of her brothers. She was, after all, the baby of the family and the only girl. Her brothers adored her and spent endless hours playing house, school, and dress-up with her. But they also taught her how to throw and catch a ball. By the time she was in first grade, her brothers invited her to play on neighborhood ball teams with their friends. This was a high honor and she knew it. She was the only girl in the neighborhood allowed to play with the older boys.

Karl didn't know how to relate to girls, so he paid very little attention to Emily when she was young. The attention wasn't negative—it just wasn't there. By sixth grade, however, Emily had become a fierce competitor in her own right. She excelled at every sport. When she was awarded the most valuable player (MVP) plaque at the middle school sports banquet, she finally had her father's attention. Emily had gymnastics lessons, viola lessons that later turned into piano lessons, and an opportunity to play all three sports in grade school: volleyball, basketball, and cross-country.

At the end of sixth grade, Emily called me into her bedroom for a mother-daughter talk. She told me she didn't want to disappoint her father by not continuing with basketball and cross-country, but the only sport she really wanted to play was volleyball. Her coach had been talking to some of the better players about an indoor volleyball club, which would enable them to play ball during the off season. We were sitting next to one another on her bed, our backs pressed against the cold wall, the ruffle on the canopy providing a modicum of privacy, our brown and white Sheltie stretched across our laps.

Emily, leaning closer to me, yet trying not to disturb Muffin, put her hand on my cheek and gently turned my face towards her so our eyes met. "Mom, if you and Dad pay for club ball, I know I can earn a college volleyball scholarship. Ms. Rinehart talked about it today. I know I can do it, Mom. I *know* I can." My throat closed shut as I fought back the tears. This was one very talented and very determined young lady. "I promise I will talk to your father," I said.

After meeting with several noted volleyball coaches in the area, Karl and I agreed to fund club ball for our daughter. Even though her brothers had not had a similar opportunity, they supported her efforts and became her cheerleaders at weekend tournaments.

Parenting/Money

In addition to parenting differences, money issues continued to be huge areas of disagreement between Karl and me. Although each child was involved in sports and music, every activity had to be justified; money was always a factor. By this time I was working outside of the home thirty hours a week as an editor for a local publishing company. Because it was considered a part-time job, the money wasn't terrific, but the trade-off was that I could come home during my lunch hour and begin dinner preparations. While we weren't wealthy, with my extra income, we had some discretionary money and could well afford to support the children's activities.

When Craig was in fifth grade and Mike and Tom were in third grade, they took on the responsibility of a neighborhood paper route. The three boys shared a route that involved approximately 100 houses. There were no busy streets to cross. Every morning they would leave the house together at 6:30 and return home together just before 7:00.

When Karl and I talked about how they should handle their money, he favored the boys contributing a certain percentage of their earnings to the household food fund. I rejected this idea, declaring it punitive. Instead, I suggested taking 50% of the boys' money and establishing savings accounts in their names for use during high school or college. The other 50% would be theirs to spend as they saw fit. Reluctantly, Karl agreed to this idea.

More and more I challenged Karl's logic and authority, knowing that each rebuttal widened the chasm between us. He refused to give up on the "money for food" idea, though. During the dinner hour, whenever requests were made for certain foods to be added to our unending store list, he reminded the children of how poor he was when he was growing up, how he had to work to help support his family after they arrived in America, and how they (our children) had life much too easy.

Sometimes there was a wistfulness in his tone and sometimes there was an angry edge to his voice when he allowed himself to reflect on his childhood. And, always, there was a distance between Karl and the rest of us. He was such an important part of our family, yet he preferred detachment to engagement.

During these years, Karl and I believed we had to be all things to our children. We functioned as Scout Leader, Den Mother, Brownie Leader, Soccer Coach, Sunday School Teacher, and the children's pseudo teachers in the evening when they did their homework. In retrospect, I wish we had opted to be just parents. The parenting role is intrinsically prestigious, full of intrigue and drama. Why did we feel the need to clutter our lives with activities that, in the end, may not have mattered at all?

CHAPTER 17

A Family Sport

We faced the same challenge every family faces. How do you keep everyone tightly connected to one another as each person grows and changes? What is the magic formula for holding family members together? We attended church together, we ate most of our evening meals together, and we continued holding family meetings. Was there something we had overlooked?

By the time the boys were in high school, tennis had gained widespread acceptance. Tennis gear was relatively inexpensive, the potential for injuries was minimal, and the game offered excellent cardiovascular benefits. Because of Karl's love of tennis and his desire to teach his sons how to play the game, I decided to learn the fundamentals of the sport. Maybe tennis was the glue that would hold our family together.

Continuing education classes for men, women, and children were offered every weekday evening and every Saturday morning at the high school. Karl was the instructor of choice for many reasons: he was an excellent player, a competent coach, and passionate about the sport. Boxes of trophies stored in his basement workroom attested to his athletic skill.

I hesitated signing up for one of Karl's sessions, but, with his encouragement, I signed up for an intermediate tennis class with Karl as the instructor. He was confident my two semesters of college tennis qualified me for the intermediate class. I was neither physically nor emotionally prepared to compete with the other women in the class, all of whom had already mastered the rudiments of the game. I couldn't return their volleys. I lofted the ball with my forehand, swung at air with my backhand, and smashed the ball into the net on my serve. After the first few sessions, Karl managed a few complimentary remarks. "Everyone has a bad day. Just keep your eye on the ball. You'll do better next week."

In addition to my inability to keep the ball in play, I didn't look the part of an athlete. My faded blue jean shorts, baggy grey tee-shirt, and black and white Keds were in stark contrast to the pastel tennis dresses (complete with matching panties and low-cut socks) and the Adidas and Nike footwear worn by the other women.

By the fourth week it became apparent that every session was a bad day for Katherine Kreher. Embarrassed by my inability to adjust my level of play to meet his expectations, Karl would say, "Maybe you're just not cut out for tennis. You might want to enroll in a beginner class with Doug Miller. Why don't you take the dogs running every morning to improve your stamina?" I dropped out of class.

Months later, after taking beginner lessons with Doug and adhering to a fairly strict exercise routine, I thought I was ready for some mixed doubles. Karl agreed, scheduling a doubles match with several of his friends from the physical education department. This time my shorts matched my tee-shirt and my overly large feet sported a pair of white-on-white Rockport tennis shoes. Unfortunately, I still lofted the ball with my forehand, swung at air with my backhand, and smashed the ball into the net on my serve. We all agreed to go out for pizza before the second set was finished.

A few years later I tried again—this time, on my own. I joined a highly rated indoor tennis club and won a trophy for the best player in the *B+* women's league. I was seeded #2 for the league playoffs. Most people don't know the reason the trophy came to rest on the top shelf of my bookcase is the #1 seeded player required eye surgery just before the final match. I offered Anita the trophy. She deserved it—she had outplayed me all season—but she politely declined, saying I had played a good match. Having achieved a recognizable level of competence in tennis, I decided the game was not for me. I chose to be a passionate and dedicated spectator at all of the children's sporting events. Tennis became the family sport for everyone except me—at least for a while.

Although boys' high school tennis was a spring sport, serious training began in late winter. Karl and the children, however, played all year long on indoor courts. When Craig was a senior, he was determined to work especially hard so he could help his dad's varsity team qualify to go downstate for the high school tennis championships.

Craig spent most of his free time on the tennis courts practicing his serve or in the gym running laps. The remainder of his leisure time was allocated to playing his saxophone. He was the oldest and determined to be the best. His frustration with his own personality traits led to frequent outbursts. "Mom, I'm tired of Dad telling me I don't have the 'killer instinct.' When he says that, I want to punch him. I know he's my father, but I'm tired of him telling me I don't want to win. I want to win, Mom; I'm just not as good as Mike." Craig would turn away, so I could not see his tears.

Two events occurred during tennis season of Craig's senior year that caused him to put away his tennis racquet for the next four years. The first incident took place about midway through the season. On a beautiful Saturday morning in May, Lincoln was playing Benton, a long-time tennis rival. Emily and I had walked over to watch the matches because all three boys were scheduled to play.

When we arrived, Craig and his opponent were in the middle of their first set in a best of three series. After watching for about fifteen minutes, I realized that Craig's opponent had made several questionable calls; many of the spectators on the bleachers were also voicing their concern over the bad calls. I suggested to Karl that he appoint a line judge for the match. He laughed and said, "Still protecting your baby? Let him grow up and be a man." Had any other parent asked for a line judge, the request would have been granted.

I could see by the droop of Craig's shoulders and the number of first serves he began to miss that he was losing concentration. When his opponent yelled "long" on a critical serve that was clearly in, Craig threw his racquet down on the court so hard it bounced up into the air. Catching the rebounding racquet in his right hand, Craig lunged towards the net and screamed, "That was good. My serve was in." Had Craig been someone else's son, Karl, as coach, would have simply said, "Son, you're through for the day." But this was not just anyone's son—this was *his* son.

I happened to be standing near the entrance to the courts. As I glanced over at Karl to watch his reaction to this outburst, I saw him rip open the snaps on his warm-up jacket, feverishly working his arms out of the sleeves. With three long steps he was at the fence, rage electrifying his body. Instinctively I moved forward, turning to face him, blocking the entrance. Karl would have had to knock me down to get inside the courts.

"Get out of my way." He was breathing hard, his voice low. "I'm going to kill him."

"You won't touch him," I said. "You'll let the match continue. His opponent has cheated on at least a half dozen calls. You've stood at the sidelines watching, doing absolutely nothing to help your son. Look at the crowds—they're angry. You need to appoint a line judge and allow this last point to be replayed."

The emotion drained out of Karl's body just as quickly as it had come. Slowly, he backed away from me. I knew Craig would be chided for his behavior after the match, but I also knew Karl wouldn't dare lay a hand on him. Not now. Not with other students, coaches, and parents milling around, most of whom had witnessed the animated exchange between us.

The second incident that occurred was Mike had been selected to represent the school in the #1 singles spot. Mike had worked hard that season, but so had Craig. Craig had beaten Mike in singles as many times as Mike had beaten Craig. And yet Mike was chosen to go downstate. "Your brother has the mental edge," his father told him. "You just don't have what it takes."

Perhaps Mike did have the mental edge. He was incredibly focused when he played the game, intent on hitting the yellow ball and nothing else. Determined to play well in the tournament, every immovable object became a backboard: the garage door, the windowless side of the house, the ground to ceiling wooden planks just to the left of the high school courts. He practiced fiendishly, tossing the ball with his right hand, firing it over the net with his left.

Tom, like his brothers, had played tennis for many years. His success was more erratic because his heart was never truly in it. He played tennis because it was *expected* that he play tennis. In his junior year, he cracked. He had had enough of his father's chiding. "Get up on your toes, Tom. Get the lead out of your feet. If you'd quit eating so many cookies, you could move faster. Run, Tom. *Move*, would you?"

During a typical after-school practice, subjected to just such a tongue lashing, Tom laid his tennis racquet gently on the ground and walked off the court. When his father rebuked him later that evening for being a quitter, Tom studied the patterns in the kitchen linoleum, saying nothing. Three days later when his father asked him to rejoin the team "for the sake of the state championship," Tom, again, said nothing. It would be six years before Tom would pick up a racquet again.

While Emily learned the fundamentals of tennis very quickly, she was immersed in the world of volleyball. She often accompanied her father and brothers to nearby courts for the camaraderie of the activity rather than for love of the sport itself. Content to shag balls during warm-up and sit cross-legged at one side of the net and keep score during the games, Emily always cheered for the underdog. "You can do it, Tom. You'll get the next one. It's okay, Craig. Good try."

Tennis could have been the catalyst that brought six disparate personalities together. Instead, it showcased our differences.

CHAPTER 18

Band for Two

Fortunately, Craig and Tom had another outlet: they both loved Symphonic Winds and the Marching Band. The Symphonic Winds was an elite collection of dedicated musicians who rehearsed their musical selections until a level of perfection determined solely by the director had been achieved. In contrast, everyone in the high school band program was allowed to participate in the Marching Band. In addition to learning the music, members of the Marching Band had to learn a fairly sophisticated dance routine while, at the same time, balancing heavy (and often awkward) musical instruments. The Marching Band typically practiced on the football field over the lunch hour, filling the adjacent neighborhoods with lively strains of Sousa marches. These back-to-school routines, coupled with cooler weather and the changing of colors, made the fall a special time of year for local residents.

Getting the boys ready for each year's Marching Band season required extraordinary patience and a ready checkbook. We typically ordered Craig's shiny black Corfams out of a catalog because of his long, narrow feet. The sleeve length of the white pleated shirt and black jacket had to be thirty-six inches and the extra long unhemmed pants required some minor sewing adjustments by Mom.

Tom was easier. He was a full three inches shorter than his brother and wore a common size eleven shoe instead of the oversized thirteen that his older brother required. His sleeve length was in the normal range as was the inseam of his trousers.

The challenge for Tom was to find a cover-up for his birthmark that wasn't affected by the intense heat of the sun. Still self-conscious about his birthmark, Tom would pull the brim of his military style band hat low over his forehead. Even so, the right shade and consistency of the cover-up was critical; Tom seldom left the house without applying one or two coats of his favorite concealer. It was a small price to pay to help him feel better about himself.

Band kept Tom whole during high school. Since his twin brother had chosen sports over music, Tom was spared the continual comparison between him and Mike—at least in this one area of his life. School had been a challenge for Tom; he typically came in third out of three sons. He pretended a *C* was good enough, but I know he was disappointed with his academic efforts. Unable to get enough attention in positive ways, Tom resorted to turning in homework assignments late, not showing up for class, and isolating himself from his brothers and sister.

Had his musical ability been more fully supported in these formative years, it is likely Tom's life would have taken a different direction. He had a passion for music, a respect for musicians, and he could compete and excel in this arena.

Perhaps the most significant benefit of Lincoln's music program, however, was that Craig and Tom's joint participation in high school band helped forge the close bond that exists today between these two young men.

CHAPTER 19

Family Celebrations

Cultural differences, opposing parenting views, the polarities of money management—all chipped away at the core of Karl's and my relationship. Yet another major stressor for us was how family celebrations should be handled. Our family was growing, and it became increasingly common to have mass get-togethers in back-to-back months. Because our large paneled basement could readily accommodate a large group, we typically hosted the party.

My family had always recognized birthdays, anniversaries, graduations, and every traditional holiday throughout the year. We viewed these milestones as occasions to honor the special person, rekindle friendships, remember good times gone by, and rehash petty sibling disagreements. The birthday celebrations of my childhood were joyful events carefully planned by my mom and two aunts three months in advance of the special date. I loved the fuss made over my brother and me; had I been a grade school feminist, I would have picketed in the school yard to change birth*day* to birth*week* or birth*month*.

Karl's world was different. In Karl's family, birthdays and holidays were ordinary days. No paddle balls, squirt guns, and jump ropes as prizes for classmates. No odd-shaped balloons to untangle from the lower branches of cigar trees. No pastel candles poked into too-sweet butter cream frosting on a homemade chocolate layer cake. No hugs or well wishes from Mom and Dad. Instead, a pair of socks, a shirt, or money towards shoes from his mother. A silent nod from his father. That was all.

Karl said he dreaded family gatherings because of the additional expense and work. He was right on both counts; every party cost us money and time. Yet I knew these reasons were superficial ones. I had determined the underlying reason years ago, but we were married ten years before he could put his feelings into words. Each birthday, each holiday, reminded him of what he had never experienced as a child. The painful memories of his past prevented him from enjoying the happy moments we were able to provide for our children.

Knowing *why* he disapproved of family celebrations, however, did not keep me from adding confirmation and graduation parties to the kitchen calendar. These events were significant, and I was determined to "mark the moment" for each child.

While all of these special events were as financially and physically draining as the routine celebrations, some were emotionally draining as well. Craig's and Emily's eighth grade graduation parties were easy on us emotionally. They had done well in grammar school, but neither had been nominated for the Most Outstanding Boy or Most Outstanding Girl award. Mike and Tom's eighth grade graduation was somewhat different.

Weeks before the twins' graduation, the principal of the junior high school had called to say Mike had been selected as one of five nominees for the Most Outstanding Boy award. During the graduation ceremony, the President of the local American Legion chapter would present this award to one boy. The winner had not yet been chosen; both teachers and students were encouraged to cast their votes.

Mike had worked hard for this award, consistently making the honor roll and participating in every sport as well as all junior high band activities. He was definitely deserving of the award. Tom was not a contender. Even though he knew he hadn't worked hard enough to deserve the award, he was hurt that he hadn't been nominated.

Having twins often presents bittersweet moments. That evening, getting dressed for the graduation ceremony, both sons were nervous about wearing their new suits, shirts, and ties, and walking across stage to accept their diplomas. Mike kept repeating, "It's okay if I don't win, Mom. At least I made it to the top five." But I knew how much he wanted to win the Legion award. I hugged him hard and told him what a great job he had done with his life so far and wished him luck. I promised him my applause would be just as loud whether or not he won the award. When Tom finished dressing, I gave him a body-wrap hug and told him I was proud of what he had accomplished in grade school. I reminded him of the band scholarship he had won the year before and told him that high school represented a brand new opportunity for him to shine. He gave me a half-grin and said, "Yeah, I guess so."

There was little conversation in the car during the ride to the school that evening. Paper flowers and hand-made banners decorated the stage of the junior high gymnasium. I felt we had truly reached a milestone in our lives. After tonight, we would only have one child in junior high. All three boys would be in high school in the fall. The graduation class had special seating; Mike and Tom sat next to one another because the graduates would be called in alphabetical order.

After the opening remarks by the principal and good-luck speeches by several teachers and students, the President of the American Legion came forward bearing two wood-framed plaques. He described the history of the award and what it represented: leadership, honesty, hard work, and concern for others. "We will present the plaque to the Most Outstanding Girl first. Alison Wentworth, will you please join me on stage?" Alison claimed her plaque amidst much applause. The President paused slightly and then continued. "I am also very proud to present the Most Outstanding Boy award to Michael Kreher." I was on my feet in an instant, applauding loudly, so excited for his success. Then I glanced over at Tom; hunched over in his seat, a single tear rolled down his right cheek. In this moment, I had it all—the very best and the very worst of motherhood—joy and sadness pummeling my senses simultaneously.

After the boys' graduation party that June and my mom's birthday party in July, I had the remainder of the summer to think about Karl's 40th birthday coming up in September. For many people, turning forty can be life-changing. It symbolizes a rite of passage. It is an occasion accompanied by good luck wishes, laughter, and poking fun at the unrelenting aging process. This milestone birthday allows us to reflect on our lives, to realign our personal and professional priorities. We reminisce over lessons learned, and, if we are lucky, we acknowledge that life has been good to us.

Karl had been trivializing birthdays more than ever this year—just in case we were thinking of throwing one of those "stupid surprise parties" for him. The only thing worse than a birthday party, he would say, was a *surprise* birthday party. It was now the end of August, about a month before Karl's birthday, and I still hadn't decided what to do. During our years together, Karl had mastered the art of burying his real feelings. What if he secretly wanted a party but didn't know how to ask for one? Maybe he didn't think he deserved one.

Divorce had been an occasional topic of conversation between us over the past two years. Should I host a party to honor someone I had thought about leaving? The neighborhood expectation was to surprise your spouse with a party when he/she turned forty. Karl was, after all, a prominent figure in the community and a respected teacher at the local high school.

Finally, I turned to our children for advice; all voted for the intrigue of a surprise. Then I sought my mom's advice. Ever politically correct, Mom was neutral, offering money, but no guidance. I then asked for input from each of my close friends. They all encouraged me to have a party. Still, I wavered.

Secretly hoping for a reciprocal mid-life birthday bash, I decided to hostess the "party of parties." I invited the entire high school math department, most of the athletic department, spouses, plus a few neighbors—forty-four people in all. No family members were invited. His mother would have worn her stern look of disapproval and his brother would have been jealous of the attention showered on Karl. Since I wasn't inviting his side of the family, how could I invite mine? Just friends, that was the final decision.

Renting a hall to have a catered affair or taking forty plus guests out to dinner was beyond our means, so, except for the cake ordered from our favorite bakery, all food items came from Katherine's Kitchen. I spent the better part of two weeks cooking and freezing sauerkraut and Polish sausage, roast beef au jus, sweet and sour meatballs in gravy, assorted fruit breads and cookies. I quadrupled recipes and stored the food in the basement freezer. Every piece of Tupperware and Rubbermaid was pressed into service. I thought I had been super organized, but on the day of the party I assumed the multiple roles of head cook, waitress, and scullery maid.

August and September were typically busy months for us: end-of-summer tennis tournaments, back-to-school shopping, mandatory inoculations, and school registration. Karl dedicated his waking hours to lesson plans and the local tennis courts. Oblivious to my culinary efforts, he suspected nothing.

The party was scheduled for the last Friday evening in September. The children came home from school eager to help with last-minute chores. Having kept the secret from their father, they were enormously proud of themselves. They showered, dressed, straightened their rooms, and played soccer in the front yard until the first guests arrived. Craig directed our friends to inconspicuous parking spots on side streets. Mike walked the guests to the front door. Tom ushered everyone downstairs where Emily was busy spreading cheddar cheese on Triscuits and Wheat Thins. I prayed I had made the right decision and that Karl wouldn't be angry with me.

Karl came home that evening forty-five minutes late. A critical three-setter had detained him. What did it matter that his family was ostensibly waiting to take him out for his birthday dinner? We could wait.

Once inside the front door, Karl headed for the kitchen, opened the refrigerator door, and reached for a bottle of Gatorade. The children grinned at one another behind their father's back; they followed him to the top of the basement stairs. Predictably, Karl had rolled up his sweat-soaked towel and tee-shirt, preparing to deposit the damp wad directly into the washer in the laundry room. As he rounded the bottom of the stairwell, the roar of SURPRISE was deafening. Stunned, as if struck by an unforeseen attacker, Karl leaned heavily against the carpeted wall, his face ashen.

A few of his friends came forward to shake his hand and pat him on the back. What must he have felt in those first few moments? Fear? Joy? Anger? Betrayal?

When he finally spoke, all he could say was, "Wow! Wow! How did you all get here? Who did all this for me?" He sounded pleased, almost little-boyish. All the work and worry had been worthwhile.

While Karl mingled with his colleagues, the children and I served up endless bowlfuls of food. Most people drank wine or slush (a concoction of green tea, brandy, orange juice, and lemonade) with their dinner. By the time the last plate was cleared from the tables, the din of conversation had escalated, the room appeared to have shrunk, and the air felt thin.

Raucous applause broke out at the far end of the basement and a chant of "speech, speech" gathered momentum. Karl, giddy with anticipation and alcohol, chose to stand against a wall between the two inside dinner tables. Limited space restrained his normal pacing, but nervous energy radiated through every nerve in his body. Karl began by thanking everyone for coming and asking their forgiveness if he was slurring his words and making a fool of himself. "I'm having a good time. I love you all."

As he opened each gag gift (golf balls, tennis balls, a black wooden cane with a horse's head for a handle, a trash bag in the shape of a corset, a tee-shirt with K>39 on the front), he referenced various high school tennis, basketball, football, and golf events. His comments were peppered with expressions like "be tough" and "we never lose because we're the best." A few friends closest to him handed him a series of mixed drinks camouflaged in beer cans. The more he drank, the louder and funnier he became, at times screaming, "But I have to go to the bathroom!" He was totally vulnerable and the crowd loved it.

Jock-like movements and a clenched right fist punctuated every comment, his right forefinger periodically pushing up the glasses that kept slipping down on his nose. "Will you ever be able to forgive me? What will you think of me on Monday? This is the only time I've ever been this way." Wild hilarity alternated with sobering remorse. At one point he remembered to thank me for all the preparation and planning. He asked for a round of applause on my behalf, walked over to where I was standing, and gave me a full body hug. "In case you've forgotten how to do it...." More laughter.

The last gift was a caricature of a tennis player in heavy pursuit of a ball with these words inscribed on the bottom: "Will this person still be able to compete in the future? Only time will tell." Karl thanked everyone again and hurriedly excused himself to go to the bathroom.

When he returned, unsteady on his feet, the boys helped him over to his cake so we could sing happy birthday. Karl read the birthday verse printed on the frosting. The children and I had written this poem two weeks earlier.

"Dear Dad,

Now that you are growing old,
You've had to slow your pace.
It's now our turn to outrun you
In any kind of race.

For all the gray that's in your hair,
I guess we get the blame.
Don't feel sad about your age;
We love you just the same.

We tried to find that special gift,
Like a Migi, small and sporty.
Instead, we settled for this cake
With a wish for a Happy Forty."

With tears streaming down his cheeks and a choked voice, he hugged me again, hard. "Thank you. Thank you all for coming. This means so much to me. What a great party!"

Several hours later, the guests began to leave. When about a half dozen remained, Karl excused himself again to go to the bathroom. This time he didn't return. Worried about his alcohol consumption, I climbed the stairs, calling out his name. I found him sprawled out on the floor in our tiny bathroom, the back of his right hand flung carelessly across his forehead, semi-conscious.

The next day Karl complained of a headache and wondered aloud how he would face everyone on Monday. He said he hated the party and would never forgive me for planning it without his permission.

CHAPTER 20

Issues of Fairness

After Karl's life-changing birthday party, the distance between us widened. Embarrassed by his vulnerability and atypical drunken state, he retreated to the safety of the television room and basement work area. The daily demands of four math preparations, coupled with his two-night-a-week junior college class, appeared to justify his self-imposed isolation. I loved Karl—he was my husband—yet I felt I wasn't really a part of his life. For the first time in our marriage, I began to wonder whether he had a mental disorder. His mother had experienced panic attacks. Had she ever been properly diagnosed? Was there some type of genetic imbalance that we were not aware of?

Allowing myself to consider that part, or all, of Karl's inappropriate behavior could stem from mental illness affected my thinking. On the positive side, if Karl had a mental illness, it could be diagnosed and treated. It also gave me license to continue to make excuses for his abrupt mood changes and unprovoked spurts of anger. On the negative side, if Karl had a mental illness, what could it mean for our children? And if he refused diagnosis and subsequent treatment, what would that mean for the two of us?

Since Karl's day-into-evening schedule allowed little time for family, I handled the household and childcare tasks. After writing documentation for software programs eight to nine hours a day, I drove the children to music, tennis, and volleyball lessons. I shopped, cooked, cleaned, washed, mended, dictated spelling tests, puzzled over story problems, proofread sermon reports, and shored up sagging psyches. I fielded questions about sex, taught each child to drive a car, and whispered "I love you" over and over to our four children. This was my five-day-a-week routine. I loved it and I hated it.

I loved being a mom; I especially loved being *these kids'* mom. They were unique individuals, each a special blessing and challenge. On the one hand, I gave thanks every day for my children. On the other hand, I was tired and resentful because I had no time for myself—no pampering, no pleasure reading, no time to be alone.

It came down to an issue of fairness. How much time did Karl need each week to satisfy his cravings for recognition by playing ball games, watching sporting events on television, and teaching junior college? Why didn't he notice I had no time for fun or relaxation? I felt guilty for wishing I had chosen a gentler, more nurturing father for my children and a more compassionate husband for me.

One night at dinner I reached the breaking point. In a loud, almost militant, voice I announced that from this day forward, I would not be silent about issues regarding fairness. When I disagreed with something their father said, I would voice my disapproval. I explained that my past reluctance to speak my mind was because I didn't want dinnertime to become a battleground. But no longer did I want my silence to indicate approval of their father's behavior or thought process.

Unfortunately, Karl was hearing this information for the first time right along with the children. He had a very annoying habit of licking whatever utensil he was using when he was thinking about a retort. He began licking juice off the spoon he was using to eat his dish of fruit cocktail. His eyes narrowed and his jaw tightened. "So that's how it's going to be from now on around here. Well, we'll see about that." He carefully placed his spoon in the empty dish, pushed back his chair, and disappeared into the basement for the remainder of the evening.

Mealtimes became more intense as Karl began slinging verbal potshots at me. "I bet *you* had a hard day today." "How much money did you spend at the grocery store *this time?*" "Why did you buy the kids new tennis shoes? There was nothing wrong with the ones they had." His tirades exhausted me.

The word *divorce* made its way into our conversations more frequently. At first, there were only casual references to a divorce. I would say, "Nothing I do meets with your approval. You would probably be happier if we were divorced." During another conversation, Karl would say, "The divorce statistics are climbing. Maybe we should add ourselves to those numbers."

Threats and accusations continued. I wanted Karl to be more understanding, less violent; more loving, less judgmental; more parental, less punitive. Karl wanted me to be more authoritative, less understanding; more "by the book," less compassionate; more action-oriented, less patient.

I begged Karl to go for counseling, either privately or through our church. By this time the children and I, both individually and collectively, had gone to see a psychologist recommended by our pediatrician. Part of Karl's reluctance to join us was his embarrassment at not being able to fix the problem. Raised to be stoic and independent, he resisted intervention when medical problems surfaced. How, then, could I expect him to be receptive to psychological help?

In the fall of 1981, finally acknowledging that our marriage was in trouble, Karl signed us up for a Marriage Encounter weekend sponsored by one of the local churches. The blurb in the Sunday bulletin read, "Sign up now for a marriage enrichment weekend and learn how to make a good marriage even better." The very name of the workshop, Marriage Encounter, carried with it much less stigma than the word *counseling.* Perhaps anonymity was a factor—it was not going to be held at our church where many people knew us. He must really care about me after all, I thought. Walking the dog that evening, I allowed the tears of relief and hope to flow—I had prayed so long and hard for this moment. All I wanted was some small sign that we could work through our differences. I looked forward to, yet dreaded, this weekend.

Neither of us was prepared for the demands of the two-day session. Questions we responded to cut to the very core of male/female relationships, from perceptions learned from our parents to how we currently felt about one another. We journaled our innermost thoughts and shared them with each other and the fourteen couples attending the workshop with us. "What are your fondest memories of your mother? Your father?" "How do these memories manifest themselves in your current relationship?" "What do you like/dislike most about your partner?" "What would you like your partner to do that he/she is currently not doing?" "What would you like your partner to stop doing?" The probing questions pummeled us.

Each couple shared stories of unmet expectations and painful recollections of childhood disappointments. Karl accused me of talking over him; I accused him of not listening to me. Karl told the group his family never came to watch him perform in school activities and that, as a young child, he had been told to sit quietly and not speak until he was spoken to. I told the group my parents weren't able to spend time with me when I was young because they both had to work; an aunt and uncle watched over me. As a child, I had been denied fishing trips with my father because I was a girl.

I liked Karl's work ethic; he admired my skill with words. I disliked his detachment; he disliked my preoccupation with family. I wanted him to pay me more compliments. He wanted me to pay him more compliments. I wanted him to spend more time with me and the children. He wanted me to spend more time with him. I wanted him to stop punishing the children. He wanted me to stop interfering with his punishment of the children.

That Sunday evening everyone stood shoulder to shoulder in the center of the small classroom. We each lit a white candle and waited expectantly for the moderator's final words of wisdom and forgiveness. We reaffirmed our love for our partner and repeated the age-old marriage vows. We promised each other and the workshop leaders that we would pray together and continue writing in our journals and sharing our most private thoughts.

Although the time we spent in children's activities seemed all-encompassing, Karl and I agreed to spend thirty minutes together in conversation every evening after the news. I was incredibly excited by the progress we made during this renewal weekend. For the first time in years, I truly believed our marriage could last. I loved Karl, and with love, I believed everything was possible.

Eleven days into our new routine, Karl walked up the basement stairs after the 10:00 news. Throwing his journal on the kitchen table next to me, he said, "I quit. I'm too tired to write this late at night and the whole thing is stupid anyhow." Stunned, I closed my Marriage Encounter folder, turned off the kitchen light, and sat down in the rocker in the darkened living room. Within minutes I heard Karl's even breathing; he was asleep. I quietly made my way down the hallway to our bathroom, carefully sidestepping the floorboards that creaked. I brushed my teeth, washed my face, climbed into my side of the bed facing away from him, and, noiselessly, began to cry.

This time the crying didn't stop. Feeling the onset of a headache, I glanced at the bright blue numbers on the clock: 11:50. I was exhausted and needed some rest. I wanted to sleep, but couldn't. It was now 12:15. At 1:05 I tiptoed to the bathroom to replenish my tissue supply. Quietly I blew my stuffed-up nose and then felt my way back to bed. With the top sheet and comforter drawn tight under my chin, I yielded to my sadness and allowed the tears to come again. I must have fallen asleep while I was still crying.

Suddenly I felt someone shaking me hard. "It's 3:00 in the morning. What's the matter with you? You must be dreaming; you're moaning and shaking the bed. How can I sleep?"

My eyes felt itchy and swollen. "I think I'm having a nervous breakdown. You don't really want to be married to me. You keep telling me the children and I are weights around your neck. Sometimes I just want to run away from everything—from you, the kids—everything. I love you, Karl, but you're so far away. I don't know how to bring you close to me."

"Yeah, yeah, yeah," he said. "I've heard all this crap before. Maybe you should go to the hospital to have your nervous breakdown. At least then maybe I can get some sleep."

I turned my dampened pillow over, edged closer to my side of the bed, and cried more quietly the rest of the night. I knew this was the beginning of the end. The truth was he didn't care about me. And he didn't care about the kids. What was the point of staying?

I was too emotionally drained to see the situation for what it was. The signs of his depression had been gradual, yet so obvious: prolonged sadness, decrease in appetite, unprovoked irritability, loss of energy, withdrawal. Yet I couldn't see it clearly. It was all about me, my sadness, my loss, my loneliness. Life was just not fair.

CHAPTER 21

Germany

The trip to Germany in August of 1982 was a desperate, and costly, attempt to save our marriage. After lengthy discussions about finances, we planned a fourteen-day trip to Germany, Austria, and Switzerland. With Karl's refusal to continue the communication techniques learned during the Marriage Encounter weekend, I wondered why we thought a vacation without the children would bring us closer together.

Using the trip as a ruse to improve our relationship, however, was not its sole purpose. For years Karl had been complaining that his money always seemed to be spent on the children, rather than on himself. Here was a chance for him to be the main character in a play of his own creation. One of his dreams had always been to return to his heimat (hometown), so I suggested he plan an itinerary that would make the trip memorable for him.

After we booked flights from O'Hare to Düsseldorf for $600 per person, we applied for our passports. We planned to spend most of our time in Germany, crossing the borders into Austria and Switzerland for occasional day trips.

I was frantic with last-minute preparations: pick up Mom so she could stay with the children while we were gone, make a list of critical phone numbers, decide which neighbors would be back-up drivers for the children's activities, and cook and freeze enough meals so my mother could enjoy the remaining summer days with the children.

The boys planned their days with Grandma: favorite games of Bunco and Rummy and frequent trips to the movies, malls, and local restaurants. It seemed as if they told every neighbor on their paper routes that we would be out of the country for two weeks. We received calls from people we hadn't spoken to in months telling us to have a safe trip. Emily, however, was unusually quiet. She loved my mom, but Emily and I had never been apart before. She was eleven and very attached to me. One day at work I drafted an itinerary for her, listing the towns and castles we would explore. After she posted the schedule and a map on her bedroom bulletin board, she seemed less tense about our leaving.

The flight from Chicago to Düsseldorf was arduous. I had never learned how to sleep on airplanes. The seats were too narrow, the backs too stiff, the arm rests too hard. We chose a late morning flight, so it was early evening in Germany when we landed. Overcast skies and a light drizzle could not detract from the natural beauty of this bustling German town. In less than nine hours, we had been transported to another world.

The next day we explored Düsseldorf on foot and engaged many of the residents in casual conversation—auf Deutsch, of course. They were proud of the antique stores, galleries, and pubs that lined their cobblestone streets. The following day we drove to Hannover, the city of gardens and museums, to visit two of Karl's cousins. It was an awkward meeting that began with stiff handshakes and ended with brief embraces and hollow promises of their visiting us in America. The speed of the banter and the heavy accents accounted for my missing most of the verbal exchange during the visit. So engrossed was Karl in the conversation, he had forgotten the extent of my German had been gleaned solely from textbooks and stilted classroom dialogue.

I remember walking into total blackness when we left their apartment. Not one lamplight was lit. Hand over hand, we felt our way to our rented BMW. When Karl opened the car door, the tiny light inside the vehicle shone like a beacon of safety against the backdrop of night.

The next day we traveled to Goslar and Astfeld, tiny villages where Karl grew up. He had carried the memories of the nearby meandering brooks and the gracefully sloped Harz Mountains in his head and in his heart all these years. The rivers and peaks remained untouched, but the open fields and one-room schoolhouses Karl knew as a boy had yielded to concrete structures, otherwise known as progress.

Despite the many opportunities Karl and I had to share confidences, there was painfully little conversation between us during the day and even less contact between us in bed at night. In fact, one evening after I made some romantic overtures, Karl suggested I see my gynecologist to have my hormones checked when we returned home. Just when had I become so physically unattractive to him? Had he found someone else? I was ready to go home. I didn't care that we had one more week of adventures in this beautiful, faraway land.

The inns we visited were small, yet impeccably clean. The rooms, sparsely furnished, shared a communal bathroom located at the far end of a dimly-lit hallway. By the end of the second day I realized the importance of limiting the intake of liquids past 8:00 p.m.

We traveled to Füssen to visit the castles. I was struck by the intricacies of the artwork and tapestries created by humans blessed with genius. Baden-Baden was beautiful; shops and taverns lined the narrow, picturesque streets and Viennese waltz music filled the air. We drove to Innsbruck on a Saturday morning and discovered most of the shops were closed. My grandparents on both sides were Austrian, yet I had made no attempt to trace my ancestry prior to the trip— an oversight I will always regret. A tram ride to the top of the Zugspitze provided us with the most magnificent view of the entire trip.

Savoring the final days of our vacation, Karl insisted we stop in Heidelberg and Wiesbaden on our way back to Düsseldorf. We agreed to call a halt to the continual bickering we had engaged in throughout the trip so we could enjoy the timelessness of these European towns. Should we buy souvenirs for the children? My mom? Ourselves? How often should we call home? Who would do the ordering off the menu? Whose turn was it to go into the bank to exchange currency? Such pettiness. I was sick of it. I just wanted to go home.

Three distinct impressions remained with me long after the trip was over. First, I wondered why all Germans had a death wish; otherwise, why would they drive their new Mercedes-Benz vehicles on the Autobahn at speeds in excess of 100 miles per hour? Second, I remembered the scratchy toilet paper found in every public washroom. And, third, I realized I couldn't continue in this marriage much longer, not even for the sake of the children.

Our conversations were intermittent and insignificant on the return flight, each of us preoccupied with our separate thoughts. The children seemed genuinely glad to see us, yet they sensed the increased tension between us. Craig wanted to know how his dad reacted when he saw his cousins. Mike asked me if his father and I had "settled anything." Tom asked, "Did Dad get angry while you were gone, Mom? Did the two of you argue very much?" Emily was just happy to curl up next to me on the couch and listen to stories about the trip.

It felt good to get back into a familiar routine. The name of the game was Keep Busy—I knew the rules all too well. The children were back in school and Karl was gone from morning to evening, leaving me, once again, to shuttle four young bodies from place to place. I vowed to do the best I could each day and prayed for right outcomes between Karl and me.

On a Sunday afternoon in late fall, I received a phone call from my brother. He announced he had filed for divorce. We all knew there had been rough spots in his marriage, but none of us thought he and his wife would divorce. Yet here it was. He had met someone interesting at work, and he needed to move on with his life.

When Karl returned from his tennis match, he found me lying on our bed, crying, my make-up streaked and my nose red from tissue. I told Karl the news about William. I felt bad for my brother and his family, but I was really crying for me, for Karl, for all of us. Why couldn't we do something to help ourselves? I didn't really want a divorce.

Karl sat down on the edge of the bed, not touching me. He took his shoes and socks off and rubbed the back of his neck without saying anything. Then he turned to me and said, "I don't want a divorce. I know we've talked about it, but I really don't want a divorce. I still love you." I turned my face into the pillow and cried harder. He patted my leg and walked out of the room, closing the door behind him.

CHAPTER 22

Katherine's Career

During our eighteen years of marriage, juggling the activities of four children, mediating six strong-willed temperaments, tending to endless home repairs, and negotiating money issues had frayed the already thin cord of our relationship. Like many of our married friends, Karl and I had begun to move separately through life.

But what would I do if I ended up alone? How would I support myself and the children? On the outside, I pretended it didn't matter that my teaching career had ended prematurely; on the inside, I mourned the loss of my lifelong goal. I always imagined I would retire as the head of a high school English department. Two major events prevented my dream from becoming a reality. The first had to do with daycare issues. Having four children in four years narrowed my options. My mom worked full-time and was unable to help us during the week. Sending the children to daycare was cost prohibitive. The second event was the economy; the country was facing a nation-wide reduction in teachers, making it difficult for me to return to the classroom.

Whether or not I stayed with Karl, I had to find a full-time job—Craig was just a few years away from choosing a college. Within the next two years all three boys might be away at school. Karl and I had failed to plan for multiple college expenses. Panic gripped my gut.

Yet the weekly church sermons promised hope and abundance for those who followed in Christ's footsteps. Surely my work in the church (teaching Sunday school, leading several youth groups, and participating in a lay ministry program) would count for something. God has given me choices. Let my choices be good ones, I prayed.

The boys were in high school and Emily in junior high. After so many years of putting everyone's needs before mine, I felt guilty thinking about what I wanted to do with the rest of my life. Did I really deserve to have a life of my own?

I wanted a job that mattered—not just any job. Karl would say, "Why can't you be happy being a secretary?" While I didn't dislike administrative work, I wanted something more— I wanted to teach. Gradually, reluctantly, I loosened my grip on our family unit and looked for business opportunities that would make use of my writing skills.

My first job as an editor ended abruptly when the company folded. My second editorial position with a well-known publishing company consisted of writing documentation for a series of software programs targeted for high school administrators. The company supplied me with a home computer and printer. I set up my office in the laundry room and went to work each morning in jeans, a sweatshirt, white cotton socks, and no make-up. I would work for two hours before the children awakened, stop for breakfast, work another four hours until noon, take the dog for a walk during lunch, and finish my work day by 3:00. The job was perfect! I was heartbroken when, two years later, the company sold its entire computer division to a major toy manufacturer.

I told myself I deserved a vacation that summer, yet I was far from idle. I cleaned cabinets, closets, the garage, and the basement. I sorted through years of photos with no names or dates on the backs and emptied file drawers packed with children's report cards, lesson plans from my early teaching days, and household receipts.

Having satisfied my nesting instinct, I applied for a job at a nearby manufacturing company that fall. Responding to their ad in the local paper, I signed up for the temporary secretarial pool. Karl's suggestion had come to pass—I would be typing labels and answering telephones. This is just an interim position, I told myself. When a full-time teaching position becomes available, I will give two weeks' notice and leave. A few months later I was offered a full-time position as Training Coordinator in the Corporate Training department. I accepted, confident I would be called back to the classroom the following semester.

I stayed with Alchem for seven years; not one school district called me. By spring, though, I was teaching classes on writing and grammar skills for our sales and customer service departments and my manager, with the help of the Vice President of Human Resources, was creating a career path for me. I was earning less than $30,000 a year, but my success and newly-acquired independence left me euphoric. I had taken control of a tiny part of my life.

When I began working at Alchem, my wardrobe consisted of two pairs of polyester pants and three paisley polyester blouses. I devised a plan that, initially, Karl did not support. Twice a month I took $100 out of my paycheck and spent the entire amount on *me*.

Along with building a professional wardrobe, I began building a network of professional friends—women who worked in nearby departments. We began a tradition of going out for dinner on the last Friday of each month. Mostly we talked about work. We loved the visibility of being housed in the building where all the important meetings were hosted and free lunches were the norm. We hated the good old boys' network and the salary inequities, yet we accepted the glass ceiling as a way of life at Alchem.

Karl disapproved of these once-a-month dinners. Throughout our marriage, it was acceptable for him to play golf, tennis, and basketball with his friends, stop for burgers or pizza, and come home whenever he chose. Yet it wasn't acceptable for me to have dinner with my female friends once a month.

I now felt I had something important to say during the dinner hour. My work-related, dinner-time stories often involved men since almost everyone I worked with was male. Within six months Karl was accusing me of having an affair with a coworker. "How do I know you're really having dinner with Denise and Joan? How do I know you don't have a lover?"

These accusations were preposterous for so many reasons. First, I felt caged in *our* marriage. Why would I want to get involved with someone else? Here I was, trying to find the courage to end an emotionally abusive relationship; finding a replacement for Karl never entered my mind. Second, even though our marriage was unstable, I believed in the sanctity of marriage, the sacredness of the marriage vows. While my love for Karl had waned over the years, I would never have cheated on him. Third, what kind of an example would I be setting for our four children if I were involved in an extramarital affair?

Unfortunately, Karl couldn't keep his accusatory comments between the two of us. He accused me of infidelity in front of the children. Didn't he realize the effect his insulting remarks would have on the children? It was humiliating to have to defend my innocence while my sons and daughter listened in nearby bedrooms. I deserved more respect and trust than this.

Of course, this was a core problem. Karl had difficulty respecting women in general, so how could he show *me* any respect? Nor did he respect my need for achievement and personal growth. For the past few years I had talked about going back to school to earn my master's degree. Each time I broached the subject with Karl, he would itemize a list of upcoming expenses. "How can you think about going to school? We need to replace the furnace, the Olds needs tires, and my big life insurance premium is due next month." I couldn't refute his logic—there were always unexpected bills to pay.

I clung to the belief that even though I had been denied a teaching career, there was another purpose for my being here.

I just hadn't found it yet. During a growth plan discussion with my manager, I asked his opinion on the best universities in the area offering a master's degree in human resources. Human resources offered more opportunities than training; hopefully there would be a greater selection of available jobs if I became a generalist.

My manager promised to discuss my career goals with the Vice President of Human Resources. A few weeks later at a staff meeting, our Vice President announced that I was going back to school to pursue a master's degree in human resources. He congratulated me on my decision, the group applauded—those seated closest to me gave me high fives—and suddenly I was going back to school! I called for an application and catalog that afternoon.

Since Alchem offered educational assistance to its employees after they had been with the company six months, money was not as much of a factor as I had originally thought. I had to come up with the initial payment, but tuition was 100% reimbursed if I received a grade of C or higher. That left books, a nominal expense each quarter, and the cost of commuting, an equally insignificant amount since I had chosen a university with a campus close to work.

Karl was angry when I told him I was planning to return to school after the holidays although he couldn't put into words why he was angry. Perhaps he was worried I might be more successful than he was—or earn more money. Perhaps he was afraid he would be required to be at home more. Perhaps he feared he was losing control of me. In fact, he *was* losing control over me. I knew that my pursuing a master's degree would further jeopardize our marriage, but I didn't care. I was going back to school and that was a very exciting thought indeed.

Some of my friends who were not as achievement oriented as I was thought I was crazy. One friend said, "You're too old to go back to school. By the time you finish your degree, you'll be forty-five years old!"

I replied, "In three years I'm going to be forty-five—with or without a degree."

Another friend said, "Why don't you just join a bridge club or sign up for a sewing class? Why make life harder than it needs to be?"

"I want to see if I can still succeed in the classroom," I said. Maybe she was right. Maybe I did make life harder than it needed to be. Getting my master's degree would definitely involve some sacrifices, but I knew I had the desire, determination, and discipline to make it happen. Besides, it was good for the children to see their mom setting a goal and working towards achieving it.

Karl found reasons to spend more time away from home. Instead of creating lesson plans at the dining room table, he would stay after school to prepare for the next day of teaching. Instead of joining us for dinner, he scheduled more tennis matches for 5:00 or 6:00 p.m. Instead of spending weekends at home with us, he finished his house projects early and spent Saturday and Sunday afternoons at the library. The quiet is relaxing, he would say.

These days Karl seldom attended a family meeting. He would arrive home around 9:30, reach for a can of pop, and head for the basement to watch the evening news and sport highlights. Sometime between 10:30 and 10:45, he would slowly climb the stairs, deposit his empty can in the kitchen sink, and go to bed without saying goodnight to me.

As Karl and I withdrew from the family unit, each in our own way, the children withdrew from us and from one another.

CHAPTER 23

Under the Influence

Working a full-time job made it difficult for me to know what each child was doing after school. Emily was usually the first one home because the boys were involved in sports or band activities. Although each child challenged the house rules, Mike blatantly scoffed at the school code of ethics for athletes.

Soon after graduating from eighth grade, Mike packed up his drum set, choosing to concentrate on the familiar rotation of sports: cross-country in the fall, basketball in the winter, and tennis in the spring. Mike excelled at every sport, but he didn't always excel at using good judgment.

During Mike's freshman year in high school, he fell in with a crowd of athletes who had discovered liquor. Smoking and drinking were not sanctioned in our household—nor were they sanctioned by the high school. For holidays and birthday celebrations, family members who enjoyed drinking brought their own wine and beer. I had hoped that Karl's and my collective stance against alcohol would send a strong enough message to our children on the use/abuse of this drug. I was wrong.

On a Friday evening in January during a home varsity basketball game, Mike, who played on the junior varsity team his sophomore year, had left the house earlier than his brothers to meet up with a friend before going to the game. Since Craig and Tom were playing in the pep band that evening, Karl was planning to drive them and their instruments to the high school. We lived an easy six blocks from Lincoln High, but the horns were cumbersome to carry. Emily had invited a friend for a sleepover. She and Dana were in the far corner of the basement listening to Olivia Newton-John and paging through teen-age fashion magazines. Karl, too tired to attend the game, decided to stay home and watch a movie.

Retreating to the family room downstairs, we turned on the television and adjusted the volume to block out the strains of "Hopelessly Devoted to You." I took my favorite seat in the rocker; Karl and the dog curled up on the couch. Before the first commercial, they were both snoring. If only we could talk, I thought. There was so much history between us. I really didn't want to leave this man—we had spent half a lifetime together. With effort, I focused my attention on Robert Redford and Mia Farrow.

About an hour and a half later, I heard muffled noises upstairs. That's strange, I thought. It's too early for the game to be over. The creak of the rocker awakened Muffin, but not Karl. She pushed past me up the stairs, increasingly agitated by the ruckus in the hallway. As I reached the top of the stairs and crossed through the kitchen to the hallway, I saw Mike lying face down on the floor. He was vomiting, and the stench was overpowering. "I'm sorry," he slurred his words. "Forgive me, Dad. I'm sorry. I'm so sorry." Craig grabbed his ankles and Tom his wrists. Together, they eased him down the hallway towards the bathroom.

"He almost walked off the end of the bleachers, Mom. Tom and I caught him just before he fell. Pete came over to the band pit to tell us to take him home. He's very sick. We don't know where he got the liquor." Just then Karl appeared in the kitchen doorway, apparently having heard the end of Craig's explanation.

These days Karl's rage could accelerate from zero to a hundred with very little provocation. But here was *real* provocation. "Drinking? At a school function? What the hell's the matter with you?" With the toe of his paint-spattered house shoe, he pushed at Mike's legs. Kneeling close to Mike, he raised his hand above his head. He slapped Mike on his back—hard. As he raised his hand again, I grabbed his arm, knocking him off balance.

"Let me at him. Let go of me." He pushed me backward with such force the back of my head hit the wall. Craig grabbed my shoulder to steady me just as Tom stepped in front of his father to prevent any additional physical harm to me.

"I'm sorry, Dad. I'm sorry, Mom. Forgive me, please. Please forgive me." There was Mike, lying in a pool of vomit, while his mother and father engaged in a shoving match.

"Are you crazy?" I screamed. "He's drunk. Can't you see he's sick? Don't you dare hit him again! He's sick." I straddled Mike's body, looped my arms under his shoulders, and gently moved him closer to the bathroom. Dampening a washcloth with warm water, I bathed his tear-stained face. With help from my sons, I positioned him over the toilet, encouraging him to vomit some more.

The vomiting, crying, and apologizing continued for a long time. Exhausted, his body finally purged of the poison, he curled up on his right side in a fetal position on the bathroom rug and slept. Tom carefully lifted Mike's neck and shoulders so I could slip a pillow beneath his head. Craig spread his afghan over Mike's legs to keep away the draft of the air vent. We dimmed the light, deciding he should sleep in the bathroom for a while in case he needed the toilet again.

Emily and Dana emerged from the basement, tiptoed down the hallway to Emily's bedroom to change into their pajamas, glanced nervously in the direction of Mike, and scurried into the kitchen to scavenge for snacks.

Craig and Tom returned to the high school to collect their horns and sheet music. Karl and I sat down at the kitchen table to talk. Actually, I talked and he listened, not once meeting my gaze. "We need to agree on how to deal with this," I heard myself say calmly. "We've been over this so many times. Force is not the answer. Don't you see that hitting him is not the answer?" Abruptly, Karl stood and left the room. The conversation was over. It had turned into another mini lecture by Katherine.

The next morning Emily and Dana peeked in on Mike, who was sleeping in Tom's bed. Eyes half-open, the scent of alcohol still on his breath, he continued to apologize to anyone who would listen to him.

No one spoke about the incident for two days. The following Monday, Mike was given an in-school suspension for being drunk while on school premises. He could attend classes but was barred from extracurricular activities and team practices for a week. Mike was humiliated. The public disgrace was a far greater punishment than anything his father or I could have meted out.

We discovered the parents of Mike's friend had been out of town for the weekend. Mike and Pete had unlocked the liquor cabinet, downing two bottles of beer and a fifth of whiskey between them. They had then walked to school to watch the basketball game, not realizing how drunk they were. Had Pete not realized the potential danger of Mike's bizarre behavior that evening, the incident might have ended tragically. Public humiliation was bad, but an accidental death would have been worse.

CHAPTER 24

The Trip to Milwaukee

Craig graduated high school in June of 1984 with plans to attend college in Milwaukee the following fall. Influenced by his dad and other high school math teachers, Craig planned to major in biomedical engineering. This particular university offered one of the few specialized programs in the Midwest.

That summer all the boys had part-time jobs. Craig and Tom worked at a local gas station, and Mike worked at a nearby golf course taking care of the greens. Emily played volleyball twice a day and became the chief babysitter in our subdivision. Karl and I looked at homes in neighboring suburbs, trying to decide whether to invest more money in our house or start out fresh with another home. We were both tired of redecorating the same rooms over and over again. Yet neither of us was excited about the prospect of moving. Why buy a house when you're contemplating a divorce?

On a beautiful Friday morning in late August, Karl and I packed up the station wagon with Craig and his belongings and headed for the Milwaukee campus. I insisted on driving because I knew I would be the one picking Craig up on weekends when he chose to come home. If I drove to a destination once, I could *usually* find it the second time.

I headed north on 294; within minutes the expressway turned into 94. It was an easy drive—no rush hour traffic and no construction. Although I was moving too slowly for Karl, he was trying hard not to chide me on my driving.

When we veered off onto the Kilbourne Avenue exit toward the Civic Center, I took the 6th Street ramp heading south. Instead of turning right onto Wisconsin Avenue, I turned left. Suddenly I was heading east instead of west. The mistake cost us an extra few minutes, but we were not under a deadline. Karl suddenly snapped, "If you could just learn which way is east and which way is west, you wouldn't have made a left-hand turn at that intersection. I told you to go west, but, no, instead, you turned east. The sun always rises in the east. See? It's 11:00 in the morning. We're heading *into* the sun, so that means we're heading east. Get it?"

I could feel perspiration form on my upper lip. I willed myself to remain calm, but years of restrained silence had given way to strident self-righteousness. "I am so tired of your making me look like a fool in front of the children. So, big deal. I made a wrong turn. So what?" By this time I had turned around and was heading back towards the campus.

"All you women are the same. Really stupid when it comes to directions."

I jammed on the brakes in the middle of traffic, demanding an apology. Craig, in the back seat, opened the door and started to get out. "I'll meet you guys at the dorm. I don't want to listen to this crap any more."

Straining to face Craig, I yelled, "Don't you dare get out of this car. I will drive you to your dorm." He slammed his door, slouched against the back seat, and stared out his window.

We drove the last few blocks in silence. After unpacking the car and setting up Craig's room, we took him out for lunch at a corner coffee shop. Conversation was strained. Karl told his son to be successful and uphold the Kreher name. I told Craig to have fun and make some new friends. When I kissed him good-bye, Craig turned away from me, but not before I saw the tears streaming down his cheeks.

CHAPTER 25

The Decision

The following day, a Saturday, I awakened early, knowing intuitively it was time. It was time to end this destructive relationship. By staying with Karl I was silently telling the children it was okay to be a victim and that life was meant to be tolerated, endured. It was up to me to break this chain of anger. Hans, Lena, Karl, me, our children—it had to end.

I showered and dressed before Karl's alarm clock buzzed. When he walked down the hallway and saw me sitting at the dining room table staring into space, he knew something was wrong. Without an invitation, he sat down across from me. "Well, what is it now?" he asked. "Make it quick—I'll be late for my match."

"I want a divorce, Karl. I'm tired of pretending that everything is okay. Everything is *not* okay. I'm unhappy, you're unhappy, and the children are unhappy. We need to end this farce we call marriage. I want a divorce."

He pushed his chair back abruptly, nearly tipping it over backwards. "I'm not going to deal with this now," he said. Gathering up his tennis gear, he headed out the front door.

I called a family meeting that evening with the three younger children to tell them about my decision to divorce their father. They were sad, yet visibly relieved. They tried to act grown up and not show their emotions, but I knew they were scared. What would this mean for them?

I had instructed the children not to tell Craig about the divorce; I wanted to break the news to him myself. Craig was coming home for the weekend so he could watch his dad and brother play in the annual Labor Day tennis tournament. I would have to find time to be alone with him.

Late Friday evening I asked Craig to go grocery shopping with me. The children were used to late night trips to the supermarket, so I don't think he suspected that I had bad news to share. I deliberately parked far away from the lights above the store entrance. "Craig, your father and I have been at odds with one another for a long time. This decision has been a difficult one for me, but I've made up my mind; I'm leaving your father. Your brothers and sister already know. I didn't want to tell you on the phone, so I waited until now. I love you so much. Your father loves you, too. I am so sorry to hurt you like this."

Craig hunched down in his seat and stared into the darkness. No tears, no emotion, just silence.

CHAPTER 26

It's Over

The local Labor Day tennis tournament was a huge event in our town. Karl and Mike were playing singles in separate divisions. At his father's invitation, Mike was also slated to play doubles in the father-son division. This was the first year Craig and Tom had not entered the tournament.

Play started early Saturday morning. As I dressed in shorts, tee shirt, and sneakers, I thought about the family dynamics of this past week. What must Craig and Tom be thinking? How could Karl have singled out Mike as a partner? Why hadn't he drawn the names out of a hat? It was so obvious that Karl wanted Mike as a partner so they had a better chance of winning the trophy. As I crossed the highway and walked the few short blocks to the high school, I felt a pressure in my chest. Probably nerves. How would our friends react when they found out I had asked for a divorce?

The next day the scene was the same. I arrived at the courts around noon and stayed until 3:00. At 4:30 Karl stopped home to take a shower and put on fresh clothes. Old clothes, of course. He always wore old clothes to tennis tournaments because he wanted his opponent to feel further demoralized when beaten by someone who looked like a transient.

Karl's matches were finished for the day, but he was going back to the courts to watch more tennis. He opened the refrigerator and reached for a can of pop. He took a few steps towards the sink where I was working and said, "Maybe we can talk about this some more."

"It's over," I said. "It's really over. There's nothing more to say."

He slammed the just-opened can down on the counter and said, "You're right. It's over." He crossed the living room, opened the front door, and disappeared.

It's over. It's over. The words rang in my ears. It's finally over.

CHAPTER 27

The Separation

The elation I felt that weekend was short-lived. I never really wanted to be divorced. I didn't believe in divorce. When two people care about one another, they should be able to talk things over, work things out.

The next few days went by in a blur. Karl stuffed shirts, pants, underwear, shoes, and toiletries in a suitcase, insisting he would be back by the end of the week. "I hate you. I *hate* you," he raged. "This is my house, too. You have no right to kick me out of my own house. I'm calling a lawyer tomorrow. We'll see who gets to stay in this house."

He was right, of course. It was his house, too, but we couldn't live together during the separation—it would be too hard on the children—and also on us. I refused to leave because I didn't think the children were safe in his care. Even though I was an adult, his mercurial behavior frightened me. I can only imagine how his mood swings must have felt from the perspective of a teenager.

Those first few nights Karl stayed with friends—husband and wife math teachers he worked with at Lincoln. Around 9:00 each evening, he would call to say he was coming home. "Okay, Katherine, the joke is over—you've carried this too far."

"This is no joke, Karl—this is for real," I would say.

Former neighbors who lived around the corner had just divorced and moved to another state. Since the closing on their home was a month away, they had given us their house keys and asked us to take in their mail. At the end of his first week away from us, Karl decided to move into our neighbors' empty house.

"By next week you will have come to your senses," he said. "You don't earn enough to support yourself and the children. You'll soon come begging for money."

He disassembled the spare bed frame stored in the basement and packed his car with more of his belongings, including the full size spring and mattress. Two nights later, around 11:00, the children heard a noise in the driveway. Peeking out their window, Mike and Tom called out, "Mom. Dad's back. I think he plans to stay. He's carrying the mattress on his back!"

In a loud whisper I hissed, "Don't anyone get out of bed!" As I opened the door, a rush of pre-winter air pushed through the screen. I made a mental note to remind the boys to put in the storm windows.

Karl had propped the mattress against the house brick; his right elbow leaned into the mattress, the palm of his right hand cupping the back of his head. "I'm coming home where I belong," he announced. "No more games, Katherine. Let me in."

Be calm, Katherine, I heard myself say. Talking to myself always helped me stay in control of my thoughts. "It's late, Karl; this is not a good time to talk."

"We *will* talk *now*," he insisted, glaring at me.

"It's late," I repeated.

"We need to talk *now*." His voice was shaking.

"I'll call the police if you push me any further." Again, the threat of exposure.

"I'm not finished with you yet," he growled, retreating down the driveway, the angle of the mattress on his back forcing an uneven gait.

The children were to endure a second loss. As if the absence of their father were not enough of an emotional strain, they were forced to deal with the passing of their childhood pet.

Eighteen months earlier our veterinarian had told us Muffin, our ten-year-old Sheltie, had only six months to live. She had a growth on one of her hind legs that had begun to change in shape and size. The vet tried to remove the tumor, but it was attached to the bone. "I removed as much of the malignancy as I could. Six months—tops. It's not good news. I wish there were something more I could do for her."

Soon after Muffin's surgery, the children began talking about getting another dog. A few months later, on Emily's birthday, I surprised the children with a six-week-old puppy from our local shelter. She was part black Labrador and part Shepherd. Because of her shiny black coat, we named her Bear. We hoped Bear's nonstop energy would extend Muffin's life.

On this beautiful fall day, almost eighteen months after Bear joined our family, Muffin could no longer stand up. The cancer had spread. Her hind legs would no longer support her Collie-mix top-heavy torso. I scooped Muffin up in my arms and carried her to the back yard. When I brought her tired body through the kitchen door for the last time, she whimpered softly, refusing her morning treat. She licked my fingers, my hand, and my arm. I called the children together and told them today was the day I would be taking Muffin to the vet to be put to sleep. We had set the limits of her suffering on the day of her surgery. When she couldn't get up by herself to go outside or when she cried out at our touch, we would put her down. The children said their teary farewells to their long-time pet, lingering until the yellow school bus rounded the corner of our street.

Two weeks had gone by without hearing from Karl. On this Friday morning, however, I left a message for him with the math secretary. "This is Katherine. We have a family emergency. Please ask Karl to call me as soon as possible."

Karl was angry to learn I had left a message at the school. "Haven't I told you before never to call me at school unless there's an emergency?"

"This *is* an emergency; Muffin is very bad. I'm taking her to the vet this morning. I just wanted you to know." There was a moment of silence.

"Okay, you did the right thing, then. Do you want me to go with you?"

"That's up to you. You need to do whatever is best for you"

"I can be there at 10:30; wait for me."

I fixed myself a cup of tea, sat down on the kitchen floor close to Muffin so the length of her body leaned against my leg, pulled Bear onto my lap, and cried. Another ending. Sometimes life sucked.

When Karl arrived, he wrapped Muffin in a lightweight quilt and gently laid her on the back seat of his car. Although it wasn't cold outside, he tucked the edges of the blanket around her, stroking her soft tan and white fur one last time. Fighting back more tears, I avoided looking at either one of them.

We were ushered into a back room—the clinic had been expecting us. "Five minutes," the assistant said softly. "You have five minutes." I pressed my cheek gently against Muffin's jaw as she lay motionless on the icy metal table. "I love you, sweet dog." I whispered. "You have been a devoted friend and loving companion for ten years. We will miss you. I love you." I continued to hold her when the vet came in to administer the shot. Death came instantly—and so did my tears.

Karl and I walked out of the dimly lit animal hospital into blinding sunlight. Without a word, we walked to his car. Karl turned onto the highway to take me home. When we reached our subdivision, instead of heading in the direction of our house, he made a left onto Pine and drove past the neighborhood park. The play area was deserted. He pulled over to the curb near the swings and turned off the ignition.

Shifting in his seat, he leaned towards me. "You did this to her. Because of you, Muffin is dead. You've killed a part of me the same way you killed her. Who are you to say I'm not good enough to be your husband any more? I hate you, Katherine. I will always hate you."

I opened my door and started to get out. Grabbing my arm, Karl forced me back into the seat. "You'll leave when I tell you to leave. I haven't told you to leave yet." He restarted the engine, jerked the steering wheel to the right, and sped around the corner. The residential speed limit was fifteen miles per hour, but he didn't care. The speedometer read fifty as he pulled into our driveway and slammed on the brakes.

"Get out. Get *out*. You've ruined my life."

I got out of the front seat as quickly as I could and leaned against the row of shrubs that lined our driveway. I was afraid to cross in front of his vehicle; neither did I dare walk behind it. Best to wait until he pulled out of the driveway. He put the car in reverse, pushed his foot against the gas pedal and backed out of the drive, not once looking in his rear-view mirror.

Safely inside the house, I poured myself a glass of cold water. I knelt down to rub Bear's ears and tummy—she would miss her old pal. After putting away Muffin's collar, tags, and bowls, I reapplied my makeup and dressed for work. I had told the children they needed to go to school that morning. Life goes on in the midst of death. I decided to follow my own advice. If nothing else, work would take my mind off Muffin and Karl.

CHAPTER 28

The First Few Months

K arl had accused me of ruining his life. Did he not see that he had ruined mine as well?

Karl took his anger out on the children, refusing to acknowledge the boys' presence in the hallways at Lincoln and choosing not to respond to Emily's frequent phone calls. He wouldn't call her back out of fear I might answer the phone. He didn't invite them to dinner or offer to spend a Saturday afternoon with them. Nothing. Only silence. The children were devastated. *They* hadn't divorced their father; *I* had divorced their father.

The children were seventeen, sixteen, sixteen, and thirteen at the time we separated—old enough to make important decisions regarding their well-being. During one of his calmer moments, Karl had agreed the children should decide which parent they wanted to live with. In August of each year the children could re-evaluate their situation and decide whether to stay at their current residence or move in with the other parent. The children had to abide by their decision for one year. This agreement was definitely in my favor because I was staying in the primary household. If the children lived with me, they could stay in their respective schools and maintain their current friendships.

I was quite sure Craig, Tom, and Emily would elect to stay with me; I was not so sure about Mike. Karl was, after all, Mike's hero, but I was scared for Mike. What would happen when he was the sole object of his father's anger? When he hadn't lived up to his father's expectations? He was sure to take his father's spiteful words personally. I needed to talk to Mike alone—and soon.

Inviting Mike to use his newly-acquired driver's license to pick up pizza for dinner one evening gave me the opportunity I needed. "Mike," I said, as we moved along in traffic, "I know we've struggled a bit over the years. Part of my frustration is that you have learned some of your father's ways. You treat me as if I'm an idiot just because I'm a woman. You could only have learned that from your father. Break the chain, Mike. Start thinking for yourself. You don't have to do as your father has done. I love you. I know I've made some mistakes with you and your brothers and sister, but I love you, Mike, and I want you to stay a part of our family unit. Dad needs counseling. His flare-ups are getting worse and they're more frequent, yet he refuses to help himself. Don't allow misguided sympathy to affect your decision. I know you love your father, Mike, but you need to think about what's best for you."

By the following Sunday, Mike had decided to stay with us. His brothers and sister had also put pressure on him to stay. I knew there would be more push-pull between Mike and me, but I was up to the challenge. I loved this child and hoped I could get closer to him without Karl's constant influence and interference.

The impending divorce was hard on all of us, but I was especially concerned about Emily. At thirteen, she was too young to have to deal with this much emotional trauma. She pretended she was just fine, but I suspected otherwise. She spent more time in her room and less time with her brothers and me. She completed her chores without second and third reminders. In early December I asked Mike and Tom what they thought about my taking Emily to northern Wisconsin for a long weekend.

"That's a cool idea," said Mike. "I think you and Em should go."

"I agree, Mom," Tom added. "I'll look after Mike so he doesn't fall off any bleachers while you're gone." Mike didn't laugh at Tom's comment. They loved to needle one another.

Hotel rates were low in Door County because it was winter, gas prices were down, and we could bring a cooler for pop and snacks to cut down on food expenses. We decided to go.

Three days before we were scheduled to leave, the Upper Peninsula had eight inches of snow. "They have plows, and I just had new tires put on the station wagon. We'll be safe," I assured my mom.

Leaving on a Thursday morning made us both feel like we were playing hooky, which we were. We cranked the volume on the car radio and sang along with the vocalists on the light rock stations. When we arrived at the hotel, we asked for a list of restaurants that were open year round. We drove fourteen miles to have grilled chicken for dinner. Back at the hotel we turned up the thermostat, donned matching sweats, and watched *Grease* together. When the movie ended, we read magazines until we couldn't stay awake any longer.

For the next two days we talked girl talk. Emily told me how sad she was that Dad was gone, how much she missed Craig, how guilty she felt about going to see Dr. Wesley because the visits cost so much money, what her friends had said to her about the divorce, her fears about money in general (Can you really support all of us, Mom?), and how much she was dreading Christmas this year. Her concerns were my concerns, her sadnesses my sadnesses. The weekend was a success—it reopened the lines of communication between us.

Christmas was just three weeks away, but our attempts to engage in the holiday rituals failed. I baked cookies, wrapped presents, and decorated the house. Despite my efforts, we were not feeling joyful. I had hoped to recreate the peacefulness of my childhood Christmases. But the

Christmases of my childhood had a mother *and* a father in the background. This year the father was missing.

Not that Karl had ever been totally engaged during other holiday celebrations. When the five of us settled in around the tree on Christmas morning, we had to call out to Karl three or four times. "Come on, Dad. We're ready to open presents." Then we would wait.

Thirty to forty minutes later, Karl would saunter down the hallway to the living room and say, "What's the big deal? It's just another day." Looking directly at me, "So how much did you set us back this year? I don't even want to look at the charge account statements."

Regardless of which gift he opened, he would say, "I already have enough socks." Or, "I don't need any more ties." Or, "The wallet I have is just fine." The focus was always on money. Sadly, the focus was on money this Christmas, too, because there was less of it to go around.

On Christmas Eve the doorbell rang. When I opened the door, there was Karl standing on our snow-covered porch. Looking thinner than before, he handed me a huge bowl of fresh fruit. "Just thought I'd wish all of you a Merry Christmas. Tell the kids I love them." He turned and walked away. I set the bowl on the kitchen table and, through my tears, read his note:

> "Katherine,
>
> I hope you have a great Christmas. I miss you and the kids. I will always love you.
>
> Karl"

CHAPTER 29

Papers and Presentations

In January of 1985, before the divorce was final, I went back to college after having been away from school for twenty years. Within weeks I discovered being on the teacher side of the desk was more fun than being on the student side. Once again, I felt compelled to prove myself worthy. A compulsive overachiever, I settled for nothing less than a straight *A* average, sacrificing precious hours of sleep to achieve this goal. Fear of failure spurred me on. Relentlessly, methodically, I pored over every text, memorizing headings, bulleted lists, and all data highlighted in bold.

Balancing home, work, and school was tricky. I decided to take only one course at a time, which eased my burden enormously. I had finished my undergraduate work in three years instead of the conventional four. I was determined not to be in a hurry this time. Besides, my undergraduate grade point average suffered because of the extra hours I took each semester. A grade point average of 3.5 out of 4.0 wasn't good enough for my master's degree. I was going for a 4.0; taking one course a semester would make that goal more attainable.

Most nights, at 10:30, I was just beginning to open my books. I disciplined myself to spend two hours each evening writing papers and keeping current on reading assignments. I slept from 12:30 to 5:30; then life began all over again. On rare occasions I was able to steal a few hours of homework time from Alchem. More than once, though, I spent precious weekend time completing school-related projects.

I tried to keep school responsibilities separate from family activities. But there were times when I needed input from the children. One such incident occurred soon after I began my graduate studies. I had finished a rather lengthy research paper on the impact of experiential activities on the retention of learning and was scheduled to deliver a fifteen-minute presentation the following week.

One evening at dinner I said to the children, "I need your help. I haven't given a presentation for a grade in many years. I need you to tell me what works and what doesn't work. And I want you to be honest—don't be afraid you're going to hurt my feelings."

I must have sounded pretty pathetic because each child agreed to attend the 3:00 Sunday afternoon practice session. "You bet, Mom." "Yup." "No problem." "Got it down." I was especially looking forward to Craig's feedback since he was planning to come home from school that weekend.

At 2:45 on Sunday, the children began to file past the refrigerator, preparing mid-afternoon snacks to give them the necessary stamina to endure Mama's words. They filed into the living room balancing plates of assorted foods in both hands.

Craig sprawled out on his back next to the piano, the bench straddling his stomach, his plate and pop can balanced precariously on top of the bench. Mike monopolized the couch; he had draped one leg over the upholstered arm and stretched out his other leg across all three cushions, thus preventing his twin brother from joining him. I hadn't even begun my speech, yet he was already glancing at the clock, impatiently waiting for the next fifteen minutes of his life to end.

Tom finally settled down in front of the coffee table, one hand propped under his head and the other clutching Bear's oversized middle. Emily had turned one of the straight-back dining room chairs around so she was facing me. She carefully arranged her legs and feet beneath her, extending her arms and hands straight out in front of her to make sure the tips of her fingers didn't touch. That third coat of Heart Throb nail polish seemed to take forever to dry.

Finally, I was ready to begin. Willing the telephone not to ring, I addressed my offspring in my most professional tone, pretending they were, indeed, members of my first graduate level class. "Good evening. I'm here tonight to share the results of my research with you on the impact of experiential activities on the retention of learning." Within minutes, I sensed my children drifting away from me on a sea of profound boredom.

Undaunted, I continued, gesturing, nodding, smiling, turning to face them squarely at appropriate places, encouraging their mental participation in this lengthy monologue. The presentation ended with a three-minute summary. To their credit, not one of them fell asleep. Nor did the telephone ring.

"At this point in my speech, I would like to facilitate a question and answer session. Who has the first question for me?" I asked, certain no one would respond. No one did. "Well, then, let's move into the evaluation phase," I continued. Stepping out of my role of the student, I said, "It's me again. Mama. Fifteen minutes on the nose! What did you think?"

Except for occasional chewing motions, no one had moved from their original positions. Collectively, they had been a most attentive, polite audience. More silence. "So what did you think?" I repeated, more urgency in my tone.

Still nothing.

After several more moments of silence, Craig lifted the piano bench carefully from his chest, rolled over on his side, pulled himself up on all fours, crawled over to where I was standing and said, "Mom, you talked for fifteen minutes and never moved your upper lip. How did you do that?"

"Craig, you listened to me talk for fifteen minutes and that's all you noticed? That my upper lip never moved?"

"Don't get mad, Mom. I don't want to hurt your feelings. I just want to know how you did it. It's kinda cool, really."

I learned several important lessons about feedback that evening. First, when you ask for feedback, don't be surprised if you hear something you're not expecting to hear. Second, you need to prepare your audience for the kinds of feedback you want to hear. For example, I should have given my teenagers checklists containing information I wanted feedback on: Did I talk too fast or too slow? Were my visuals helpful? Did I have any distracting mannerisms (other than my stiff upper lip, of course)? Third, I learned that while in certain situations children might be an ideal source for feedback, in other instances you need to find an audience with a working knowledge of your subject matter.

My final presentation went well—no thanks to my silent critics. In fact, all of the subsequent courses went well and I ended up with my sought-after straight *A* average. I must admit, though, occasionally Craig's comment about my stiff upper lip comes back to haunt me.

CHAPTER 30

The Lenten Service

Sometimes we choose a position of leadership; other times, leadership is thrust upon us. In an instant we must decide whether or not we want to assume the responsibility of this new, undefined role. We know that leadership requires something of us; it obligates us to make decisions that affect the welfare of others, forces us to take risks, and mandates that the words we speak are in perfect alignment with our value system.

I found myself in an unwanted position of leadership in the spring of 1985. The head pastor at our church had invited six parishioners to give a talk on "The Cross in My Daily Life" during the Wednesday evening Lenten services. As we filed into the pastor's study for a pre-Lenten meeting, we were invited to sit anywhere we wanted. Various Scripture readings had been placed around the long mahogany table.

I sat down and began to read a passage from Romans, Chapter 5, verses 1 through 11. The message was about suffering producing endurance, endurance building character, and character leading to hope. Since all of my waking moments were focused on my upcoming divorce, I wondered how to link this topic to Romans, Chapter 5.

Maybe I could talk about how the divorce would make all six of us grow stronger and closer together. Divorce a positive step? An unorthodox message, to be sure. How would it be received by the congregation? How would my delivering a sermon about the intimate details of our family life affect the children? I left the meeting that day intending to call the pastor and tell him I was simply not up to the task. Instead, messages of hopefulness and survival began to take shape in my head.

I spent the next three days drafting and revising a sermon text. I then tape recorded the speech and slipped the audiotape and a hard copy of the sermon into the pastor's mail slot at church. I expected changes to the text, but the manuscript was returned to me unmarked. Our pastor encouraged me to speak from the heart and assured me our members would take comfort from my words and experiences.

To this day, I can still remember every detail surrounding that evening in early March. In the grip of anxiety, I had bitten every nail down to the quick and anguished over what to do if I had to go to the bathroom in the middle of the sermon. The closer Wednesday evening came, the more I chewed my fingernails and camped on the toilet.

I wore a two-piece green and black knit dress, low-heeled black pumps, and a gold and pearl chain around my neck. On the outside, I looked composed, confident. On the inside, I was panicky, nauseous. The children, unusually boisterous that evening, had showered before dressing for the 7:00 p.m. service. My mom called just before we left the house to wish me good luck.

The scene from the pulpit was daunting. My three younger children huddled nervously in the last pew to the left of the center aisle; only Craig, away at college, was missing. Their father, curious about the content of my sermon, sat in the fifth pew from the front to the right of the center aisle. He was accompanied by a female colleague from the high school where he taught. The church seemed crowded for a Lenten service. Palms sweaty, throat dry, doubting my ability to deliver God's Word, I began my sermon by reading the Bible passage that had prompted me to draft this message.

"We rejoice in our sufferings knowing that suffering produces endurance and endurance produces character and character produces hope and hope does not disappoint us because God's love has been poured into our hearts through the Holy Spirit which has been given to us.

This verse from Chapter 5 of Romans is the basis for my sermon tonight. I will explore the three most important roles I have played in my life—that of a mother, daughter, and wife—as they relate to suffering, endurance, character, and hope."

From a mother's perspective, I shared personal stories of how my children had dealt with suffering as teenagers. From a daughter's perspective, I shared the suffering I went through when my father died. I had saved the most intimate suffering until last, the suffering I endured in the role of a wife.

I then launched into the reasons for the divorce, more to justify my actions to myself than to the congregation at large. I shared stories of how all four of the children, each in his/her own way, had assumed responsibility for the divorce. Craig blamed himself for showing his emotions too much, Mike blamed himself because he frequently challenged the curfew rules, Tom blamed himself because his grades were mediocre, and Emily believed that the volleyball demands on our time had weakened our marriage. I assured the congregation that the children were not in any way to blame for our failed marriage.

There were stories about the suffering and subsequent growth Karl experienced and my belief that our family had grown closer together during these past troubling months. I told everyone how often I had prayed for guidance during this time and how God helped me help Karl. I closed with these thoughts:

"I would like to tell you this story has a fairy-tale ending and we will all live happily ever after. It is true I think we will live happily ever after. But it is also true we will be getting a divorce in just a matter of days. The exciting thing is we are caring for one another and treating one another with respect, concern, and love.

And, so, I leave you with this final thought from Romans, Chapter 5: Hope will never disappoint us, for God's love has been poured into our hearts through the Holy Spirit, which has been given to us. Amen."

The parishioners had been exceptionally quiet and attentive. Had I embarrassed them by this outpouring of highly personal family details? Had I confused them by my outward calm intended to camouflage the pain they surely heard in my words and my voice? Were they shocked our pastor had allowed someone to speak out in favor of divorce from the pulpit?

I remember the stiffness in my legs, two wooden planks holding up my frame. I had forgotten to flex them during the sermon, so intent was I on the task at hand. I looked out at the congregation for the last time. A few people dabbed at their eyes with tissue. Two women, one older and one younger, cried openly.

I pulled the chain on the pulpit light and turned to exit down the side aisle when my attention was drawn to a movement on my right. I froze as I saw my husband moving towards me down the middle aisle, tears streaming down his face. I remember touching the corner of my right eye gently, checking for tears, terrified of the pain in my chest. If I began to cry, it would be a long time before I could stop. Karl stood at the altar steps, waiting for me to join him there. "I love you so much," he said softly. Then he hugged me hard. When he stepped back, he took my hand and we walked down the center aisle together toward the back of the church.

Many people, some strangers, stopped to say thanks on their way out; others hugged me wordlessly. The phone calls began the next day—to the pastor and to me. Some applauded my courage while others chided the pastor for my actions and message.

Four parishioners sent me letters. The first was from a friend; it was dated March 7. On the front of the card was a caricature of a young girl holding a raised glass of wine, the word *LIFE* printed in black letters on her yellow sweat shirt. She smiles as she is pummeled with rain. The caption beneath the picture read, "So, what's the decision?" When I opened the card, my eyes caught the words *Go for It* in bold print. Inside the card was this handwritten message:

> "Dear Katherine,
>
> As I said last night, thanks for sharing your faith with us at St. John's. I could relate to your role as a mother, daughter, and wife. Our three boys are so different from each other and each has his struggles and joys. My father is in good health, and so has a life of his own.
>
> Chris and I have had similar trials the past few years. However, it was my family of strong German ancestry that had no communications skills. I did not know of such things as feelings, let alone sharing those feelings with loved ones. I've grown a lot, and I like the change that has resulted from our struggles. We continue to struggle and to grow.
>
> Good luck in your new roles.
>
> Cindy"

The second letter was from our female pastor, who was also a close friend of mine; it, too, was dated March 7.

> "Again, thank you for your message last night. It was helpful to hear how God continues to support you and your family in the midst of your struggle with the divorce and how God has helped you to have a sense of hope. So many of us need to be reminded of that.

Enclosed is a copy of a confirmand's sermon report from last night. This is only one example of how helpful your shared story was to others.

God bless you, Katherine.

Pastor"

This is the confirmand's sermon report:

THE MOST IMPORTANT IDEA FOR ME IN THIS SERMON WAS

How other people suffer besides me. Like Mrs. Kreher. She has problems with her kids (how they have problems and how they aren't responsible for the divorce).

Mrs. Kreher has problems not just as a mother but a daughter. Her father has passed on and her mother is in pain and has gone through emotional pain so that hurts Mrs. Kreher. As a housewife, she has suffered by her divorce.

THE SERMON MADE ME THINK ABOUT

"I'm not the only one who went through problems and it made me think of my mom's divorce from my first father. I felt it was my fault by being born in the first place. I mean, it's like he didn't want me to be born. And when I was, he left."

About a month later, I received this letter from our senior pastor:

"Dear Katherine,

As our Lenten season draws to a close, I wanted to stop and, once again, say thanks for your gift to us. Your sermon was strong, constructive, uplifting. I continue to hear words of appreciation for it from our people. I shall never forget your eloquence on the cross as suffering love in intimate relations.

Peace,

Pastor"

The opportunity to preach this sermon was a defining moment for me. I realized I had touched Karl, my children, and the members of our congregation in a very personal way. I experienced firsthand how the power of the spoken word, when delivered with clarity and conviction, can influence people's lives. On that Wednesday evening in 1985, I was a leader. I took a risk and spoke from my heart, hoping my message would impact our parishioners. I will never know how many people thought about my words after that evening. I would like to believe that a thirteen-year-old boy had been set free from his past. I would like to believe that he finally realized he was not responsible for his father leaving after he was born. I would like to believe that suffering does, indeed, produce endurance, endurance builds character, and character leads to hope. On that Wednesday evening in 1985, I was filled with hope for a better life for my children and for me.

CHAPTER 31

The Divorce

Another defining moment in my life had arrived—the day I had been anticipating—the day I had been dreading. So much had happened since September when I made the decision to dissolve this marriage: Muffin's death, Craig leaving for college, my pursuing a graduate degree, and the lingering impact of the Lenten Service.

During the past nine months Karl had tried so hard to win me back. In the twenty years we were married, I seldom received a greeting card for a special occasion and gifts were infrequent. Since October, however, I had been the recipient of a variety of carefully chosen gifts: an antique vase from an upscale boutique, a burgundy pantsuit from my favorite dress shop, and countless colorful floral bouquets. Just before Christmas, Karl even volunteered to use some of his vacation days to drive my mom to the Mayo Clinic for an evaluation of her ongoing back problems. On the surface, he appeared genuinely contrite for the mistakes he had made.

Our court date happened to fall on a particularly fragrant spring day, plants and blooms washed anew by an early morning thundershower. Had circumstances been different, I might have opted for a vacation day. Driving into Chicago in the middle of the week and strolling along Lake Michigan with a close friend at my side seemed like a delightfully frivolous outing—which is just what I needed.

I had slept fitfully the night before, unable to fall asleep between the loud snaps and white bursts of lightning. Since 4:10 a.m. I had lain in bed thinking about how different life would be from now on. No one to answer to. No one to take a back seat to. No one to ridicule my shortcomings. Yes, life would be different and definitely better.

It was almost 7:00. Time to shower and dress for the day. What does one wear on the day of a divorce? My black suit, perhaps? Or my new blue dress? After our court appearance, we were having lunch at Berghof's on Adams Street to mark the day of our divorce. Oddly enough, I was concerned about how I looked. I chose the blue dress and fussed with my hair and makeup, consciously rejecting the idea of applying mascara. I knew I would cry before the day was over—most likely more than once.

The best time for a good cry was in the shower. Red-tinged eyelids and slightly distended nostrils could be attributed to the pelting of hot water. So, on this happy-sad morning, standing in the tub of our tiny pink and gray tiled bathroom under a steady stream of too-hot water, tears of relief and tears of sadness flowed freely down my cheeks.

As usual, Karl was punctual. With Emily's bedroom window partially raised, I heard his new white Nissan pull into the driveway. Throwing on a terry robe, I unlocked the front door just as he walked up the porch steps.

Bear, sensing the familiarity of her former owner, wagged her tail expectantly, awaiting her due: some vigorous scratching behind the ears, a belly rub, and a perfunctory pat on the behind to signal the end of her master's show of affection.

I quickly slipped on my clothes, reached for my new go-with-anything purse, gave Bear fresh water and two large dog biscuits, and led the way out of the house into the cool morning air. It was 8:15; we had less than two hours to reach the Civic Center.

The trip downtown was anticlimactic. I'm not sure what I had expected. Karl wondered aloud how we ever reached the point of divorce without his realizing the marriage was heading in that direction. Silently I studied the cars and trucks weaving in and out of the lanes, choosing not to rehash old issues. Karl looked drawn, his oversized nose and heavy brows more pronounced than usual.

"I really thought you would change your mind, you know. You've always been the type to let off steam and then forget about what made you angry. I thought this was just another one of those times. You pushed against me too hard this time—that's why we're where we are now."

He vowed he would never remarry—the pain of the divorce had been too great. He would never allow himself to be so vulnerable with another woman. He had worked so hard, and what he had given to all of us simply wasn't good enough. What did I really want, anyway?

He was partially right, of course. He *had* worked hard for us. Maybe too hard. He had been so caught up in the world of sports and home improvements that he had forgotten what was most important—to love and be loved by his family. He had expressed his love by bringing home twice-monthly paychecks, lining his bookshelves with gold-plated statuettes, and spending endless hours caulking, sanding, and painting.

I had hoped to replicate my parents' marriage. They had been in love during their entire thirty-four year union until my dad died at the age of sixty-one. I'm sure they occasionally disagreed, but my brother and I never witnessed an angry exchange of words. They treated one another with respect and truly enjoyed being together. Theirs was a comfortable, nurturing relationship.

Unexpected construction on the expressway made us late for our 10:00 appointment with my attorney. I say *my* attorney because Karl had chosen not to have an attorney represent him; he balked at having to pay professionals for their services. Lawyers, doctors, accountants—Karl was skeptical of the value they brought to a situation. Even though my lawyer had made it clear to Karl that he could not represent both of us, Karl had adamantly refused separate legal counsel throughout the divorce proceedings.

We walked quickly from the underground parking lot on Michigan Avenue to the imposing structure housing Chicago's legal system. Martin Ross of Ross & Associates was waiting for us outside the courtroom. He told us the judge had a full schedule that morning and to answer his questions as concisely as possible.

We sat near the rear of the courtroom and waited impatiently for our names to be called. As I looked around the room, I thought, "We look smarter than most of the people in this room. Why is this happening to us?" But we really weren't smarter—better educated, better dressed, yes, but definitely not smarter. Like everyone sitting in this courtroom, we hadn't been smart enough to resolve our differences.

Finally, only five people remained in the room: the judge, the court reporter, Martin, Karl, and me. I was very nervous, still wondering if I were doing the right thing. My mouth was dry; I was hoping I wouldn't have to say very much out loud.

"Karl Kreher and Katherine Kreher—please come forward." The judge ordered us to state our names, explain the reason for the divorce, and agree to uphold the directives in the divorce decree. Years of unhappiness distilled into a few micro-seconds of promises that would never be honored and agreements that would later be challenged.

Feelings of anger, sadness, exhilaration, and relief washed over me simultaneously.

Having lunch together at Berghof's after the hearing was decidedly *not* a good idea even though it had been *my* idea. We ordered German Rhine wine and a beef stroganoff special the waitress recommended. The exchange between us was superficial, as if nothing historic had just occurred. We talked about Karl's plans for the summer and improvements that needed to be made on the house over the next few years. We conducted ourselves in a very civilized and courteous manner. I struggled to keep the conversation light, not wanting to show Karl how dark my world looked right now.

When I returned home that afternoon, I began ripping up the brown and beige tweed carpet in the living room, dining room, and hallway, carpeting worn thin by years of child-and-dog traffic. Hours of sanding and staining the hardwood floors underneath would bring them back to life. The project marked a new beginning for me. I felt a strange, yet strong, desire to leave *my* mark on the house.

Looking back on this chapter of my life, I can see how this massive task was a socially acceptable channel for my frustration and overwhelming sadness. How odd that I had chosen a home improvement project as an outlet for my discontent. I used to get so angry with Karl for busying himself with home projects to work out his daily frustration with the children, his students, and me. Now here I was, immersed in my floors, a radio blaring country ballads in the background, trying not to think about the past, the present, or the future.

CHAPTER 32

Health Challenges for
Grandma Rose

By the end of June, less than two months after the divorce, I was physically and emotionally worn out. The initial excitement of studying for tests, writing papers, and preparing for group presentations had faded. The divorce had been difficult. Here I was in the middle of a huge house project; scraping glue from hardwood floors had proven to be a tedious, time-consuming, and thankless task.

On a warm summer evening a week before my forty-second birthday, the phone rang around 10:15. I lifted the handset from the cradle on the first ring, said hello, and then waited. I heard slurred sounds, unnatural pauses, and tentative attempts at conversation. Something had happened to Mom. She said she felt unsteady when she walked and her right hand and arm felt numb. She had difficulty dialing my number and her garbled speech frightened her. Would I come over right now?

"Ma," I said, forcing calmness into my voice. "I love you. You're going to be all right. Listen carefully, Ma. Here's what I want you to do. Are you on the kitchen phone? Yes? Good. Move away from the kitchen steps, Ma. When you hang up the phone, walk slowly to the front door, the *front* door, Ma, okay? Unlock the door. Then sit down in the living room and wait for help.

I'm going to dial 911 first and then Ben next door. Ben will come over and sit with you until the rescue squad arrives. I'm leaving the house right now; I'll meet you at the hospital. Ask Ben to lock up the house. Ma, did you understand everything I said? Okay. I'm going to hang up now and make those calls. I'll see you in half an hour. I love you, Ma. You're going to be just fine."

The short ride to the hospital seemed unduly long. I thought about speeding to attract a police escort but decided against it. Mom was too young to have anything seriously wrong with her, I told myself. Yet she had smoked most of her life, refused to modify her fat-laden diet, and seldom exercised. I willed myself to stay in control of my emotions.

As I pulled into the emergency parking lot, I saw an ambulance parked just outside the double doors in the circle drive. Mom had probably ridden here in this vehicle. Breaking into an uncharacteristic sprint, I reached the entrance and pressed the oversized silver button. The double doors swung open, revealing two paramedics talking to a registration clerk. They looked up as I approached and asked if I were Katherine. I nodded and waited for them to give me a report on Mom's condition. They said they thought she might have had a small stroke, but the doctors were examining her; I would be able to see her in just a few minutes.

Ten minutes, then fifteen, crept by. Still nothing. By this time the paramedics had left, so I asked the receptionist if she could check with Mom's doctor to see how much longer it would be before I could see her. Within minutes I was standing at my mother's bedside. Dressed in a blue and white print gown, propped up against pillows, Mom looked shrunken and tired. She was hooked up to screens that buzzed, blipped, and beeped. The right side of her face, especially the eye and cheek areas, drooped a bit. She forced a half-smile, apologizing for bothering me so late at night.

I stooped to hug her, kiss her forehead. "Ma, I'm sorry I couldn't get here any faster; I wanted to be here when you arrived. Do you want me to call William?"

"No," she said, "let's wait until tomorrow."

The doctors wouldn't know the results of the tests until tomorrow anyway, so I agreed we should wait. Mom was moved to a private room that evening because the hospital was overcrowded and all the double rooms were occupied.

When she had settled in for the night, I pulled up a chair next to her bed. We talked in whispers until the drugs overpowered her. Mom explained she had been watching the news and eating a banana when she decided to go to the kitchen for a glass of ice water. She barely reached the sink when she felt weak and had to lean against the counter for support. She managed to sit down at the kitchen table but felt sweaty and dizzy. When the fogginess cleared, she walked the few steps to the phone to call me.

I spent the entire night watching Mom. A lifetime of Mom stories played out in my head. She was such a great lady. She was my best friend, my champion, the epitome of what I wanted to be for my own children. I always thought I fell short as a mother. I was so driven, impatient, and ambitious. Mom was different; she had always been content in her marriage, her greatest happiness rooted in family relationships and simple pleasures. She liked to sit on the front porch in the evenings and talk to neighbors. She savored the last cigarette of the day and a cup of coffee (milk only) after dinner.

Mom enjoyed the predictability of her day job. She started out as a factory worker at a small wheel cover company just a few blocks from home. Within a few years she was promoted to the position of payroll manager. Friends and family members who worked for larger, more well-known companies tried to lure Mom away with promises of higher hourly wages and more lucrative retirement plans. Mom politely, but firmly, refused their offers. The four-block walk afforded Mom the luxury of having lunch with Dad every day because he worked the second shift. Nothing was more important than spending time with your husband, Mom would say.

By morning I was both agitated and exhausted; I feared the worst. Mom's doctor arrived early and confirmed that she had, indeed, had a slight stroke that affected the right side of her body. The only word I heard was *stroke*. What exactly did that mean? Would her precise speech and beautiful smile return? I wanted Mom to be just as she was before, perfect.

The doctor kept her in the hospital for three days for further testing—just as a precaution, my brother and I were told. When the doctor visited us the morning of the third day, she had a specialist in tow, an oncologist. They had found cancer in Mom's left lung. Since the tests indicated the cancer had not spread beyond the lung area, the medical team unanimously recommended removal of the infected lobe. After scheduling a consultation for the following week, we left the hospital with booklets describing treatment options for lung cancer patients. William and I were stunned by this news.

After several days at home, Mom's speech had markedly improved and the numbness in her limbs had disappeared. It was hard for us to imagine her facing a life-threatening surgical procedure. I refused to think about the possibility of losing Mom. I knew my parents weren't invincible—my Dad had died eleven years earlier. I forced myself to think of mundane issues: work, school, the children, summer activities. But my mind refused to focus on the trivial. I felt sick every time my thoughts drifted to Mom. Did she know how much I loved her? Had I said "I love you" enough times?

The surgery was scheduled for the second week in July. My brother William, Aunt Sophie (Mom's only living sister), and I arrived at the hospital early that morning so we could wish her well before she was wheeled into the elevator. "Don't worry about me. I'll be just…," she said as the doors closed on her final words of comfort.

The three of us walked down a flight of stairs to the cafeteria; we ate bagels, drank coffee, and waited. Two hours passed, then three, then four. When the doctors finally appeared in the doorway of the visitors' room, they motioned us into a small sitting room. The good news was Mom's surgery had been successful and they were confident the cancer had not spread to the right lung. The bad news was Mom's right lung was not working up to capacity and she had sustained another stroke during the surgery, this one much more severe than the first. Once again, we were numb with disbelief. We had prepared ourselves for the surgery, but we were not prepared to deal with a compromised right lung and a second stroke.

Mom spent the next two weeks in intensive care. Each day she was weaned away from another machine, but she was weak and unresponsive to our touch and the sounds of our voices. The doctors couldn't promise that Mom would live— nor could they describe how her life might play out if she *did* live. With her future unknown, we were all actors in a stage play with an ending yet to be written.

Mom's progress was painfully slow. We prayed, we cried, and we planned Mom's funeral. William bought a new suit. I took my black dress to the cleaners.

At the end of the second week, Mom was transferred to a regular room. She no longer required the constant care of the ICU wing, but neither was she able to talk or walk. She seemed to be getting stronger but still needed help feeding herself and using the bedpan.

Another month elapsed. We celebrated mom's sixty-seventh birthday in her hospital room. We brought balloons, presents, a chocolate cake with fresh strawberries and whipped cream, and candles. Mom scribbled *thank you* on a pad of paper with her left hand.

By the end of Mom's sixth week in the hospital, we were told we could make plans to take her home. Her doctors wanted to know what provisions we had made to take care of her at home. "She will require a great deal of care and physical therapy."

The timing could not have been worse. I hadn't healed from the divorce, and my oldest son was about to begin another year of college. I saw my master's degree slipping away and worried I might not be able to fulfill my fall training schedule at work. On top of all this, my floors weren't done. All of my bedroom furniture was crammed into our tiny living room, and the house reeked of stripper fluid and varnish.

My brother and I had two choices—Mom could stay with William or Mom could stay with me. It was an easy decision— Mom would come to stay with me. The twins, juniors in high school and able to drive, could rearrange their schedules so Grandma Rose would never be alone for more than two hours at a time. My manager approved my request for an unusual work schedule. I would start work at 7:00 a.m., take two hours for lunch from noon to 2:00, and stay until 6:00 p.m. each day.

Three therapists visited Mom at home several times a week: one for speech, one for upper body, and one for lower body. Mom still couldn't talk, use her right arm and hand, or walk. She would need to relearn basic sounds, exercise her useless right arm and hand, and take baby steps for the second time in her life.

The weekend before Mom's release from the hospital, Mike, Tom and I finished sanding, staining, and varnishing my bedroom floor. The boys helped me move the bedroom furniture back to its original position. Only the hallway and living room floor remained undone.

Since Mom could not go to the bathroom alone, I decided to move her into my bedroom, which had its own adjoining bathroom. At least I would hear her if she awakened at night and needed my help.

Aunt Sophie also came to stay with us those first few weeks. Just under five feet tall, silver-haired, and demanding, my aunt was an explosion of energy. She shopped, cooked, vacuumed, dusted, and kept Mom entertained during the day.

The frenetic activity of three teenagers, however, tried her patience. Not having children of her own, she was unused to roughhousing, late-night phone calls, and a refrigerator door that seldom stayed closed for more than twenty-two minutes.

Aunt Sophie was an enormous help to Mom. She hovered over her even though the doctors had assured us that Mom was no longer in danger of dying. Mom would simply have to undergo a very lengthy rehabilitation process.

The near-normal schedule we had achieved was broken when I received a frantic phone call from my aunt late on a Tuesday morning. Mom was having trouble breathing, and Aunt Sophie didn't know what to do for her. Trying to calm my aunt on line 1, I accessed line 2 to call 911 and have a rescue squad sent to my home. Then I made one more call. I phoned the high school, told the office secretary there was a family emergency, and asked her to send both of my sons home immediately.

Gathering up my papers and briefcase, I hurried to my car and pulled out onto the highway, ignoring the posted speed limits. I parked on the street, not wanting to block the ambulance in our driveway. My sons pushed through the doorway together to greet me. A paramedic stood in the foyer. "I don't know what to do first: reassure you that your mother is okay or apologize for ruining your floors."

The evening before, I had varnished half of the narrow hallway floor, but it had not had time to dry properly. Black rubber wheel tracks from the metal gurney ran the full length of the hall. Mom was resting comfortably in the portable hospital bed in the middle of the living room, tears running down her cheeks. She was pointing to the hallway floor with her left hand and trying to form the words *I'm sorry.* I crossed the living room and hugged Mom, holding back my own tears. Thank goodness she was okay.

Feeling a huge sense of relief, I turned away from Mom and took in this bizarre scene. The dog, barking wildly in the side yard, lunged repeatedly at the screen door. Bear knew there were strangers in her house; she was letting us know she didn't approve of the intrusion. My aunt fluttered between the kitchen and dining room, dabbing at her eyes with a tissue. The boys, receiving assurances that Grandma was just fine, made sandwiches at the kitchen table. The phone rang continually with inquisitive neighbors offering to help. The paramedics needed to leave. Would I please sign these forms?

I didn't return to work that afternoon. Instead, I offered up prayers of thanks and pondered how I could repair the hallway without resanding and restaining the entire length of flooring.

By the end of two weeks, Aunt Sophie's patience had been severely challenged. We agreed that Mom was doing well enough that Aunt Sophie could return to her home in Chicago. Reluctantly, she said good-bye to Mom. For as long as I could remember, my Aunt Sophie's departures from family gatherings had been predictable rituals. She would say *bye* six, seven, sometimes eight times, in quick succession. She would throw kisses and continue to wave even when she could no longer see the person she was waving to. Saying good-bye to Mom was especially emotional. I'm sure Aunt Sophie wondered if she would see her sister alive again.

Grandma Rose would stay with us for two years. During this time, she received excellent care from three home health therapists and taught her children and grandchildren the true meaning of courage in the face of adversity.

CHAPTER 33

The Letter Years

The letter years began in 1984 after we separated and lasted until Karl's death in 1994. For long periods, perhaps six to nine months, the only form of communication between us was letter writing. I was forbidden to call him at school (my voice upset him), and he generally hung up on me if I called him at home (my voice made him sad). While letters gave each of us an opportunity to express our feelings without the other person interrupting, it was a tedious and cumbersome process for resolving issues. There were many times when I simply needed an answer to a question.

"The sewer is backing up again. I've called Don's Plumbing. Are there other services I should call where you think I can get a better price?"

"Emily needs new volleyball uniforms. Since Grandma Rose and I are paying for her club dues, will you pay for her clothing?"

"Craig's last day of school before Christmas break is Thursday, December 19. That is a vacation day for you. Can you pick him up so I don't have to take a half day off work?"

All simple questions. All needing his input. While the divorce contract was fairly specific on some issues, there was a clause that read, "Karl and Katherine shall work out the details of their daily existence in the best interests of the children." This was a challenge without the use of the telephone.

The summer following our divorce Karl's letters sounded fairly positive and rational, and I actually thought he was making some headway bridging the gap between him and the children. That August Karl made plans to revisit his homeland. One of the first letters we received during his trip to Germany was addressed to all of us; it was both reflective and wistful, somewhat reminiscent of his apologies following an outburst.

"Dear Katherine and Children,

I hope this short note finds everyone healthy and happy. I'm sure your mother (Grandma Rose) must feel much better being out of the hospital.

I'm sitting in my rented car looking at the mountains, Katherine, thinking back to 1982 when you were here with me. I loved you then and I love you even more now. Your friendship and love are what I need and I wish it were possible to have it again someday. I have funny ways of showing my affection, but it is buried deep in my heart.

I sleep alone at night thinking of you and how special you are to me, but your feelings aren't the same. I know I hurt you many times over the years, but I wasn't aware enough to see that. In time, perhaps, your anger will subside and forgiveness will follow. I know that you love me as much as I love you.

Yes, I am still hurting and so are you, but the healing process is slowly beginning with me. I am a different person who recognizes feelings that people have, people like you. I want you most of all, Katherine. You are my best friend and I need you. You are very special to me.

Nothing is ever easy, but if we are both willing to try, there is a chance to come together again. I love you today more than ever before. You aren't perfect, Katherine, but I am willing to accept you as you are.

You must also accept me as I am, or the relationship will not work.

I miss my three sons and daughter. Please tell them I love them and wish them well. They are so special to me; someday I hope to show them how much they mean to me. Spending time with them is about the only way to do it.

Until later on this week, I remain your friend.

Love you,

Karl"

In another letter addressed to *The Kreher Boys*, he wrote,

"Dear Craig, Mike, and Tom,

How are you guys these days? I'm hoping you are being helpful to your mother. Things are probably pretty hectic at times and she needs you very much. I know I can count on you because you have always been dependable.

Pretty soon school will begin for all of us. Craig, you will be going back to college and Tom and Mike, you will be in your last year at Lincoln. I hope to help you in any way possible and perhaps the relationship between father and sons can improve some. I love you all so much.

Your Father

P.S. Say hi to Grandma for me and also to Mom."

At about the same time there was a separate letter addressed to Emily. She was surprised at the warmth of it since her father was not typically demonstrative. She was the only child Karl had invited to accompany him to Germany. We could only speculate on why all four children had not been invited. Airfare to Europe was at an all-time low, and he had the funds to pay their travel costs if he had wanted them to join him.

"Dear Daughter,

I'm sitting here in the post office in West Berlin writing this letter to you. I keep thinking of you and I wish you were here with me—someone to talk to and share things with. Speak to me, Emily. I want so much to hear your voice. I can't wait to see you and give you a big hug and kiss. You are very precious to me, Emily. I feel so proud to be your father.

See you soon and love you so much.

Your Father."

And, finally, a fourteen-page two-sided letter sent to me in the same week. In addition to a description of the day-to-day events of his trip, he included a commentary on his perception of the divorce. He hoped I would admit I made a mistake. Didn't he know I never believed divorce was a *good* option? I simply knew it was a *better* option than staying with someone who continued to create abusive situations.

"Dear Katherine,

I thought three weeks would be so much time, but the days have passed very quickly. I've taken over 130 pictures so far. When I get them developed and organized, I'd like to share my trip with you. I only wish you were along with me because I miss you so much.

How is your mother? My prayers and thoughts are with you, Katherine, as you try to do as much as you can for her. You do love her so—I know that for sure. I hope she is doing much better these days.

I have thought about us quite a bit on this trip. One of your comments that continues to haunt me is, 'The marriage wasn't fair.' Katherine, life isn't fair and keeping a tally sheet on our marriage wasn't the way to develop a relationship. I did this so you get to do that. Everything must be fair. If, indeed, I am correct that you had this mental tally sheet, then no wonder you became so resentful. Maybe if you had not been so compulsive about keeping track of things and being fair, perhaps....

Well, Katherine, we have been divorced now officially for about three months and separated for almost a year. How does your decision rest with you? I would never expect you to admit you might have made a big mistake. I'm sure that you will always come up with more reasons for the divorce—you are something else.

As for myself, I wish you had never done it. Yes, Katherine, you made your choice, but we both lost heavily. I love my family very much and I am lonely for your company; you will never know how much you hurt me by divorcing me. I'd like you to know that I love you very much. I'm being very sincere with you. If, indeed, your feelings for me are still indifferent and you no longer wish to work on our relationship, then I'm ready to accept that decision.

Just as I have learned to love you so much, I can, if I must, learn not to love you. You appear to have turned your feelings off for me, and I have learned how I can do that as well. The choice is ours to love or not to love. Until we see each other again, I remain at least a friend, your friend, your best friend. Yes, Katherine, I still want you, but I don't need you.

With my love and affection,

Karl"

In all, Karl wrote five letters to me that August. Each letter was more heartbreaking than the one before, each filled with assurances that he loved me and wanted to be my friend. In earlier conversations about friendship, Karl had said husbands and wives could not be friends—they could only be husbands and wives. Yet here he was, once again saying the right words, saying the words I had wanted to hear all these years: "I love you, Katherine, and I need you. I want to spend the rest of my life with you." All these declarations of his love for me spoiled by the final words of his fifth letter, "Yes, Katherine, I still *want* you, but I don't *need* you."

CHAPTER 34

Who's in Charge Here, Anyway?

K arl returned home from Germany shortly before the school year began—just in time to wish Craig good luck as he began his sophomore year at college. Craig was loading up the station wagon with crates of clothing, books, and food items when his father stopped by for a visit. We both cautioned Craig to take his studies more seriously. Craig hovered around a *C* average, a dangerous place to be with specialized and more challenging engineering courses awaiting him his junior and senior year. He had spent too much time practicing with the Pep Band and partying with his friends after each victory.

Life in the Kreher household never quite returned to a normal state if, in fact, it had ever been normal. Nevertheless, Grandma Rose, Mike, Tom, Emily, and I fell into a routine that worked for us. Mom and I were always the first ones up in the morning.

No one was able to shower in the bathroom off the master bedroom because the large white plastic squares posing as wall tiles needed replacing. Taking a shower in the back bathroom meant wiping up the floor in the basement laundry room. Thus, the tiny pink bathroom off the hallway became a highly coveted area. Coordinating our daily showers was critical to being on time for work and school.

Because I have always been a morning person, I awoke at 5:30, flipped the switch to *brew* on the coffee pot, and ushered Bear out the kitchen door. Then I helped Mom shower; three months passed before she was stable enough to handle this simple task by herself. I finished dressing Mom and helped her back to bed so she could rest until I brought her breakfast.

While the boiling water saturated the coffee grounds and Bear was outside sniffing under the pine trees enjoying the early morning chill, I took the second shower of the day. Afterwards, I served Mom coffee and wheat toast with grape jelly and counted out her pills. I always put on my makeup and curled my hair in the bathroom off my bedroom, leaving the pink bathroom available for the children. This also gave me an opportunity to engage Mom in conversation. I would talk; in response, she would smile and nod, encouraging me to continue chatting.

Mike and Tom alternated turns for the third and fourth shower of the day. While neither son was a morning person, each had learned a communication skill set that included, "Mornin', Mom, didja sleep well? Um-hmm, that's good." Or "Gotta busy day today? Um-hmm, that's cool." A feeble attempt at civility, but definitely an attempt, which is more that I could say for Emily.

Emily took her shower last. The final bus stop was directly across the street from our house, which meant she could sleep longer than anyone else. The penance for getting more sleep, however, was she had to clean the shower stall, carry all the wet towels down to the basement, and start a load of laundry—every day. Emily made no attempt at civility in the morning. From her bedroom, directly across from the hall bathroom and kitty-corner from my bedroom, she would half-smile and half-wave to Grandma Rose.

The slam of the door and the rush of water told us Emily had begun her day. With the bathroom tidied up, she would retrace the ten steps to her dresser mirror, where she deftly applied eye shadow, mascara, and lip-gloss, and teased and sprayed her hair. Considering she was an athlete, she had a huge head of hair, made even larger by gel and mousse. In junior high, Emily had earned two nicknames: *Springs* because of her ability to jump and *Hair* because its volume dwarfed her narrow, heart-shaped face.

With books and purse balanced under her right arm (like her brother Mike she was left-handed), she paused momentarily over the kitchen sink to eat two buttered pieces of white toast with Cheese Whiz and drink a cup of coffee with extra cream and two heaping teaspoonfuls of sugar. Our eyes met briefly, heads bending forward slightly to acknowledge one another's presence. Then she was gone. From start to finish, hers was a routine that took twenty-seven minutes. Like clockwork, twenty-seven minutes.

That fall, when Mike and Tom became seniors, a strange phenomenon occurred in our household. Almost simultaneously, each twin decided he should be head of household. I'm sure their collective reasoning made sense to them. It almost made sense to me. They were upper classmen. They were tall and strong. They were in charge of outside work—putting up and taking down the heavy wooden storm windows, washing and storing screens, trimming the hedges, and mowing the lawn—all of which required a degree of muscle and bulk. They had also risen to the challenge of helping out with Grandma Rose. But only parents can be parents. Since neither Mike nor Tom could be the parent, there were times when I had to practice tough love.

Mike

I became obsessed with the possibility of losing Mike. That's how the scenario played out in my head—I would be losing Mike. We had promised the children they could choose the parent they wanted to live with each August before the school year began. Once the decision was made, however, they had to stay with that parent the entire year, thereby reducing the possibility of playing off one parent against the other.

Ultimately, Mike decided to stay with us every year. No doubt peer pressure from his siblings factored into his decision as well as proximity to the high school. I would like to think that Mike, even though he identified strongly with his dad, also stayed because of me. While he didn't agree with all my parenting techniques, he knew how much I loved him, and I knew how much he loved me. Much later, when Mike and I would talk about the years following the divorce, he would say that he could have convinced his dad to go for medical help if he had lived with him.

Mike pushed the envelope. Like many school athletes, Mike had acquired a fondness for alcohol: beer, wine, and, sometimes, hard liquor. Neither Karl nor I were drinkers, so we harped on the dangers of drinking and driving, citing countless newspaper articles describing the addictive nature of alcohol and the horrible consequences that could occur when drinking preceded driving. Yet peer pressure has a strange pull of its own.

On this particular New Year's Eve, I had given Mike permission to go to a friend's house for a party. I had phoned the parents the week before, and they had assured me they would be home the entire evening.

About 6:00 p.m. on New Year's Eve, snow began falling, so a few of us parents had arranged to drive the boys to the party. By 10:00 that evening, the snow had become heavier, making visibility poor and the roads treacherous. New Year's Eve had always been a holiday I disliked. Being on the road was especially risky. Even if *you* hadn't been drinking, what guarantee was there that the other person was sober? At 1:30 a.m., Mike's curfew, the phone rang. The parent who was supposed to pick up Mike and two of his friends called to say Mike had left the party at 11:00 with two friends and gone to another person's house.

I was furious. Mike knew that roaming was not acceptable unless he called home to let me know he had gone somewhere else. I had the phone number for one of his friends; I dialed the number, waking the mother. She said she had no idea where her son was because he was supposed to be staying with his father for the weekend. She said she assumed everything was just fine. She did, however, provide me with the phone number and address of the boy whose house they had gone to.

I dialed the number. No answer. I dialed the number again. Still no answer. I looked out the window and saw nothing but white. It was now almost 2:00. Craig and Emily, asleep for almost an hour, were oblivious of my predicament. Tom, watching a movie in his bedroom, was still awake. He noticed how twitchy I had become.

"Let's go get him, Mom," Tom said.

"But, Tom, we could get stranded or have an accident on the way."

"Not with me driving, we won't. Come on, Mom. I'll back the car out."

Tom pulled the old station wagon out of our driveway, turned onto the slick highway and half-drove, half-slid to the next town. At no time did our speed exceed twenty miles per hour. Luckily, we passed few cars on the road. When we were within two blocks of our destination, we saw three figures walking toward us in the middle of the street. None of them wore hats, gloves or boots. Talking loudly and elbowing one another, the boys were unaware of our vehicle approaching them. We slowed down and pulled over to the curb. Tom lowered his window as we approached and recognized Mike as one of the three.

"Come on. Get in. You boys must be frozen," I hollered, motioning them to get in the back seat.

"Mom, what are you doing here?" Mike asked.

"Do you know what time it is?" I replied.

"But, Mom, it's New Year's Eve. Chill out!"

"I *am* chilled out, Mike. In fact, I'm freezing. Damn it, get in!"

Mike climbed in the back seat, letting in a waft of frigid air. The other boys, neither of whom I knew, ignored my invitation for a ride.

No one said much on the way home. I smelled the stench of alcohol mixed with the sweetness of Juicy Fruit gum behind me. Why do teenagers think they can camouflage alcohol with chewing gum or breath mints?

I grounded Mike for two weeks.

After the New Year's Eve incident, the tension between Mike and me increased. He began coming home late. The children had a fifteen-minute leeway on their curfew, but, beyond that, they were grounded. Historically, Mike arrived home within the fifteen-minute grace period, but now he was coming home twenty, twenty-five, and even thirty minutes late. According to Mike, there was always a good reason: the driver needed to take someone else home first, the party started late, he had to help the host clean up. On and on it went.

The second time he was more than thirty minutes late, I said, "Look, I'm tired of these excuses. You need to be home within fifteen minutes of your curfew or you'll be grounded the following weekend."

The next weekend he came in late and drunk; I grounded him. Mike complained about life being unfair, but he stayed in both Friday and Saturday evenings and worked on homework assignments.

The following weekend he broke curfew again. He came home more than thirty minutes late; I grounded him again. This time he balked, telling me I had no right to keep him home when all his friends were allowed to go to parties and drink. I told him his friends weren't *my* children and I didn't much care what they did. He stomped around the house that weekend, letting me know how much he disliked being disciplined.

In mid-February, after several more incidents of his coming home late and drunk, I finally said, "I've had it. One more incident and you're off the basketball team for the remainder of the year."

"You can't do that to me, "he challenged. "It's a school sport and I have to play or the whole team will suffer."

"I *can* and *will* take you off the team if you don't cooperate," I responded calmly. "Watch me."

Mike was extraordinarily polite all week. That Saturday night, however, he evidently could not control his drinking. He came home late again. As always, I was lying on the couch in the living room, waiting up for the boys to arrive home safely. When Mike walked in, I said, "Hey, Mike. I'm glad you made it home okay. You're late. We'll talk in the morning."

"There's nothing to talk about," he retorted.

"We'll talk in the morning," I repeated calmly and walked down the hallway to my bedroom. During my years as a parent, I learned never to argue with a child when a) you are tired, b) you are angry, or c) the child has been drinking. In this particular situation, all three conditions applied.

The next morning I went to the 9:30 church service. Before I left, I placed a note on the kitchen table: "Family meeting at 11:00; your presence is required. Love, Mom."

When I walked into the living room at 10:50, the two boys and Emily were sitting in the living room waiting for me. I hung up my coat and bent down to scratch Bear's ears. For several weeks, I had been mentally preparing a short speech to address how the boys, especially Mike, were trying my patience more than usual. While I didn't like the idea of any of them going to live with their father, I was ready to accept that scenario as a possibility. I told my three younger children I loved them and emphasized that, from now on, all house rules would be strictly enforced. No second, third, fourth, or fifth chances. I asked if anyone had questions. No one did. Then I said, "Now I need to talk to Mike alone." Tom and Emily made a quick exit.

I moved next to Mike, who was sitting on the sofa. "I love you, Mike, and I'm not sure what is going on inside your head, but what has been going on inside this house between you and me is going to stop. It needs to stop now. You're through with basketball for the rest of the year, Mike. I've tried to cut you some slack on this curfew issue, but you're just not getting it. You need to accept the fact that I'm the parent and you're the child. End of story. I don't care how many pounds you can lift, how fast you can run, or how many baskets you can make in a row. You are still my son and you will do as I say as long as you live with me." I paused, hoping he would comprehend the full impact of my comments.

"I plan to call my boss at home tonight to let him know I'll be late for work tomorrow. I will stop by Lincoln first thing in the morning and talk to Mr. Stuart, Coach Meyer and Coach Sullivan. They will support me, Mike; they may not like what I'm doing, but they *will* support me. I talked to Mr. Stuart several weeks ago and told him you may not finish out the season. He said he would talk to you about your routine of coming home past curfew. Did he do that, Mike?"

Mike, carefully studying the weave of the sofa fabric, nodded his head.

"So Mr. Stuart warned you and I warned you, but you didn't think I would follow through on my threat. You think you should be able to call your own shots. I'm not afraid of you, Mike. Sometimes I think you want me to be afraid of you and your angry outbursts. I love you, Son. I want you to continue living with me. Having the four of you as my children has been the very best part of my life. But right now, this minute, I am not having the best time of my life. My heart goes out to you, Mike. You are a troubled young man. You keep your feelings bottled up inside of you until suddenly you unleash your frustration in a stream of threats and insults. That's not healthy. Talk to me, Mike. I'm your mother. What's going on? What are you thinking?"

Mike, dressed in cut-offs and a torn jersey, got up from the couch and headed towards the bathroom. I heard him take a tissue from the box and blow his nose. When he came back into the living room, he said, "I've got nothing to say to you, Mom. I just wish you would reconsider. I haven't done anything that awful. I'm not a bad person." He disappeared into his bedroom and closed the door.

I wiped the tears from my eyes with my fingertips and decided to fix myself a cup of tea. I was dreading tomorrow. It could be an ugly scene if his father decided to join the meeting.

Monday morning I left the house forty-five minutes early. I pulled into the high school parking lot just as Joey, the custodian, was unlocking the front doors. We waved to one another, but on this particular morning I was not interested in making small talk. I headed straight to the administration office. Mr. Stuart had just arrived; he shook my hand warmly and asked me how I was doing. I told him I could be doing better and asked him if he had some time for me. He invited me into his office and closed the door.

"I'm pulling Mike off the team for the rest of the season," I said. "His behavior hasn't improved at home, and I'm out of options."

Mr. Stuart rested his clasped hands on his oversized oak desk, leaned forward, and spoke softly. "You know the team could lose the state championship without Mike."

I followed the activity of our sports teams closely and knew that what Mr. Stuart was saying was probably true. "I would be sorry if that happened," I said. "But Mike leaves me no choice. He has had plenty of chances; we've had many talks about his coming in late and challenging my authority, and, quite frankly, I'm at the end of my rope."

"I respect your decision," he replied. "Let me call in the coaches, and we'll explain the situation to them." He made a few phone calls. Within ten minutes, the varsity and junior varsity coaches joined us in Mr. Stuart's office. Two minutes later Karl appeared. One of Mike's friends had told Karl he had seen me in the front office.

The varsity coach was antagonistic. Looking straight at Karl, he challenged my authority to make this call. "Karl, are you in support of this idea? I've never heard of anything so crazy. Without Mike, we don't have a chance at the state championship."

Karl shifted in his chair, cleared his throat, looked straight at me, and said, "If you can't control Mike, why not have him live with me? I'm sure I can do a better job of parenting."

I wanted to laugh out loud and scream at him at the same time. Forcing an even tone, I reminded him of the agreement that the children could only change places of residence in August. This was February and, therefore, no living arrangements would change any time soon.

After about fifteen minutes of discussion, the junior varsity coach, silent until now, commended me for setting and enforcing consequences for Mike's behavior. He agreed the bigger parenting issue was more important than winning a state championship. The meeting ended with Mike not being allowed to suit up for practices or games. He could, however, sit with his teammates and help coach as long as he met his curfew the remainder of the season.

Word traveled around the school quickly. By noon everyone knew Mike's mom had come to school for a special meeting. Humiliated and hurt, Mike refused to talk to me that evening. And the next evening. By the end of the week, he was talking to me through Tom. "Tell Mom we need more orange juice, will you, Tom?" he would say with the refrigerator door in its normal open position. "Ask Mom if I can have a ride to school tomorrow. I need to be there half an hour early." The situation would have been comical had it not been so sad.

From his seat on the bench, Mike watched his team lose the state championship. In the end, I was blamed for the loss. Actually, I did feel bad the team lost, but I didn't feel bad about the position I had taken. I was disappointed in *me*—it had taken me too long to take a stand.

Tom

Tom had been a rebel since junior high. He desperately wanted to be noticed by his father. His academic scores were average and he was not as quick and agile as his brothers, both marks of failure according to his dad. Tom might have pursued a career in music, but his father scoffed at the arts, saying he wouldn't spend his hard-earned money paying for one of his sons to play a horn in college.

With Karl continuing to disapprove of his future plans, Tom began focusing on his birthmark again. Most mornings, while getting ready for school, Tom would curse his forehead. "F___ my face. F___ this birthmark. I hate my f___ing life."

He was using a heavy pancake makeup on his forehead that had to be blended into the surrounding skin. If the cream were applied carelessly, the outline of the birthmark was more pronounced. When Tom perspired during gym class, the beads of sweat caused the makeup to run. When he spent too much time outdoors, the skin surrounding the birthmark tanned, making the birthmark appear pinkish in color and more obvious.

Tom still enjoyed tinkering; it was a welcome diversion for him. He loved working with tools and signed up for every shop class at school. Occasionally he was able to reassemble an item after taking it apart.

With Grandma Rose living with us, we had three cars at our disposal. I was driving the new Chevy station wagon Karl and I had purchased just before we divorced. Mike was driving Grandma's 1974 Opal, and Tom, by choice, was driving the old beat-up wagon.

Late one Friday afternoon, I received a frantic phone call at work from Karl, who had stopped over at the house to collect a few items he had left behind. "Where are your children?" he yelled.

"What did you say?" I heard myself ask, trying to process this request. His question made no sense.

"Mike, Tom, Emily. Where are they?" This seemed like such a stupid question to me since he was at the house packing up his math texts and I was twenty minutes away at work.

"You better come home right away. All four car doors from the old wagon are lying on the back lawn. Betsy Schultz just called to say Tom, Billy, and Emily just picked up Dana to go for a ride. She noticed there were no doors on the car. Don't you have any control over these kids? Maybe you ought to quit your job. And Mike didn't show up for practice after school today."

I told my boss I was leaving early to resolve a family crisis. On the way home, I kept wondering why Karl was suddenly so concerned about the children's welfare. He had been completely disinterested in their activities for the past few years. I pulled into our driveway just behind Tom. He was sitting in the driver's seat with a huge grin on his face. "This is great! What do you think, Dad?"

With slow and deliberate steps, his father walked over to the car, bent down close to Tom's face, and whispered, "Are you trying to get everyone killed?"

"Oh, no, Dad. Look, we're all wearing seat belts." Karl stepped back onto the lawn, told Billy to go home, and ordered Emily and Dana to call Dana's mother and tell her Dana was okay.

"Tom," I said, trying to control my voice, "what do you think you're doing?"

"We were just having some fun, Mom. I saw this program on TV a few weeks ago, and these kids were driving around in a car like mine without doors and I thought it would be a cool thing to do. It really *was* cool, Mom. Want to go for a ride?"

"It is definitely not cool, Tom. And, no, I do not want to go for a ride. You are now without a car for two weeks. That's not a very cool thing, either. How are you going to get the doors back on?"

"No problem, Mom. I took them off—I can put them back on." Tom pulled the car into the back yard, turned up the stereo in the garage, and began working on the doors. He managed to reattach the doors, but they never worked quite right.

Teenage boys seldom let on that they are upset about a punishment. It wasn't cool to whine. Tom refused to talk about his punishment. With the doors back on the frame, Tom parked the wagon in the garage, and there it sat for two weeks.

We had another incident with the old wagon, which hurried its demise. In addition to the shower routine in the morning, we had another routine in the evening. I always parked my car in the garage. The boys parked their cars in the driveway in the order in which each of them left for school the next day—the first one out in the morning parked at the end of the driveway.

One evening, however, the three vehicles were not lined up in the driveway in the proper order. I had an early morning meeting the next day, which meant I would have to move the other two cars in the morning before I could pull out. Tom had parked the wagon closest to the street and Mike's car was in the middle. The next morning I unlocked the driver's side of Tom's car, slid inside, and inserted the key in the ignition.

The vehicle turned over on the first try, but I stared in puzzlement at what was in front of me. The steering wheel was missing. The steering column and the three spokes of the wheel were still there, but the wheel itself was gone. Furious, I walked back inside the house to find Tom in the pink hallway bathroom with the door locked. Mike, knocking quietly on the door, whispered, "Tom, you jerk. It's my turn to take a shower first today." Tom, hearing my footsteps in the hallway, didn't respond.

"Tom," I said. No answer. "Tom," I said, a little louder. No answer. "Tom, you're in deep shit. Unlock this door and talk to me."

Just then the toilet flushed, the doorknob turned slowly, and a sheepish Tom emerged from the bathroom.

"Explain," I said.

"Would you believe I saw it on another TV show?"

"No, I wouldn't. Here's the deal. I'm taking your car keys to work with me today. You've just lost your driving privileges again. Tonight we find a junk dealer who will take the car off our hands. You and Mike can share Grandma's car—if I ever decide to let you drive again."

"No way!" yelled Mike, the pulsating shower spray muffling his voice. "Just because he's a jerk doesn't mean I have to be punished, too!"

Watching the junk dealer haul away his station wagon three days later made a lasting impression on Tom. He treated our vehicles with greater respect and sat down with his twin brother to draft a workable plan to share the use of Grandma Rose's Opal.

CHAPTER 35

No Take Backs

At a distance, Emily watched the grief her brothers were giving her father and me. She saw firsthand the shoving, name-calling, and resistance to help with household chores. Fortunately, she chose a different path and stayed focused on her volleyball goals. I only remember her veering off course in high school once—and I was to blame for the mishap.

The summer after her freshman year in high school, Emily began dating a young man named Jake. He was every mother's delight: bright, clean-cut, and respectful; he was absolutely crazy about Emily. Jake was a frequent visitor in our home. Whenever I would greet him at the front door, he would always say, "Hi, Mrs. K. How are you? It's good to see you. Is there anything I can do for you today?" I loved Jake and even though he and Emily were young, I allowed myself to fantasize about the possibility of Jake being my son-in-law some day.

On a warm Saturday afternoon in July, I decided to make five pounds of meatballs (Grandma's recipe) and a huge pot of angel hair spaghetti—the heat never seemed to affect the children's appetites. With the meatballs simmering on the back burner, I hurried to the grocery store, returning with three plastic bags of salad fixings and fresh Italian bread. Jake had decided to join us for dinner. Within five minutes of our sitting down at the table, the children began teasing one another and pretending to flip meatballs and spaghetti at one another. Before I could get the words "Stop this nonsense" out of my mouth, the first meatball flew across the kitchen table. Then another and then another. Some of the meat and red sauce landed on their clothing, the kitchen walls, the tile floor, and Bear's back.

I suppose I should have seen the humor in all of this, but all I saw was more work. I had already spent several hours making the meatballs and I had no intention of spending several more hours cleaning up the kitchen. Losing control, I yelled, "If I had it to do all over again, I would never have had children. I'm going for a walk—a *long* walk. By the time I get back, this kitchen damn well better be spotless!"

I reached for a paper towel, swiped it across the orange stains on Bear's black fur, picked up her leash, grabbed my sneakers, and headed for the front door. Sitting on the front stoop tying my laces, I heard the noise and laughter from the kitchen increase in volume. I sought out my friend Kitty—we often commiserated on the dubious joys of parenthood. When I returned home, the kitchen was in pristine condition. The children had stored the leftover food in Rubbermaid containers and washed and dried the dishes. I could see the three boys playing a game of horse in the back yard.

Jake had gone home after dinner. Emily, who, according to her brothers, had retreated to her bedroom after cleaning up her share of the mess, was nowhere to be found. After about ten minutes, the boys and I began to look for her—inside the house, downstairs in the basement, around the corner at a friend's house. Her brothers rode their bikes through the neighborhood, calling her name. After phoning a few of her girl friends, I set out by car to try to find her. Then I remembered Jake had come for dinner. I dialed his number; Jake's mom answered the phone. She told me Emily was safe, but that she wasn't ready to come home just yet. Jake's mom asked permission to keep Emily overnight. Emily had taken my hurtful words to heart. She believed that I sincerely regretted having had four children.

When Emily returned home the next morning, her face was still blotchy and swollen. She walked past me, avoiding my eyes, closing her bedroom door ever so softly. Sometimes I can still hear Emily's muffled whimpering. I don't remember how many months it took to heal the wounds I had inflicted. Maybe wounds as deep as these never heal. How many times would I need to assure her that my words were spoken out of anger, that not once had I ever regretted being the mother of these four children. How many times would I have to say, "I love you, Emily," before the memory of that awful afternoon dimmed. It was a hard-learned lesson for me—bitter words spoken in a rage can *never* be erased.

CHAPTER 36

Ron

Ralph Waldo Emerson once said, "A friend may well be reckoned the masterpiece of nature." Ron was such a friend.

Six months after the divorce was final, Alchem sent me to Baltimore and Atlanta to deliver a customer service program I had developed for our sales and service branches. The program was highly experiential, which meant it was fun to facilitate. Workshop attendees engaged in small group activities, role plays, paper and pencil activities, and games. I had set the stage for high energy and enthusiasm in the classroom.

I flew out to Baltimore on Halloween, the day before my presentation. I landed at Baltimore Washington International airport about 1:30 in the afternoon, early enough to rent a car and meet everyone at the plant. Some of the customer service representatives were dressed in costumes and masks; bowls of shiny red apples, miniature candy bars, and caramel popcorn balls decorated each work station.

As I greeted everyone individually at his/her desk, I commented on a picture hung on the wall, a piece of memorabilia on a shelf, or the tidiness of the work space. The last person I met was a long-time Alchem employee, Ron Hanson. Observing the friendly banter between him and his coworkers, I surmised he was the office jokester.

When I reached his cubicle, he stood up, extended his hand, and introduced himself. I shook his hand and looked around his work area. No pictures, no plants, no memorabilia.

A heavily used zip code directory lay open on one side of his desk. On the other side were a sheaf of papers with illegible scribbling next to columns of names, a telephone, a cup of coffee, and a partially eaten candy bar.

"Where are all your mementos?" I asked.

He grinned sheepishly. "I have no life, so I have no pictures."

As I finished my rounds, I made mental notes of the information I had gleaned during these brief, yet intimate, moments with each person—fodder for establishing a spirit of camaraderie and drawing some laughs during the training session the next day. The workshop was to be held in a conference room at the hotel where I was staying, so I decided to set out my materials before dinner. If I moved quickly enough, I would have time for a hot shower and seven hours of sleep, the most blessed of all gifts for a trainer.

Surprisingly, my last thoughts before falling asleep that evening were of Ron in his faded jeans and pilled, light blue sweater. Beneath the self-deprecating remarks, I sensed a man who was quick-witted, down-to-earth, and compassionate.

Facilitating workshops always gave me a natural high. I am definitely an introvert, but when I'm in front of a group, I am transformed into a gregarious entertainer, feeding upon the energy of the group. Most days I'm good—some days I'm even *very* good. On this particular day I was very good. Everything worked. The material flowed well, my transitions were smooth, the activities were entertaining yet educational, and the group was thoroughly engaged. Even the afternoon session, which can sometimes drag for those suffering from food coma, passed quickly. I knew the ratings on the evaluation forms would be impressive.

Following the program, I met with the business unit manager to review the day's activities. Since my return flight wasn't scheduled until Sunday morning, I took my time retrieving my markers and repacking the sets of extra handouts. As I made my way to the elevator, I was surprised to see Ron waiting for me.

"You mentioned your flight wasn't until tomorrow. If you have no plans for the evening, I'd like to take you to dinner."

Plans? What plans? I didn't know a soul in Baltimore. I had been looking forward to a check-in phone call with my children, a hot shower, and a pay-per-view movie in my hotel room.

"That would be very nice. Thank you. I'd like that," I heard myself say.

He suggested an Italian restaurant in another part of the city. He planned to go home to shower and shave, promising to return to the hotel by 7:30 to pick me up.

At 7:20 Ron rapped on my door. I opened the door, unprepared for this new Ron. He had traded in his comfortable work clothes for a pair of freshly shined cordovan loafers, gray-brown dress slacks, an off-white, button-down collared shirt, and a brown tweed sport coat. He looked very handsome; I could detect a mixture of scents: soap, peppermint, and musk.

We talked nonstop the entire evening—about our families, our careers, our hobbies—and the divorce. I found myself describing painful details I had not shared with anyone. Here was a gentleman I felt I could trust who was both non-judgmental and willing to listen.

When we returned to the hotel, he walked me up to my room, stepped inside to switch on the light, took me in his arms, and kissed me. I kissed him back. It would have been easy to yield to his increasingly demanding caresses, but my professional side resisted. Breaking the embrace, I thanked him again for the evening and told him I was suddenly very tired and needed to get some rest. It had, in fact, been a tiring day. Training was like that, energizing and enervating at the same time.

The next morning about 11:00 my phone rang. Instinctively, I knew it would be Ron.

"I just called to thank you for last night and to tell you to have a safe trip home today. Would it be okay to call you this week at work?"

"Sure," I said. I'd like that."

At first, we talked on the company tie line several times a week. Then it became a once-a-day ritual. By Christmas we were talking to one another several times a day and sometimes on weekends. We both acknowledged that long-distance relationships were futile, destined for failure, yet we continued to allow our emotions to override logic.

In January we made plans to get together. He would fly out to see me Valentine's Day weekend. My children and mother were shocked to hear of my plans. They knew I had met someone special in Baltimore, but they never thought this prim and proper woman would spend a weekend with a gentleman from another state, especially one they hadn't met.

The long-awaited weekend together was a fiasco. An ice storm delayed Ron's flight; I sat at O'Hare for four hours waiting for his plane to arrive. Since Ron had eaten only a snack on the plane, he was hungry. We stopped at an all-night diner; within two hours the food had made him queasy and given him diarrhea.

By the next morning, Ron had recovered from the food poisoning. We drove to a nearby forest preserve and spent most of the day walking the trails and talking. We discovered we had quite a lot in common: a fierce commitment to our respective families, dedication to a hard work ethic, the ability to talk about feelings with one another without fear of censure. I had found someone I could push against verbally and intellectually. We differed on political, social, and religious issues, yet we respected the opinion of the other person. I encouraged him to dream about and plan for his future, and he taught me to live more fully in the present.

We spent many more long weekends together. Our favorite vacation spots were Door County and Madeira Beach. Door County because we loved the serenity of the pines and lakes and Madiera Beach because we could set up housekeeping for a week where no one could find us and walk along the Gulf shoreline as often as we wanted. Because Ron was not burdened with parenting responsibilities, he did most of the flying and most of the paying. I offered to pay for meals and airfares whenever possible, but Ron assumed responsibility for most of our travel expenses.

Aside from the precious gift of his presence in my life, I appreciated his ability to see each situation within the framework of a broader perspective. When I complained about any of the children, he was able to reframe an incident in terms of the overall maturity of each child. When I expressed concern about my mom's physical well-being, he encouraged me to think about the progress she had made thus far.

Ron offered me unconditional friendship and emotional support at a time in my life when my self-worth was at an all-time low. I was physically exhausted; my life consisted of going to work, studying for exams, caring for my mother, doing housework, helping with homework, and preparing meals.

When I met Ron, I was emotionally worn out. I was angry that the lives of my friends seemed so much easier. *They* hadn't been forced to choose between their husbands and their children. Clearly, they had made better life choices. Why hadn't I listened to my father? In his gentle way, he had warned me Karl and I would have problems in our marriage, but I thought I had all the answers. I believed that love conquered all—that if you loved someone enough, you could work through your differences.

It frightened me sometimes to realize I had been crying without remembering exactly when the tears had begun to fall. The time I spent with Ron was therapeutic. He helped heal my wounds.

As our relationship blossomed, I felt an increasing need to close the circle. I wanted to be a whole family again. Ron had never experienced parenthood, never owned a house, and never lived more than twenty minutes from his childhood home. Yet, somehow, I expected this man to marry me, move 1200 miles from his parents, and find a new job in the northwest suburbs of Chicago.

CHAPTER 37

Yet Another Divine Intervention

Ron came to visit several more times before I introduced him to Mike and Emily. Ron and I stayed at local hotels when he was in town—there was just too much commotion at home with Mom's therapists visiting her several times a week, Mike commuting back and forth on weekends from college, and Emily totally absorbed in achieving her volleyball goal.

Tom had joined the Army right after high school graduation and Craig, finding himself on academic probation after his sophomore year, refused our offer to send him to an instate university. In what he would describe later as one of his more impetuous acts, Craig, like Tom, joined the Army. Angry at how their young lives were turning out, both sons put in for overseas duty. After boot camp, Tom was stationed in Brussels, Belgium, and Craig was sent to Vilsek, West Germany. At least one weekend a month, the boys scheduled trips that enabled them to travel through Europe together.

Mike and Emily, during our weekly phone calls to the boys, openly shared their opinions of Ron. He was described as a "geek," "a mild-mannered guy but weird," "a nonjock," and "studious—he knows a lot about the Civil War." The fact that Ron was not an athlete was the biggest black mark against him. The children simply could not understand how I could be attracted to someone so unlike their father.

Similarly, I could not understand how Emily could be attracted to the new man in her life. During the summer before her junior year, she began dating a gentleman named

Sam. Like Jake, Sam was very bright and handsome—he even had a sense of humor. Clean-cut he was not. He came to visit in worn-out khaki shorts, baggy tee shirts, and was frequently shoeless. His image did not reflect his family's social status—Sam simply rebelled against convention. More importantly, Sam, though 18, did not drive a car. Much later I learned he had received a DUI and his license had been rescinded.

One Friday evening Emily had driven over to Sam's to pick him up so he could take her out to dinner and a movie. Her curfew was midnight. At 12:15, Emily had not returned home. I called Sam's number, expecting to hear Mr. or Mrs. McGrath on the other side. Instead, I heard a groggy male voice say, "Hullo?"

"Sam?" I queried, wondering where Emily was if he had, in fact, been asleep. "I just wondered where Emily was—it's past her curfew. She's usually very good at being home on time."

"Yes, Ma'm." said Sam, a bit more alert. "She's on her way home right now, Ma'm." I heard a click, indicating our brief conversation was over.

Twenty-five minutes later, a sheepish Emily pulled the old station wagon into the driveway.

"Hi, Mom. I'm really sorry I'm late. There wasn't anything good at the movies, so we went to Olive Garden and then to Blockbusters to rent a video. We fell asleep watching the movie. Sorry I'm late." She kissed my forehead, headed to the refrigerator for some Gatorade, and waved good-night.

Three hours later I was awakened by Tom. The headlights of a squad car in our driveway had roused him. I wrapped myself in a cotton robe and hurried down the hall to the front door.

"Is this your car, Ma'm?" one of the officers asked. It was the third time I had been addressed as Ma'm in less than twenty-four hours.

"It is," I said. "Is there a problem?"

"Do you know how all this grass and mud got on the left front tire?" the second officer asked.

"No, I don't," I replied.

"Were you the last person to drive this car tonight?" the same officer continued.

"No, my daughter took the car to her boyfriend's house earlier this evening."

"Can we talk to your daughter then?" the officer asked. Clearly there was a purpose to his line of questioning.

"Yes, I can get her." Emily's bedroom window was adjacent to the driveway, so when Tom headed down the hallway to wake her, she was already dressed in a tee shirt and shorts. When I saw her arms folded across her chest, shoulders hunched, and tears rolling down her cheeks, I knew I was not going to like what I was about to hear.

By this time the officers were standing inside our tiny foyer; Bear lay at my feet, exhausted from barking at our unexpected visitors. Looking directly at Emily, the first officer asked, "Were you in the vicinity of Lake Street and Dogwood Avenue this evening? Do you know anything about the race track sign being knocked down? A resident in that area said he heard the squeal of brakes and a loud crash in his front yard. It seems a vehicle just like your wagon hit the race track historical marker and then left the scene of the accident. Do you know anything about this incident?"

Emily admitted she was in a hurry to get home because it was after curfew. She hadn't realized she was driving so fast. When she turned right onto Lake from Dogwood, the car spun out of control and hit the sign. Yes, she knew she should have stopped; she knew she had hit the sign. No, she didn't realize she had destroyed a historical marker.

The officers drove Emily and me to the police station so they could give her a breathalyzer test. Yes, there was alcohol in her system. "I only had one beer," she told the officers. We signed a number of documents, including a promissory note indicating we would reimburse the village for the desecrated historical marker and for the repairs to the lawn surrounding the marker. Emily and I both signed the note, but Emily paid the bill in its entirety. Fortunately, there had been no damage to our wagon.

The truth was that Emily and Sam had each downed several bottles of beer. They had fallen asleep on the couch watching a movie and lost track of time. My phone call had awakened them. Her judgment dulled by a combination of fatigue and alcohol, Emily had dozed off at the wheel, driven through a stop sign and over a curb, and brought the wagon to a stop after hitting the sign. Terrified, she had left the scene of the accident without thinking of the ramifications of her decision.

I have several memories of that evening: I remember being very grateful that my daughter was alive and that no one had been hurt or killed. I also remember a conversation Emily had with Sam the next day telling him she didn't want to see him any more.

I felt Emily watching me more closely over the next few weeks. I think she marveled that I retained my composure during the ride to and from the police station. She expected additional punishment from me, yet none was forthcoming. I knew the accident had frightened her—that, alone, was enough of a punishment.

This event was so out of character for Emily. Of the four children, she had the most amiable temperament and generally used good judgment. Always the mediator, she rebuked her brothers when their tempers ran hot. She was a good listener and problem solver. Although she was closer to Mike because of their shared love of sports, she loved all her brothers and encouraged them to get along. When I am gone, I would tell myself, Emily will be the one to keep the family together.

CHAPTER 38

No Roses for My Funeral

Ecclesiastes, Chapter 7, Verses 1-4 (taken from *The Living Bible*)

"A good reputation is more valuable than the most expensive perfume. The day one dies is better than the day he is born! It is better to spend your time at funerals than at festivals. For you are going to die and it is a good thing to think about it while there is still time. Sorrow is better than laughter, for sadness has a refining influence on us. Yes, a wise man thinks much of death, while the fool thinks only of having a good time now."

Grandma Rose lived another ten years after the massive stroke she sustained in 1985. Although she tired easily, she could walk short distances and had learned to feed herself with her left hand. She had permanently lost some short-term memory and continued to struggle with her speech. But despite her handicaps, Mom was able to understand what was going on around her. During my ongoing challenges with the children, she remained my closest confidante. In fact, she also remained Karl's closest confidante—even when he began to date, and marry, other women. Mom was very wise—she never berated the children or Karl. Instead, she just listened, offering me wordless hugs when the tears would come.

After Mom returned to her home with Aunt Sophie in tow, I made weekly trips to visit them; there were groceries to buy, doctors to see, bills to pay, and routine household tasks to attend to. William helped as much as he could, but he was battling various cancers and needed to focus his energies on his work responsibilities.

I will always remember one Valentine's Day visit that had an unexpected outcome. I had brought Mom and Aunt Sophie a bouquet of fresh flowers for the occasion. I carefully arranged the blooms in a vase, mixing just the right amount of tap water with the nutrients from the tiny plastic packages tucked inside the waxy wrapping paper. When Mom and Aunt Sophie had rearranged the flowers to their liking, the three of us sat down at the kitchen table to enjoy a homemade streusel cake and flavored decaf coffee. We talked of the weather, William's illness, his two daughters, my four children, and Karl.

Then we all fell silent, my mom and aunt lightly fingering the petals of the carnations, irises, and daisies. Suddenly Mom turned to me, put her hand on my arm to make sure she had my attention, and said, "No roses for my funeral." Since I already knew my mom disliked the smell of roses, I was startled by her comment. I promised her there would be no roses at her funeral. In an instant, I knew Mom was thinking about her impending death.

Four and a half years had passed since that summer of 1985 when we celebrated her sixty-seventh birthday in her hospital room, and now here she was thinking about death.

I got up from my chair, welcoming the opportunity to stretch my legs, walked over to the counter, and retrieved a memo pad and pencil from the junk drawer. As I sat down again, I said, "Mom, your overall health is good—really good—based on all you've been through. But we're all going to die sometime, and so I think you're very smart to be thinking about death. Tell me, Mom, what *do* you want at your memorial service?"

I took copious notes as Mom, with her hesitant speech pattern, listed all of the things she wanted at her memorial service. Favorite flowers were carnations, mums, irises, baby's breath, and plenty of greenery for color. She listed favorite childhood hymns: "What a Friend We Have in Jesus" and "Kum ba Yuh." She named a few familiar Scriptures to read and told me she wanted to be cremated. Most of her deceased sisters and brothers had been sealed in coffins and stored in the cold, hard ground. That was not a good option for Mom; she preferred the dust to dust ideology.

When she paused, I asked, "How about the church service, Mom? Do you want Pastor Dennis to officiate?" She looked into my face and I saw tears begin to roll down her cheeks.

"What does he know about me?" she asked. "I'm just a name on the church membership list. I send money every month, but I don't go to the Sunday services. What does he really know about me?"

"But, Mom," I responded, "I can't imagine a funeral without a church service." As I helped her wipe away the tears, without thinking, I said, "Mom, what if I spoke on your behalf—what if *I* delivered your eulogy? Would you agree to have a church service then?"

She covered my hands with hers and said, "Would you, could you, do that for me?"

"Yes, Mom, I can do this for you," I replied in slightly more than a whisper.

The conversation then took on a lighter tone. After eating a second piece of cake, drinking a third cup of coffee, and taking care of Mom and Aunt Sophie's paperwork, it was time for me to leave.

On the way home, my mind was racing with ideas and questions and doubt.

That evening I drafted the outline for Mom's eulogy. I talked about her courage—how she had learned to drive after Dad died and how she had worked so hard to overcome the debilitating effects of the stroke. I talked about her ability to forgive—like the time I lost my temper with her because she had ironed a crease into the collar of my favorite blouse. Lastly, I talked about her capacity for unconditional love—her willingness to do anything for anybody in the family, asking nothing in return.

Over the next few months, I continued to struggle with the message—and my emotions. It had to be good—no, it had to be perfect. When I thought I had finally captured the essence of Mom, I taped the speech and put my notes and the tape in a drawer.

The years slipped by. Then one day Mom said to me, "Did you ever write the eulogy you will give when I die?"

I replied, "I did, Mom—a long time ago. It's in a file folder in my office."

"Well, when do I get to hear it?" she asked. "If everyone else is going to hear it, I should hear it, too."

And so it came to pass in the spring of that year that I found myself sitting once again at the small table in my mom's tiny kitchen with my mother and Aunt Sophie. This time, next to the streusel cake and the coffee cups sat a box of tissues and a tape recorder with *the tape* ready to be played.

My mother was deeply touched by the love, the sincerity, and the warmth in my tone. She nodded her head in agreement as I told about the courage she showed while working with physical therapists for two years so she could speak, walk, and use her hands again. She laughed at the crease in the collar story and she cried when I told stories of all she had done for my Dad, for my brother, for me, and for other family members. I think I did well. No, I *know* I did well. At that moment in time, I did something very special for Mom, something no one else in our family could do.

"For you are going to die and it is a good thing to think about it while there is still time."

"Honey, no roses for my funeral," Mom had reminded me.

"No, Mom, there'll be no roses at your funeral," I had replied.

But what there *would* be is a wonderful tribute to an extraordinary woman who played a dramatic role in shaping the lives of every member of our family.

CHAPTER 39

Challenges to the Divorce Decree

At the urging of friends, Karl joined a new church and began attending Beginning Again meetings, a support group for widowed or divorced members.

Soon the children were talking about Mary, a good friend their father had met at church. Upon overhearing their conversations, I was not surprised when Karl began challenging the legal agreement we had just signed. "I'm giving you too much money," he told me. "I need to keep more for myself so I can build a new life."

The provisions of our divorce decree were standard. We hadn't accumulated much money; the two issues requiring resolution were the house and Karl's pension. We agreed that I would receive a greater percentage of the house because I had been out of the workforce for thirteen years raising the children. Karl, then, would receive a greater percentage of his pension. I would take the newly purchased Chevy wagon and Karl would buy his first sports car. The furniture stayed in the house; four children, their friends, and two dogs had given our household belongings a heavily used appearance.

Throughout the entire divorce proceedings, Karl had refused legal counsel. To minimize my legal fees, I had outlined the terms of the settlement, discussed them with Karl, and asked Martin to rewrite the statements in appropriate legalese. Then Karl and I had proofread each page of the document. It all seemed simple and straightforward.

But soon the games began.

Karl refused to have my share of his paycheck deposited directly into my checking account; instead, he would drop off a personal check to me after payday—sometimes as much as a week later. I would then go to the bank, deposit his check, and wait five days for it to clear before I could access the money. He announced he would hire a lawyer to have his share of the cost of Mike's schooling reduced because his support check and my salary equaled his salary. Never mind that I had to use my money to support five people.

We hadn't been divorced a full year when Karl wrote me a letter announcing he was marrying the woman he had met in his grieving group.

"Katherine,

As you probably have heard by now, Mary and I are planning to be married on Saturday, October 18. We are two real human beings who believe in each other as individuals. We don't pretend to read each other's thoughts, nor do we want to; instead, we plan to live together caring for each other. We will remain as two separate people who share a common goal of getting along, loving each other, and doing for ourselves as well as for one another. There is no pretense of a soul mate. Katherine, it is not real. Get your head examined and embrace reality. God didn't make us so that we can read each other's minds.

Karl"

The first letter after his marriage to Mary had a different tone to it. He had suddenly lost all interest in our family home. It was now my sole responsibility to pay for all of the repairs. If he had funds available, he might help me out; otherwise, he would simply collect his share of the house when it was sold. He didn't care what the divorce decree said;

he was only paying 50% of Mike's schooling even though his share was supposed to be higher based on his greater salary.

"Dear Katherine,

Thanks for the wedding wishes along with the card. I'm sure buying a wedding card for us was difficult for you. Yes, the day was difficult for me because of attending the funeral for your Uncle Frank in the morning and anticipating Mary's and my wedding in the afternoon. Well, both Mary and I got through the day.

As far as my mother is concerned, her health is not too good—neither is her attitude about life. Remember the victim complex you liked to dwell on so much? Well, that's the way she is; she will go to her grave that way. Mary seems to understand her and accepts her as she is. I would suggest you do the same.

As far as you and I are concerned, I feel that our best means of communication is the mail. I have worked through a lot of negative feelings about all that has happened and have no desire to hear your voice over the phone or across the dinner table. Accept the norm that hard feelings do exist between divorced individuals, sometimes for a lifetime. Through all this, I will continue to associate myself with my children as best I can with how it fits into my schedule.

I'll be dropping off some signed copies of the health insurance forms you requested. Speaking of health, perhaps you can get some psychological help for yourself as well as for the kids. I hope you fulfill your lifetime yearning for your *soul mate*. Good luck to you, Katherine.

Karl"

Letters reflecting the *I didn't get enough* philosophy continued to flow from Karl's house to mine. Soon after his marriage to Mary, he sent me a letter asking for some of our furniture—or a cash equivalent. At the time of our divorce, we agreed the furniture was of little value. Mary had taken her furniture to their new home, and Karl had recently purchased an ornate, solid oak, roll-top desk with a matching wooden file cabinet and a leather swivel chair for his home office. They didn't need our old furniture, yet Karl was convinced he had been shortchanged.

"Katherine,

I have another item of concern. It is about the costly furniture we purchased together that you now own. I feel the price of that furniture, which totaled $10,000 when new, is probably worth about $6,000 today. Yes, I did concede it to you because of the children; I want them to live in a decent home. But now that most of them have left the nest, or will be leaving soon, I am asking for my fair share.

My first offer to you is this: Whenever you sell the house and get your percentage of the sale, I would like to have either the five pieces of the bedroom set or the three pieces of the dining room set. If you cannot accept that offer, consider the second offer of withholding $100 from your child support payments for the next 30 months ($3,000). At that time the issue of the furniture will be settled once and for all.

Let me know how you feel about this idea.

Karl, Your X

P.S. How about the piano??? Is it being used?"

I wouldn't agree to either of his offers regarding the furniture. Craig was planning on moving to Las Vegas after the Army, but Mike had two more years of school and would be home during breaks and summers. Tom would be returning from the Army soon and had nowhere else to go, and Emily wasn't even in college yet.

The discussions over the worn-out furniture were ludicrous and yet so typical of Karl. He had what he needed, yet he was concerned that I might have more. In a recent letter he had chided me for keeping a mental tally on the fairness of our marriage, yet here he was keeping a written tally on the diminishing value and disposition of our old furniture.

In late 1986, I wrote:

"Karl,

It would appear that everything I have to say has already been said on the phone tonight, but that's not quite true. What I didn't say is I think it's time we began to treat one another with some respect and common decency. Hanging up on one another is a juvenile power play that I find extremely degrading.

I think our continuing to treat one another shabbily speaks ill of both of us. And while I know you hate when I bring the kids into this, I do feel our bickering wears on their nerves. It certainly wears on mine.

I have several letters from you in front of me, but since it is very late, I won't have time to respond to all of your comments. In one letter, you've withdrawn your offer to help me repair the basement wall, suggesting I do it myself. In another letter, you continue to hammer away on the 50/50 split for college expenses even though the divorce decree provides for a percentage distribution based on our individual gross earnings.

In yet another letter you demand half the furniture or $3,000 and question what is happening with the piano. The furniture is not worth $6,000; I'm keeping all of it because the children and I are using it, and you have stated in at least six different letters that you don't want it and don't need it. As for the piano, you may recall that I paid for the piano out of my continuing education earnings. You refused to have anything to do with piano payments or Emily's music lessons. Now you want her piano? I think not. The piano belongs to Emily.

I find all of this pettiness exhausting, Karl. Surely you must feel the same way.

Katherine"

CHAPTER 40

Mary: Wife #2

I wasn't surprised Karl had joined a grieving group at his new church. Although he initially vowed he would never remarry for fear of being hurt again, I knew he needed companionship. I was stunned to learn, however, that he was remarrying so quickly.

I sincerely wanted Karl to be happy and knew he had not been happy while married to me. But the speed at which he replaced me made me feel so ordinary. I realized I had simply filled the role of a wife. I had performed the duties expected of a wife, making Karl's life easier in the process. He had never perceived me as being special.

I planned to dislike Mary. I wanted her to be the typical *other woman*—selfish, demanding, meddling in the lives of our children. Then it would have been easy to dislike her. Instead, Mary was a gentle, caring person who had courageously extricated herself from an abusive relationship. She had two teenage children who were in serious need of counseling. Truancy, drugs, alcohol—her children had sought negative attention in every possible way.

The daughter of a minister, Mary had learned patience, forgiveness, and love. She counted on her faith to help her survive the hard times. Her unwavering hope for a day when her children would be healed guided her daily footsteps. She literally had put her hand in the Lord's and said, "Lead me." She was convinced He had led her to Karl, and she was truly grateful for Karl's presence in her life.

Karl and Mary regularly attended Mike's basketball games; often, after a game, Karl, Mary, Mike, Tom, Emily, and I (and assorted friends) would stop for a pizza. A home health care nurse, Mary spoke with compassion about the challenges of her patients. Yet she loved to laugh and tell stories. She took time to listen to, and appreciate, our children.

Had circumstances been different, Mary might have been a positive force in the treatment of Karl's depression.

One Friday night in late January of 1988, Karl and Mary chaperoned a high school ski trip to a local resort. Each had driven separately: Karl in the school van filled with a dozen active, noisy students and Mary in her small Pontiac Grand Am. When the evening ended, Mary, exhausted from the work week, left for home first. Perhaps it was fatigue or a seizure or the icy road conditions or a fleeting moment of lost concentration. Whatever the reason, Mary's car floated left, crossing the yellow line, smashing head on into an oncoming vehicle. Mary was killed instantly.

Karl, following close behind, was the first person to come upon the accident. Recognizing the license plates, he braked hard, forgetting the condition of the roads, spun around in a circle twice, and forced his numb body into an upright position. The students in the van were thrown about, but no one was hurt. With great effort Karl shoved open the heavy door of the van and willed his legs to move closer to the body pinned against the steering wheel of the canted white sedan. A sprinkling of blood dotted her left cheekbone; her lifeless eyes, half-closed, stared straight ahead.

Clawing at the frozen handle on the driver's side, Karl finally dislodged the chunks of ice. As the door swung open, Mary spilled out of the seat into his arms. "No," he shrieked. "No. No. No." A single word repeated over and over, at first loud and shrill, later soft and breathless.

Emily was the first child to hear the brokenness in her father's voice. She was in her bedroom studying for an exam when her father called to tell the children of the news. His words were barely intelligible. "She's gone, Emily. She's gone. I can't believe she's gone."

Mike, after arranging for advanced homework assignments from his college instructors, moved in with his father and handled the funeral arrangements. Craig and Tom, still stationed overseas, were unable to attend the memorial service.

I was overwhelmed with sadness for Karl and for Mary's children. Random, tragic acts such as these always humbled me and reconnected me to my Creator. I prayed Karl would feel the awesome presence of God's spirit. And I prayed He would allow Emily and Mike to be the physical and emotional sources of comfort Karl so desperately needed.

CHAPTER 41

A Chance for Reconciliation

The fear of being alone warps our thinking, distorts reality. I've been there. I know.

Ron and I spent a vacation week together in Florida the last week in January of 1988. For months prior to the vacation, we had talked about the logistics of getting married. So the diamond ring Ron gave me the first day we arrived was not a total surprise. What *did* surprise me, however, was my reaction to the ring. Instead of being excited and happy, I was sad and weepy. Ron was the best friend I had ever had, yet I knew we would both struggle with the changes marriage would require of us.

How would we ever resolve our differences? Ron's future looked much like his past—going to work during the day, reading or watching TV in the evenings, and relaxing on the weekends. And my future looked much like my past—setting goals, spending time with my children, and using the weekends to prepare for the demands of the upcoming week. I was finishing a master's degree and climbing the corporate ladder of a male-dominated Fortune 500 company. Lusting after the title of manager, I had no intention of relaxing on the weekends.

Ron must have been perplexed by my melancholy. After all, we were on vacation and supposed to be having fun. Here we were in Florida, in a lovely condo near the ocean, pretending that marriage was something we both wanted. I wore the ring the entire week, but by Friday I could no longer contain my emotions. Taking Ron's hand, I led him to the couch, motioning him to sit next to me.

"Ron, I love you. You have become a dear friend. You have always been there when I needed your support or advice. But this doesn't feel right. *Marriage* doesn't feel right."

I watched closely for his reaction and was amazed to see the tension leave his body. Ron admitted experiencing these same feelings. He said it would have been difficult for him to leave Baltimore and his parents. He feared he would lose me if he didn't marry me, so he had played along with our discussions of marriage.

Months later I would write in my journal, "Ron, my strong reaction to receiving your ring surprised me. I knew the thought of remarrying frightened me, but I wasn't prepared for the panic that swept over me when you slipped that ring on my finger. Caged. Trapped. That's what I was feeling. When I was married, I was convinced I had very little control over my life. With Emily leaving for college soon, I'm hesitant to give control of my life to someone else. For some time now, I have also sensed reluctance on your part to talk about marriage. You enjoy our closeness, yet you also treasure your separateness. All of these feelings surfaced while we were on vacation. I'm sorry for both of us."

Two important incidents occurred the week following our vacation. First, Karl called to tell the children and me that Mary had been killed in an automobile accident. I offered my sympathy, knowing how hollow my words must have sounded to him. Second, Ron and I learned that the husband of a mutual friend of ours had taken an overdose of drugs and died. These two deaths marked another turning point in our relationship. We began to realize how special and important our friendship was. We agreed that friendship was the foundation of a good marriage and once again set about the task of working on the logistics of our being together.

During the next few months, Ron and I brainstormed ways to blend our two very different lifestyles. Perhaps we were focusing too much on our differences rather than on our similarities. Both list makers, we spent long hours on the telephone analyzing our personal strengths and weaknesses, documenting what each of us wanted in a partner. I'm certain we overanalyzed our relationship. We saw one another a few more times during the spring of 1988, but each time a sadness, a wistfulness, dampened our spirits.

Ultimately, we agreed to date other people, yet we continued our Saturday evening marathon telephone calls. Neither of us seemed in a hurry to date other people. The temptation to see one another was strong, but it would have been difficult for us to continue seeing one another knowing marriage would never be an option. Ron could not bring himself to leave his family in Maryland, and I could not bring myself to leave my family in Illinois. I knew we would remain close friends, but I also knew the circle would not be closed with Ron.

By this time Karl and I had been divorced almost three years. We were miles apart in our thinking. He was grieving for his second wife, and I was dreaming of finding a soul mate. Would the pain Karl was feeling lead him to counseling? If he had asked me to join him in therapy, I would have said yes. I longed for a sign, a promise of renewed commitment and interest on his part. More than anything, I wished we could resolve our differences and start out fresh again. The need to close the circle had resurfaced.

In March, just two months after Mary's death, Karl called to talk. His voice heavy with sadness, he asked if I would meet him for dinner Friday evening. Without hesitation, I agreed. During dinner we talked about good times and bad times. We talked about things that mattered: how happy I was that he had met Mary and how sad I was that their happiness was not ours; how sorry he was for all the hurt he had caused me and the children and how much he still loved me.

Starting over again sounded so simple, so fated. What an extraordinary opportunity, a chance to right the wrongs in our relationship and rebuild a home for our children. Not many divorced couples come to this enviable fork in the road. We declared our love for one another and asked forgiveness for the hurts we had caused.

It seemed so simple. But was it?

Illusion fades to reality in early morning's light. I awakened Saturday morning remembering the highs and lows of his moods and the seemingly genuine apologies to his sons that followed bitter accusations and punitive actions. I remembered all of the pain, the children's and mine.

The children had mixed emotions about our dating. Craig, having been away from the family unit for a few years, was politely indifferent. Tom refused to talk about the possibility of his father coming home to live. Emily insisted she just wanted us to be happy. Mike, surprisingly, was very upset about the possibility of our getting together again.

"Mom," he said. "You and Dad are two very different people. You're just not good together. Don't do it."

Karl and I saw one another several times a week for the next few months. We talked endlessly about the years we had spent together and the mistakes we had made. We had dinner dates and attended school functions, community concerts, and church services together. We even made love several times.

Despite the mutual declarations of love and good intentions, however, neither of us was willing to compromise. I insisted on our going to counseling; he said no. He insisted on moving back home; I said no.

Mike was right—we were very different people. We weren't good together the first time. Without professional help, how could we hope to be good together the second time?

CHAPTER 42

Pension versus House

Once we decided not to get back together again, Karl refocused on the monetary side of the divorce settlement. A new theme in his letters was the push to sell the house. A clause in the divorce settlement specified I had to sell the house "…upon the minor child, Emily, finishing being a full-time student either in high school or college, whichever occurs first."

Karl interpreted these words to mean I had to sell the house when Emily graduated from high school. My lawyer, however, had added this clause to allow me to stay in the house until Emily finished college. Karl tried unsuccessfully to find a lawyer to help him refute this point.

My refusal to sell the house at his insistence became a huge source of frustration for Karl. In fact, I wasn't in a financial position to sell the house. Instead, I agreed to a reduction in his child support payments when I completed my master's degree and secured a higher-paying job at another company. I was grateful for Karl's financial support and didn't want to lean on him more than was necessary.

Karl's mood changes became more extreme in his letters. In one letter he agreed to come over and help repair some of the shingles on the roof. He ended with the words: "As all of us become older, it seems that each day grows shorter. Enjoy each day to its fullest, Katherine, because we never know when life's changes will come and how they will affect us."

Several days after he made the repairs, he sent me a letter containing an invoice. He had billed me for the time he had spent replacing the shingles.

Subsequent letters became more reflective. In late November of that year, Karl wrote,

> "Katherine,
>
> The holidays are extremely hard on me. So many memories float back again and again. It hurts so much at times. I miss the children very much. Yes, life is too short. Why do we fill it with so much pain?
>
> I keep writing Craig and Tom letters. Craig has answered most of them, but Tom has written only twice so far. I hope everything is well with them.
>
> Katherine, again I ask myself when will life become normal between us? I don't know the answer to that, but I do hope you have become what you want to be and are feeling you are now in charge of your life.
>
> I'm making it, but still struggling. Mostly, when things get tough, I give my cares and worries to God and try to let go of them.
>
> Take care.
>
> Karl"

Just before Christmas Karl wrote another letter telling me how angry he was that he still had to give me money each month. Once again he offered to swap his share of the house for my share of his pension. I forced myself to stay rational and consider all possibilities.

Giving up my share of his pension would give Karl most of our joint worth; on the other hand, I would no longer have to deal with late child support payments. Karl's pension would be administered by the Illinois Pension Fund. At this point in time, however, the Illinois Pension Fund did not recognize QDRO (Qualified Domestic Relations Order) rulings. This meant all pension monies would be paid to Karl first. When Karl began collecting his monthly pension checks, he would then write me a check for my share of the money. If I chose to keep the entire value of the house and sign away my rights to his pension, I could avoid regular contact with Karl and his playing games with my share of the money. I decided to give this option more thought.

CHAPTER 43

A 3:00 a.m. Phone Call

If only I could focus my mental energy on circumstances under my control, I would be a much happier person. Unfortunately, I am unable to compartmentalize my worries. Resolving the house/pension issue consumed me—until a more urgent situation required my immediate attention.

Craig was about six months away from his discharge from the Army when he phoned me around 3:00 one morning.

"Hi, Mom. You awake?"

"I am now. Are you all right?"

"I'm fine, Mom."

"Is Tom all right?"

"Yes, Mom, Tom is fine. I need to ask you a few questions about health insurance." Craig's voice had become softer. "Do you have a family plan at work, Mom?"

"No, I don't, Craig. You children have always been on your dad's policy because the coverage was better and less expensive than anything Alchem offered."

"Is there a way I can buy into the family plan at Alchem?"

"No, Son. The cost would be prohibitive. Besides, the plan doesn't have any provisions for children over the age of 18 unless they are in school full time."

"Do you know which insurance companies have the best coverage for the least amount of money, Mom?"

"No, Darling. Not offhand."

With the sleep-fog lifting, I finally asked Craig why he was asking these questions. Then I heard the rest of the story. When Craig and Tom were overseas, they frequently traveled to see one another on weekends. An Army Master Sergeant and his family stationed in Brussels frequently invited military personnel to join them for dinner on weekends. Tracey, the oldest of the three daughters, and Tom had become friends, so it was natural that Tom would introduce Craig to Tracey and her family. Craig and Tracey began dating about six months ago and had talked about getting married when Craig was discharged.

"Tracey's pregnant, Mom. She thinks she's covered under her dad's health insurance policy, but I just wanted to know if we have any other options. She's considering an abortion, but she doesn't know if she can go through with it."

When Karl first heard the news, he wrote Craig a long letter encouraging Tracey to have the abortion and offering to pay for a vasectomy; Craig was only twenty-two at the time. Before even talking to Craig and Tracey, Karl had determined a course of action. Get rid of the unborn child and prevent the possibility of another pregnancy. After all, children were too much work and too expensive.

Fortunately, the abortion never took place. While I was unhappy about the circumstances surrounding Connor's birth, I was happy for Craig and Tracey. They seemed far too young to assume the responsibilities of parenthood and I seemed far too young for grandparenthood, but their excitement over their new son was infectious.

CHAPTER 44

Brenda: Wife #3

Just a few months after Mary's death and our decision not to remarry, Karl joined a grieving group at a different church. Here he met Brenda, who would become his third wife. Brenda's first husband had died after a lingering illness. She had been a member of this grieving group for some time and had apparently taken an interest in Karl.

When Karl told me of his new friend, he said he would never love anyone as much as he loved me, but that Brenda made no demands of him. I, on the other hand, required a change in his behavior. He told me he was tired of trying to live up to my unrealistic expectations of what a husband and father should be. He also told me since Brenda had money and her children were no longer living with her, there would be fewer demands on his funds and his time than there had been with me.

Karl was flattered by someone pursuing him. "I have no intention of spending the rest of my life alone," he told me on several occasions.

One Sunday evening, after seeing Brenda for several months, Karl surprised me with a phone call. "Are you sure counseling is still a requirement for our getting back together? I still love you, you know."

"I love you, too, Karl, but we need professional help to work out our differences."

"Well, that's that, then. Just checking. I'm not interested in going for counseling. I like myself just the way I am."

Karl and Brenda's relationship blossomed during the fall of 1988. They were married in June of 1989, a few weeks after Emily graduated from high school. Karl seemed happy except that most of his comments about the marriage centered on his newly acquired double income status. Karl enjoyed seeing me struggle financially; he genuinely believed I deserved tough economic times as my punishment for divorcing him.

After Emily earned a volleyball scholarship at an out-of-state school, Karl often reminded me how easy it would be for Brenda and him to fly to North Carolina on weekends to watch Emily play. Brenda, an employee of a major airline, had easy access to stand-by tickets. Soon after their marriage, however, Brenda quit her job. She told Karl she wanted a traditional marriage and time to get to know him better. Karl, stunned by this turn of events, had already bragged to his coworkers about their travel plans. Now, reduced rates were no longer an option.

A misunderstanding caused Karl additional humiliation. During their courtship, Brenda had always referred to herself as a teacher. Karl had assumed she was a degreed professional. Since titles carried weight with him, he was embarrassed when he discovered she was a swim instructor at a local park district. She was, in fact, a highly accomplished swim instructor, but Karl felt deceived because the academic credentials were missing.

There was a marked difference between wife #2 and wife #3. Mary, Karl's second wife, was friendly and trusting. She told me to call Karl any time I needed to talk to him, and she encouraged him to spend time alone with our children. Brenda, Karl's third wife, was aloof and guarded. She monitored phone calls from the children and insisted on being present every time he scheduled time with one of them.

In the early months of their marriage, Brenda often called me on the phone probing for information about Karl's and my relationship. She asked indiscreet questions about how we had handled money, hoping to uncover *the real issues* behind our divorce.

Apparently Karl was resisting setting up joint bank accounts with Brenda. He also required her to pay for her car payment and car insurance premium with money earned from her part-time job as a daycare provider. Brenda challenged this arrangement stating, "In a traditional marriage, the man pays for everything."

Judging from Karl's letters at the beginning of their courtship, they were happy. On March 1, 1989, he wrote,

"Katherine,

Brenda and I rejoice in one another's company. We communicate very well and demand nothing of each other. Each gives freely to the other with only the best intentions. All of our problems are relatively small in comparison to what both of us have recently lived through. Our appreciation of each other finds us trying to please each other and live together in harmony and peace. It's a very comforting and enjoyable existence right now.

It didn't surprise me that you backed out of your initial decision to marry Ron. I'm sure you had your reasons. It didn't *feel right*. Such is life. Well, perhaps your ideal man doesn't exist in this world; maybe he will exist in the next world. That's the place where souls meet.

Karl"

Preoccupied with his upcoming marriage to Brenda, Karl appeared to have called a moratorium on his anger towards me. In mid-June, following a family gathering at our house to celebrate Emily's graduation from high school, he wrote,

"Katherine,

Thanks for a lovely afternoon at Emily's graduation party. It was nice to see old acquaintances again.

Life goes on and so do you and I. I'm sure everyone, including me, appreciated your efforts.

You've done a great job with the children. I'm extremely proud of what you have done alone. Emily is a great daughter, and we have three great sons. Keep on doing what you think is the right thing. I'll try to support you as much as I can.

Take care.

Karl"

Although at times Karl sounded rational and supportive, his battle with anger was far from over.

CHAPTER 45

Craig and Tracey's Wedding

Despite discussions about a future together, Craig was stunned to learn Tracey was pregnant. They both wanted to have the child, dismissing preliminary thoughts about Tracey having an abortion. They postponed wedding plans and focused their attention on the birth of their first child.

When Craig, Tracey, and Tracey's family returned to the States, Craig and Tracey moved in with her parents. Connor was born in the fall of 1989. That Christmas Craig and Tracey announced they would marry the following July. The service would be held at Nellis Air Force Base, with a small reception following the ceremony.

Attending the wedding turned out to be an expensive proposition because Mike, Tom, Emily and I had to travel to Nevada and stay in a hotel for several days. Mike, Tom, and two of their friends decided to plan a mini vacation that included driving to Las Vegas and attending the wedding. Emily and I chose to fly. She and I planned to meet up with Mike and Tom at a nearby hotel the morning of the rehearsal dinner.

I hadn't spoken to Karl in weeks, so I wondered how he would react to the wedding (which he wasn't in favor of) and to Tracey's parents (whom he had never met) and to me (for whom he was still harboring love/hate feelings).

Trouble began at the wedding rehearsal. Karl and Brenda wanted to sit in the front pew with me on the groom's side. I had no intention of sharing my space with Brenda, which, in retrospect, was petty on my part. I announced that I was sitting in the front pew with Connor and suggested Karl and Brenda sit in the second row.

Tension escalated at the rehearsal dinner. As we stood in line for the buffet, I asked Karl if he would split the cost of Emily's airline ticket with me. Clearly, my timing was off, yet I felt perfectly justified in asking for some financial help. The wedding fell outside the scope of anything we had agreed to in the divorce decree. After all, I was paying for the boys' hotel bill and some of their meals during the trip, plus Craig's and Connor's tuxedos. I had also purchased new outfits for Emily and me to wear to the wedding as well as a dress for Tracey to wear to the rehearsal dinner. Attempting to recoup half of Emily's airfare didn't seem unreasonable.

Karl thought differently. He reminded me that if I hadn't divorced him, I wouldn't be short of money, Craig wouldn't be marrying Tracey, Connor wouldn't have been born, and he wouldn't have experienced the pain of losing his second wife. Like I said, my timing was off.

I reminded Karl that he could have made different, and better, choices, including going for counseling, which might have made the divorce unnecessary. Brenda interpreted my comment about making different, and better, choices as a slur against her and called me a bitch.

"Maybe you're the bitch," I replied, without thinking. *Bitch* was not a word I used in normal conversation. Brenda's comment caught me off-guard since my statement about making different and better choices was meant for Karl.

She took a step closer to me. I could feel the warmth of her breath on my face. "I hate you," she whispered. "You'll pay for this." I backed up, preparing to respond to a blow that never materialized. Mike and Tom, seeing this exchange and anticipating the worst, left their places in line and moved between us. Somehow, awkwardly, the evening ended.

The wedding service was simple, yet beautiful. The sanctuary altar and pews, meticulously crafted of light oak hardwoods, commanded reverence. Cut-glass windows in vibrant hues depicted well-known Biblical scenes. Craig and Tracey, so young, hopeful, and happy, promised to love and cherish one another forever. Six-month old Conner, outfitted in a starched, white tuxedo, witnessed this historic family event from the crook of my left arm.

Pictures were next on the agenda. When Craig asked the photographer to take a few snapshots of our immediate family without Brenda, Karl was insulted and insisted she be part of every family photo. Brenda had already been included in most of the family pictures. Craig wanted a picture of himself with Karl and me and one of Tracey and himself with Karl and me. Karl was unable to understand the emotion behind these requests.

Without a word to Craig, Karl and Brenda decided to boycott the wedding reception. Perhaps it was the seating arrangements in the church, the altercation at the rehearsal dinner, or Craig's special photo requests. Whatever the underlying reason, when the announcer was ready to present the bride, groom, and parents to the guests, Karl and Brenda were nowhere to be found. Craig, visibly upset, motioned for the announcer to continue introducing the remaining members of the wedding party.

When we arrived home at the end of the week, I wrote Karl a short note suggesting we find a way to make future family events less emotionally charged.

He never acknowledged my letter.

CHAPTER 46

The Depression Deepens

Even when caught in the throes of denial, occasional periods of lucidity break through, causing us to weep for opportunities lost. Such a moment of clarity occurred in mid-July of 1992, when Karl called late in the afternoon to talk to Tom. Tom had been working overtime all week and was not home.

For seven years, Karl would abruptly end a conversation with me if the child he was trying to reach were unavailable. But today he threw me a crumb of kindness. "So how are things going for you?" Not a big crumb, mind you, but a crumb, nevertheless. I remember saying that business had been slow for the past few months, but I expected the fall to be busy.

Encouraged by his willingness to engage in small talk, I asked him if he and Brenda had everything in order for their upcoming trip to England. He began to talk. He told me about his sleepless nights, the concerns he had about leaving his home to someone else's care, his preoccupation with his mother's failing health, the regrets that had begun to surface over his part in our divorce, the sadness he felt when he thought about our children, and how much he had always loved me. If he had only known *then* what he knew *now*, how different things would have been for us.

All this in a matter of minutes from a man who had difficulty expressing his feelings.

I had always hoped Karl would own up to his share of responsibility in the divorce, but this heartfelt outpouring of remorse was almost more than I could bear. I loved this man when I married him and I loved this man when I divorced him despite the hurt and disappointment that had gone before.

I shared a fantasy with him: While he was overseas in a new environment, an inner strength would surface that would enable him to reach out for help. When he returned home, he would invite his four children to join him in therapy. While I had no desire to undermine his and Brenda's marriage, I desperately wanted him to be a father to our children. It is never too late for us to become better parents to our children.

Several days later, though, my hopes for a breakthrough were shattered. I received an unexpected phone call from Karl's new lawyer. She called to tell me Karl had given her power of attorney in case I decided to sell the house in his absence. Karl had suggested she offer me his share of the house for my share of his pension—as if this were a new idea. The lawyer demanded to know when I planned to sell the house. I told her I had not made a decision about the swap, but I would begin getting appraisals and put the house on the market next spring. Emily would be graduating from college, and I needed to move on with my life.

At about the same time, Karl began putting more pressure on Tom to move out of the house. He reminded Tom that when he was Tom's age, he didn't live with his mommy. Karl didn't seem to care that Tom had nowhere else to go.

"I don't get it, Mom. I'm not hurting Dad if I live with you awhile and save up some money. Besides, I do a lot of things around the house to make life easier for you."

What Tom said was true. He was working hard to save money so he could buy a place of his own. Tom was also a huge help around the house; he had assumed total responsibility for car maintenance, yard work, and minor home repairs. I knew Tom was planning for the next stage in his life, and I was determined to enjoy the final moments of our time together.

Karl's Heart Attack

Several days after the phone call from Karl's lawyer, the children received an early morning phone call from Brenda. While playing softball in a church league the previous evening, Karl had suffered a heart attack. Mike heard the news first. He called me immediately, terror in his voice. He, like his siblings, had never made peace with his father. Just as he had done when he heard about Mary's death, Mike packed up his books and some of his clothing and came home to be with his father.

Tom had already left for work, so I showered and made the twenty-minute trip to Alliance Foods. The supervisor led me to his office and tracked down Tom in the warehouse. Shocked by the news, Tom followed me home in his truck. By the time we arrived at the house, Mike was already there. Together they drove to a neighboring town to visit their father in the hospital. Emily, away that weekend at a college volleyball tournament, decided to fly home to see her father, but Craig, because of work and school commitments, would need to rely on health updates from his siblings.

Later Karl would describe his heart attack as a warning. He assured everyone no damage had been done; proper medication and diet would prevent future complications. I worried that he might die before we were able to talk through the pain of the divorce.

Karl's doctor recommended canceling the foreign exchange trip. Karl sounded relieved when he told me this news on the phone. We talked briefly after his heart attack. I wished him well and told him if he ever wanted to talk, I was available. When I hung up the phone, the realization that Karl was not only emotionally ill, but also physically ill, deeply saddened me.

A Visit from Brenda

One Sunday afternoon after Karl's heart attack, Brenda called to ask if she could come over for a visit. Brenda and I hadn't had much contact after Karl put a stop to her phone calls pumping me for information about why our marriage failed. The fiasco at Craig's wedding certainly had not brought us any closer, which is why her phone call caught me by surprise. I learned later she had not told Karl she was coming to see me.

Emily had returned to college and Mike was playing softball on this particular evening. Tom was at home waiting for a friend to come over, so the house was fairly quiet. When Brenda arrived, she settled in across from me on the love seat. She confided that her first marriage had been very difficult, that she had thought about leaving her husband several times. Since he had threatened to leave her penniless if she divorced him, she had chosen to stay in an unhappy relationship.

She talked about other men in her life who had left her and said she didn't want to be left by Karl. It seems Karl had been very depressed before the heart attack, sleeping fitfully at night. He had told Brenda he still loved me and missed his family. Brenda didn't know what to do. She asked if there were some way I could help him. I told her I had been trying to help Karl help himself for over twenty years, but nothing had worked. I told her to tell Karl I would join him for counseling if he took the initiative and scheduled an appointment with someone.

Then she asked a question that caught me completely off-guard. "Would you consider swapping Karl for your share of his pension?"

I sat motionless, not quite hearing, not quite understanding, her question.

"I would be willing to divorce Karl if you sign over your share of his pension to me," she continued. "I have invested quite a bit of money in this relationship, and I don't intend to lose any of it."

I took a deep breath and told her I had never heard of anything so absurd. I told her that my share of the pension was not negotiable. Since she would be divorcing Karl, she would have to work out the financial details with *him*, not *me*.

Brenda sat in my living room for over two hours, talking continuously. Afterwards, I shook my head in wonder at how this needy, unstable pair had found one another. Not only was Brenda's husband-for-pension exchange bizarre, there was something about her demeanor that evening that made me fear for Karl's well-being. At times she seemed concerned about his welfare; at other times, she sounded hardened, calculating.

I rehearsed a short script and then called Karl at school to tell him of Brenda's visit, her plan to swap her husband for his pension, and how unsettled I had felt the past few days. "Karl, it is difficult for me to be with Brenda. Please ask her to stop calling me. I do not want another visit from her. I am just not comfortable in her presence. I can't quite identify the cause of my distrust—it just seems as if we're dealing with more than one personality here." They must have discussed the incident because the phone calls stopped and she made no further attempts to see me.

Over the next few months when the children visited with or talked to their father, Karl admitted Brenda was extremely jealous of me and of the time he spent with the children. He described her mood swings in detail. They were no longer happy together, but Karl hated the thought of being part of a failed marriage again. To Karl, divorce was synonymous with being a loser.

"Tell your mother I hate her for leaving me. I will never forgive her for destroying my life," Karl told the children on several separate occasions. Karl's unhappiness always emanated from an external source; most of the time, I was that source.

Stephen Ministry

Frustrated by my inability to help Karl, I reached out to others in need through the Stephen Ministry program at our church. Stephen Ministry is an international lay ministry program designed to help parishioners through the grieving process. It was the most satisfying program I had ever been involved in through the church because of the close personal relationships formed between the lay ministers and the parishioners.

Becoming a Stephen Minister required many hours of training on the stages of grief, the art of listening, the resolution of codependence issues, and techniques to help those suffering from depression. I discovered I had missed so many obvious signals of Karl's depression during our marriage: the desire for self-imposed isolation, lightning quick mood changes, a diminished interest in one's surroundings, ongoing bouts of fatigue, wakefulness at night, and feelings of worthlessness. Karl had experienced them all.

Late that summer I sent several letters to Karl. I encouraged him to seek psychological help and suggested he get his financial affairs in order. He ignored my advice.

Karl's last letter of the year read,

"Katherine,

Please reconsider negotiating for the entire house and you won't be under any timetable to sell. In any case, I will not contribute to any repairs on the house once Emily graduates in May of 1993. I do not care to drag out the house issue any longer than necessary.

Divorces are emotionally painful—the pain can last a lifetime. Please talk to your children before they marry so that no divorces occur among them. Life has been so difficult because of our divorce.

I will continue to be in touch with my children and hope you will not use them as messengers for your requests. Please deal through the mail or contact my lawyer. Say hello to the children for me the next time you speak to them. Yes, they are wonderful children; it is sad for me not to be a part of their lives since 1984.

Karl"

My last letter of the year to Karl, written in December of 1992, was an outpouring of concern for the children:

"Karl,

Thanks for being so prompt with sending your share of Emily's Christmas ticket. I always end up putting her tickets on my charge card, hoping I can put your check against the balance. But somehow it never works out that way. The same day your check came, I had to have a plumber come to fix the back toilet so it would flush properly. I guess that's life—nothing ever works out the way you thought it would.

I have a few things on my mind, which is why I'm writing this letter. First, Mike and Tom had a nice time with you last Sunday; what they appreciate most is just having time to talk to you. I have a feeling they are both somewhat hesitant to tell you exactly what they're thinking for fear of making you angry, so anything you can do to encourage them to be open with you would be helpful.

I must admit I was relieved when the boys told me you were revising your will. What you choose to do with your money is none of my business, but I have a few thoughts on this subject that I would like to share with you.

First, I believe that whatever you and I accumulated during the course of our marriage belongs to the children. I'm thinking of the house, your pension, your inheritance, and whatever money you saved prior to your current marriage. Your pension continues to be your greatest asset, and I do believe our children are entitled to this money. Several years ago when Ron and I thought about getting married, I was planning to do just what I am asking you to do: specify that my share of the house, pension, and whatever I would get from Mom would go to the children.

Second, I feel our children face a greater challenge getting ahead in today's economy than we did thirty years ago. They will need every financial break they can possibly get to replicate our standard of living.

Third, I have serious concerns about Brenda. If all of your assets went to Brenda, she might say she would take care of your children, but I doubt she would keep her promise. Only Brenda and her two children will reap the benefits of any assets you leave to her.

There is one more topic I would like to discuss, and that is Brenda herself. She has put me in a rather awkward position. On the one hand, I feel sorry for her because it is clear she has her own emotional baggage to deal with, just as we all do. On the other hand, it is difficult for me to warm up to her because there is something about her I do not trust.

My bias against her stems from the fact that she got involved with you at a time when you were not ready for a serious relationship. You had (and still have) childhood *stuff*, marriage to Katherine *stuff*, loss of your children *stuff*, and death of Mary *stuff* to work through. She wanted security, a traditional marriage, and didn't seem to care that you were so needy.

As far as a traditional marriage is concerned, I believe the only time a marriage is traditional is when the children from that marriage are very young. You and I both have the same hard work ethic. I couldn't imagine staying home if there were no small children to care for.

Additional awkwardness in seeing Brenda comes from the possibility that anything I might say to her could be used against you during an argument. I choose not be a part of that. Finally, whether she's managing your money or not, if there are questions regarding the children or this house, I prefer to deal with you, not her.

Well, I guess I've rambled enough. I'm glad you're feeling better. It's hard to think about the holidays again. The irony is that when we were married, I dreaded Christmas because you complained so much about the money spent on presents and on food for family gatherings. Now I don't have to deal with your complaints, but money for presents and food continues to be in scarce supply.

Take care of yourself. Have a good holiday season.

Katherine"

CHAPTER 47

Resolution of Money Issues

Karl and I exchanged approximately fifty letters between January of 1993 and October of 1994. With the exception of one letter, they all dealt with money issues.

The exception was a fairly lengthy letter I sent to Karl asking him to co-author a book with me on choices, specifically choices he and I had made throughout the years that affected our children. I believed the book would be a valuable legacy for our children and grandchildren, helping them make better choices in their own lives. I listed the advantages and disadvantages of undertaking this joint book project.

In the last paragraph of the letter, I wrote, "With or without your support and input, however, I must write this book."

Within two weeks Karl sent me a cursory note; he politely, but firmly, told me he had no interest in working with me on the book project or, in fact, on any type of project.

The Quit Claim

After lengthy discussions with my lawyer on the house vs. pension issue, I decided to ask Karl to sign a quit claim on the house. Even though the divorce papers stated I would receive a portion of his pension, there was no guarantee this would actually happen. Because Karl's pension was administered through a public fund, my share of the pension had to be paid out to me through Karl, not from the fund directly. My attorney thought it highly unlikely that Karl would willingly part with his pension funds. This meant more legal fees and emotional hassle.

Karl was in a good place financially. He could take advantage of a lucrative retirement package from the high school district and continue to work or coach part time if he chose. He had often bragged about Brenda's assets, so it appeared he would continue to live a comfortable lifestyle.

I, on the other hand, was deeply in debt. I owed money on four different credit cards. The home equity loan had a sizeable balance, and I owed my mother thousands of dollars that I had borrowed to cover my share of college expenses for the children. If Karl and I were to split the proceeds from the house as originally agreed upon, I would be unable to purchase another home.

I decided to appeal to Karl's sense of fairness.

In February of 1994, Karl and I met outside the currency exchange in downtown Aberdeen Park to talk about the divorce agreement. Temperatures hovered just above freezing as we sat outside on an ice-caked bench, his black leather briefcase perched on his knees. He showed me his will and an insurance policy valued at $100,000 with the children's names listed on both documents. I asked if any of the children had copies of these documents. He said they didn't need copies because he always carried the originals with him. They were safe in his briefcase. I reminded him that a will had to be filed with the county in order to be valid.

"What I do is none of your business," he snapped. "I'm tired of paying out money to asshole lawyers."

We alternately sat and stood for over two hours, occasionally flexing our arms and legs in an attempt to keep our circulation going. After much discussion as to why he should do anything for me after I divorced him and made his life so miserable, he signed the quit claim. In return, I agreed to take a smaller percentage of his pension.

It was now after 5:00, and the currency exchange had placed its *closed* sign in the window. We walked the three blocks to the nearest bank (where neither of us had an account) to get the form notarized. I thanked Karl, gave him a quick, impersonal hug, and sprinted towards the warmth of my car.

Each of us had benefited from this transaction. I would be able to sell the house, pay off my debts, and still have a little money left over to put down on another house. Karl would retain a greater portion of his pension funds for as long as he lived.

A Letter by a Chicago Columnist

While I was grateful that Karl had signed the quit claim on our home, I was also frustrated that I was still tied to Karl through a state-administered pension fund that refused to acknowledge the terms of our divorce agreement. There must be a way to change the law, I reasoned.

In April I wrote a letter to a noted Chicago money advisor and columnist. She acknowledged the inequities in the way public pension funds were distributed and agreed to dedicate a future column to this issue.

Somewhat tongue-in-cheek, the columnist warned readers about marrying (and divorcing) public employees because of its impact on their future financial security. Without disclosing my name, she proceeded to describe my situation. The court had determined that Karl's pension fund was a marital asset and that I was entitled to receive one-third of its value, but the pension fund administrators failed to recognize the Qualified Domestic Relations Order (QDRO).

The columnist went on to say that the federal government regulated the retirement plans of most states. The state of Illinois, however, along with eleven other states, was not protected by federal regulations affecting marital benefits in case of divorce. This meant ex-spouses of teachers and other federal government employees in Illinois would not receive any pension money directly from the fund—even if the divorce court awarded those benefits.

The article went on to explain that *private pensions* distributed QDRO funds directly to the ex-spouse. The Employee Retirement Security Act (ERISA), the federal law that covers employees of corporate pension plans, exempts public bodies. Although a number of legislators had tried to change this law, the statute was still in effect at the time of Karl's and my divorce. The conclusion of the article stated that a woman who did not receive pension benefits based on her husband's years of service to an organization was often left in poverty.

Why hasn't the law been changed? A Chicago attorney sums it up this way: "The real issue is not just the lobby of the police, fire, and teachers' unions; it's the state representatives and senators who are worried about their own pensions."

If Karl had been emotionally stable, I would have received my share of the funds as planned. Instead, I was robbed of my retirement cushion because of his depression and subsequent suicide.

I have always been grateful to my lawyer for suggesting Karl sign a quit claim on the house. And I have always been grateful to Karl for signing the quit claim. But it is difficult to be grateful about a compromised outcome when you know in your heart the system has failed you.

CHAPTER 48

Steve

By the time I met Steve, ten years had passed since the divorce and my life seemed to have regained a sense of normalcy. My routine was getting up early, going to work, coming home to prepare dinner, and taking out the garbage. One evening in late April, as I lugged the overflowing recycling container to the end of our driveway, Steve, my next door neighbor, waved to me and yelled, "Hey, did you see my new car?"

He had been raking up piles of wet leaves trapped beneath the shrubs in the front yard. Steve was house sitting for my neighbor Gloria, who also happened to be his niece. Gloria's husband Brad was an upwardly mobile junior executive in a large telecommunications company in a neighboring town. Brad, Gloria, and their two children had been sent to England as part of a corporate exchange program. In addition to maintaining their home, Steve cared for their two cats.

Although Gloria had introduced me to Steve last fall, he and I had made no effort to get to know one another. "Come and see my new car," he called out again as I headed to the garage for another load of trash. After depositing two more bulging black plastic bags at the end of the driveway, I walked over to admire his new silver Tracer. Aside from the color (silver would have been one of my last choices), the vehicle sported sleek lines and offered ample leg room.

In comparison, my 1984 Chevy station wagon looked shabby. Although it was still serviceable, the tiny rust spots around the rear door handles had begun to spread like brown chickenpox. Somewhat flippantly, I remarked that I was planning on winning a car.

Steve's eyes widened. Then he said, "You must be one of those Mary Kay ladies."

Surprised, I said, "How do you know about Mary Kay?"

"I'm a photographer and I've done glamour shoots for many of the directors on the west side of Chicago. I'd like to meet some directors in this area. Whose unit are you in?"

I mentioned the name of my director and told him our next meeting was scheduled for Monday evening. He promised to put together a collection of photos for me to give to her. Steve delivered the samples the next evening. As promised, I brought the album to my director. She and a few of her colleagues were excited about the quality of the pictures and began to plan a glamour shoot.

As a thank-you, Steve invited me out for coffee. We sat in a neighborhood restaurant for almost two hours drinking coffee and talking. From the very beginning, the chemistry between us felt right. He was intelligent, witty, down-to-earth, and funny. Although he was fourteen years older, the age difference didn't seem to matter. We discussed our children, our work, and prior love interests, analyzing the causes of our failed relationships. I was amazed that Steve could provide so many insights into my relationship with my former husband and a recently estranged significant other.

Much later Steve would say he was attracted to me because of my intelligence, good judgment, concern for others, and sense of fair play. Qualities Karl had failed to acknowledge— or, perhaps, resented.

Without realizing it, I began subconsciously comparing Steve to Ron, my former significant other. Steve had Ron's sense of humor, the capacity to laugh at himself, and an uncanny ability to remember historical details. Unlike Ron, however, Steve knew what it was like to raise children and own a home. More importantly, he seemed willing to risk for love. Like me, Steve believed in soul mates. Like me, Steve was falling in love.

The next day, a Friday, we went for a walk around Lake Aberdeen. I invited him to join me for breakfast the next morning. From that time on, we spent every day together. On a Saturday evening, just nine days after we met, we dressed up in our best clothes and dined at a fancy Italian restaurant. After a dinner of gnocchi and lasagna, interspersed with laughter and whispered confidences, Steve asked me to marry him, and I accepted.

My children were shocked to hear I was getting married. Two of them had not even met Steve. My actions were the antithesis of all the advice I had ever given them as they were growing up. "Go slow. Take your time. Get to know the other person well before making any commitments."

I had abided by these platitudes in prior relationships, but they hadn't yielded long-term happiness. Karl and I dated for three years before we were married. Despite several broken engagements and serious misgivings on both sides, we had doggedly moved forward with our wedding plans. And Ron? We dated for almost five years before we were able to acknowledge that all we could ever be were friends and long-distance lovers.

This time, I wasn't about to go slow.

Steve's younger son and wife, who had joined him in the house-sitting venture, held a barbecue for us in Brad and Gloria's back yard. This gave me an opportunity to meet Steve's older son and our children a chance to meet one another. Mike, Tom, and Emily came to the barbecue, but their lack of enthusiasm was painfully apparent. Once again, Craig had to rely on his brothers and sister to give him a play-by-play description of this unexpected turn of events.

After breaking the news of our upcoming marriage to our children, we paid a visit to my mom and aunt. Mom was delighted. She knew how stressful my marriage to Karl had been, and she wanted me to be happy. Aunt Sophie took an immediate liking to Steve, telling everyone in the family how much he reminded her of my dad.

In fact, Steve did remind me of my dad. Steve was able to tell me how much he loved me. He told me how much he had always wanted to find someone just like me. He complimented me on my clothing, my makeup, and my hair. Never before had I experienced the degree of attention Steve lavished on me. We were inseparable; the most mundane of tasks offered us opportunities to talk about the past, present, and future. It was a glorious new beginning for both of us.

My children saw my relationship with Steve as a new beginning, but not necessarily a glorious one. They considered Steve's constant presence in my life a major irritation. They were all wishing Steve would just go away.

"There's no need for me to mow the lawn any more, Mom. Steve can do it," said Tom. "This just doesn't feel like home any more."

"I suppose you'll want us to clear out our belongings, Mom." This from Mike, who had claimed several closets in the basement for his athletic gear.

"He's sixty-five, Mom. Are you sure you want to marry someone that old?" asked Craig on more than one occasion.

Since both Mike and Tom were living at home that summer, they had the advantage of seeing firsthand how much in love Steve and I were. They saw adults in the parenting role treating one another with love and respect. How I wished all of my children had grown up seeing two loving parents run a household.

Slowly Tom's anger dissipated. Once he became accustomed to Mom having another man in her life, Tom and Steve became friends. Their friendship didn't surprise me. Steve, like Tom, wasn't obsessed with winning, money, or image. Steve was just Steve, a compassionate, loving human being.

Mike was another story. Steve had none of Karl's jocklike traits. Mike had surrounded himself with people who were like him—most of his friends were athletes. Yet Mom had chosen to marry a non-athlete—someone unlike Karl and someone unlike Mike. Although months would go by before Mike could verbalize these feelings, he felt by my choosing Steve for my husband, I was rejecting him. Mike couldn't see that he had most of the same qualities Steve possessed; he just hadn't been encouraged to show the softer side of himself. Steve's presence in our family gave Mike unspoken permission to be more gentle and caring.

Much later, when Craig was able to get to know Steve, Craig would be impressed with his intelligence, clarity of thinking, and upbeat spin on life.

"Mom, how does he know all that?" Craig would ask. Steve had incredible recall powers; he could remember the most minute details of every event he had either read about or experienced. He was an avid reader, had enjoyed a multitude of life experiences, and was able to converse comfortably on almost any topic. Craig, pursuing a degree in nursing, hadn't expected Steve to know about the latest research on knee replacements or emergent care or who fought and won which battles in the Civil War.

When Gloria and her family returned from England, I remember asking, "Is your uncle a genius? He has a remarkable mind; I've never met anyone quite like him."

Steve also had a gift for music. He could name any tune he had ever heard, (classical, rock or anything in between), give you background information about the composer, and then reproduce the melody on a keyboard in the same key in which he heard it. Had his father been more in tune with his son's innate ability, Steve might have become a musician or composer.

Retelling this family story always made Steve sad. Steve's father had been a talented musician in Chicago; in fact, he had recorded a number of albums for RCA. When Steve and his brother Jonathan, older by two years, were children, their father had insisted Jonathan take piano lessons. Jonathan, however, refused to practice the scales and simple waltzes. When their father discovered Jonathan had not been taking his music seriously, he immediately stopped the lessons. He was so angry with his older son for not carrying on their musical heritage, the anger spilled over onto Steve. Steve was denied piano lessons and the possibility of a career in music just because his older brother refused to practice the piano.

Emily, home from school for the summer months, had been dividing her time between work and volleyball. She was the office manager in a small office in a neighboring town. Since she was dating the owner of the company, she was able to take time off to run several summer league volleyball tournaments for high school students. Emily was enjoying her life, and she wanted me to be happy, too.

"If you love him, Mom, marry him. Steve is crazy about you. You never had that with Dad. Go for it."

And go for it I did. I promised myself I would be the best partner Steve ever had.

Steve's children were more receptive to me than my children were to Steve. In fact, his younger son and I formed a close bond right from the start.

Dealing with the challenges of these past ten years was made lighter because we shared the burden. And the joy of celebrating the good times was doubled because we experienced them together. Intuitively, we knew right from the beginning that we would be stronger together than either of us could possibly be alone.

Steve and I had learned long ago that when it comes to love and relationships, one size does not fit all. A prolonged courtship does not ensure happiness, and taking the advice of family members and friends can sometimes be disastrous. Steve and I did what we knew in our hearts was right. In the end, that was all that mattered.

CHAPTER 49

A Beginning and an Ending

In less than two weeks, we planned a wedding party for 100 guests. We chose July 23 for several reasons. First, we had made countless calls to banquet halls only to discover the Saturday and Sunday dates for the entire summer had been taken. We finally found a facility with one available date due to a cancellation. Second, July 23 was Mom's birthday. She would turn seventy-seven the day Steve and I married.

We would be married in my church, write our own vows, select special music, and choose each other's wedding clothes. After contacting a Swedish caterer from Chicago, we taste tested the entrees for the buffet and ordered two cakes: a yellow wedding cake for us and a chocolate birthday cake for Mom.

We were so grateful to have found one another and wanted everyone we knew to share in our joy. Two issues clouded our happiness. Steve was not feeling well, and my mother seemed more tired than usual.

Steve agreed to have a battery of tests run, which didn't uncover anything serious. A slight case of anemia was easily treatable.

In late June, Steve and I took my mom and Aunt Sophie shopping for new clothes for the wedding. In a tiny fitting room, I helped Mom fasten the buttons on a mauve-colored dress. Because of advanced arthritis and the stroke she had suffered ten years ago, small hand movements were difficult for her. Suddenly Mom leaned into me, struggling for air. I steadied myself against the wall, walked her out of the dressing room, and seated her in a chair near the cashier's station. Her breathing slowly returned to normal, but the incident ended our shopping trip.

On Monday, July 18, just five days before the wedding, Mom called at 10:15 p.m. to say she wasn't feeling just right. I told her I would call 911 and meet her at the hospital. "I'll be fine until you get here, Dear," she replied, resisting outside intervention.

Within minutes I was on the expressway in my old station wagon, heading over to Mom's. I thought briefly about the lightheadedness in the fitting room and tried to ignore my fears about her overall health and the telltale signs of fatigue.

Mom and Aunt Sophie sat at the kitchen table, fully dressed, their old lady purses on the floor at their feet. Mom stood to greet me, took two wobbly steps, and hugged me hard. "I love you, Honey," she said. "I'm sorry to bother you with this."

My eyes filled with tears. I knew Mom wouldn't have called this late at night unless she was really feeling terrible or scared or both.

Mom sat in front with me on the ride to the hospital, Aunt Sophie in the back seat. She tried to explain what she was feeling but couldn't. "I just don't feel right," she said.

We drove in silence for about five minutes. Then Mom grabbed my arm, turned in her seat, and said, "You must go through with the wedding. No matter what happens, promise me you'll go through with the wedding."

I was struck by the urgency in her tone and the clarity of her speech. Some of Mom's sentences were still garbled because of the stroke, but these words were spoken with a finality that left no room for discussion. Did she know she was dying? I couldn't bear to think of it.

I pulled up at the emergency entrance of the hospital, walked the white-haired sisters inside, completed the paperwork, and reparked the car. A cursory examination yielded nothing spectacular, but the doctor decided to admit her for routine tests.

The next few days were a blur. She wasn't getting enough oxygen, which accounted for the lightheadedness. An oxygen mask gave her some relief, but then her heartbeat became erratic. By Thursday Mom was semi-conscious and a blood clot had formed in her left upper thigh. She wasn't a good candidate for surgery, which left amputation as the only other option.

My brother and I struggled with our choices: death or amputation. We held one another and cried. Amazingly, Mom regained consciousness long enough to make her own decision. She said she was ready to die. Amputation was not a choice. She told us how much she loved us and how fortunate she was to have lived such a good life. With tears spilling freely down our faces, we held her, kissed her, and promised that someone in the family would be with her from now until she died.

I desperately wanted to be the one to be with her during her final moments. When my dad died years earlier, my brother was with him at the end. It seemed only right that I should be with Mom at the end of her earthly life.

The wedding was scheduled for Saturday. Should Steve and I continue with our plans as Mom had requested, or should we reschedule the ceremony? My brother, who had offered to walk me down the aisle, was shocked to learn I was thinking about moving ahead with the wedding plans. My children thought I should go ahead with the wedding because that was Grandma's specific request. Steve, lovingly, left the final decision to me.

I put myself in Mom's shoes. If I were dying and one of my children were getting married in just a few days, what would I want them to do? The answer was immediate: I would want them to go ahead with the wedding. Life is for the living; there would be time enough later to eulogize my mother's greatness.

I stayed at Mom's bedside from Thursday morning until 2:00 Saturday afternoon. Steve, his younger son, and Tom finalized all the last-minute wedding arrangements.

Aunt Sophie took over bedside duty when I left the hospital that Saturday afternoon; my sister-in-law chose to stay with her.

I hadn't slept for two days. The warmth of a hot shower and the relief of a good cry relaxed me. Thank goodness for Mary Kay. Her cosmetics added color to my lifeless skin and sunken eyes. I prayed Mom would be alive when Steve and I returned to the hospital that evening.

The wedding was at once beautiful and sad. Tears of joy mingled with tears of sadness. Most of the guests in the congregation didn't know my mom was in the hospital. More than anything I wanted Mom to be with us, sharing in our joy.

When the last guests left the hall, Steve and I, still in our wedding clothes, made the thirty-minute trip to the hospital. Mom lay motionless in her bed, the only sound the whisper of the oxygen mask regulating her breathing. Craig had lowered Mom's side rail and curled up beside her in bed. One bent arm cradled his head, the other arm circled Mom's waist. His was the night shift.

I took Mom's hands in mine and looked into her face for a long time. I must never forget the sparse eyebrows, creased cheeks, and those lips waiting for a reason to smile. Steve and I kissed Mom good night and went home. I had already said my good-byes. She knew all that was in my heart. There was nothing more to say.

The phone rang just before dawn. Mom had died in her sleep.

I know Mom willed herself to live until the wedding was over. In her own way she had been there with us: eating hors d'oeuvres, listening to 100 people sing happy birthday to her, cutting her chocolate cake. Then, relieved and at peace, she had allowed herself to die.

Within four days we were back in our church again, with most of the wedding guests in attendance. The same pastor that married us led the service. I made good on my promise to Mom to deliver the homily. With minor changes I delivered her eulogy titled "No Roses for My Funeral." I told the story of mom, her stroke, her courage, and her love of family.

Karl and Brenda attended Mom's wake, but not the funeral. It must have been difficult for Karl. Except for a brief "I'm sorry," he avoided contact with me and turned away when he had an opportunity to be introduced to Steve. Karl looked unusually gaunt and grey, the lines around his eyes and mouth more pronounced than when I last saw him. He had remained close to my mom. He would tell me later that my mom's death affected him more than the death of his own mother.

By the end of July, Steve and I were mentally and physically exhausted. We decided to postpone our honeymoon trip to Galena until Labor Day. Neither of us knew what to say to one another or how we should be feeling. Steve must have been disappointed that so much of our wedding service had been devoted to Mom's impending death. He wanted me to be happy that we were now husband and wife, yet he knew that I was in the beginning stages of the grief process.

I felt guilty when I was happy and thinking about Steve, and I felt guilty when I was sad and thinking about Mom. I laughed and cried and laughed and cried some more. How could I help my children cope with these big changes in our lives if my own emotions were not in check?

I tried to compartmentalize my feelings. During the day when Steve was at work, I allowed myself to think about Mom and cry. In the evening when Steve was home with me, I focused on how much I loved him and how fortunate I was to have met him. It was hard to keep the day feelings separate from the night feelings. Feelings are like that. They creep into your consciousness without having been invited.

I have no regrets about July 23. The wedding was beautiful. Mom's funeral was beautiful. But there is one image that continues to haunt me: the person curled up beside Mom in her bed on that final night of her life should have been me.

CHAPTER 50

Karl's Final Days

On July 29, 1994, Karl wrote the following letter to our children. The letter seemed to indicate he was trying to put his life in order. The children would soon discover, however, that Karl had done nothing to protect their financial interests.

"Dear Craig, Mike, Tom, and Emily,

I'm in my last class of summer school writing this letter to all of you. It isn't a personal letter to each of you; instead, it is a collective letter to all of you.

I'll be leaving for Germany this Sunday. I have enclosed some information regarding my flight schedule for you. I'll be visiting my boyhood friend Johann Katsen and my cousins Elsa and Wolfgang. Then I will spend about a week and a half in Austria. My return flight on August 21 will arrive in Chicago at 3:30 p.m.

The main reason for writing this letter is to tell all of you how much I have missed seeing you. Grandma Rose's funeral was a sad occasion and I will miss her very much; however, it was nice seeing all of you together. You have become a very close-knit group of family members, and I'm sorry I'm not part of that group. Your emotional support for one another is wonderful. Keep it up.

Since I'm on the outside of your family, I feel it necessary to somehow keep in touch. So this is my means of reminding myself of how special you are to me and how much I long for your companionship.

I'm told that all of you may somehow reap some financial benefits as a result of Grandma Rose's death. I am happy for that. Grandma Lena did not leave any monies for her grandchildren but instead left her estate to be divided equally among her surviving three children. Each may do what he/she wants with these monies. So occasionally I'll be sending you some checks to help you along with your finances. Please don't expect them on a regular basis because sometimes I won't be able to do it. This will be my gift to you because I love all of you so much.

In case something should happen to me on this trip, please be aware that all of you are the beneficiaries of a $100,000 life insurance policy, and you are entitled to the <u>personal savings account</u> of mine at the Lincoln Credit Union. Here is the address and phone number. <u>The account is rather large</u>. Emily is also a beneficiary of a tax sheltered account and a sum of money at my local bank.

So, my children, do well in your respective occupations and deal with life's adversities as best as you can. There will be many things coming your way. Don't forget that your father cares for all of you very much and wishes you well.

Love to you all,

Dad"

The children were disturbed by the foreboding content and sober tone of their father's letter. Craig and Emily responded with letters of their own. Mike made a phone call to his Dad, which was never returned. Only Tom made no attempt to contact his father.

A Letter from Craig to His Father

Craig's letter to his father was handwritten. The letter, along with Karl's only copy of his will, was curiously missing from the belongings found in his father's briefcase after his death.

"Dad,

After reading your last letter, I need to tell you there are some parts of the letter that really concern me. If I didn't know you better, I would think you were writing all of us a farewell letter. It sounds like you're going somewhere and not coming back. But that's not like you, Dad, so I'm going to put that thought out of my mind.

One part of your letter that bothers me is when you talk about all of us kids being a close-knit family and you're sorry you're not a part of that group. To that I say you <u>could be</u> a part of our group if you wanted to be. You can come and see your grandchildren any time you want to; the invitation is always open. For some reason that I'll never understand, you have chosen not to get close to us.

You have said over and over you are not happy with Brenda, but you don't want to divorce her because you would lose too much money. You need to divorce her, Dad. You don't deserve to be miserable the rest of your life. You need to see a lawyer even though you hate paying out money to lawyers and doctors.

Call me this weekend, Dad. I really want to talk to you.

Love,

Your Oldest Son"

Craig wanted to make sure his dad would be the only one

to read his letter. Since Brenda frequently opened Karl's mail and listened in on his conversations with the children, Craig decided to send the letter to Emily. Emily would then personally deliver it to Karl.

Although Karl did not respond to Craig's letter, the directness of Craig's words did not seem to offend him. Craig received a birthday card from his father the following month signed with his name only—Love, Dad. The words *love you very much* in the greeting were heavily underscored.

Karl's Last Letter to Me

With Karl's impending retirement, he was anxious to buy out my share of his pension. I was willing to listen and brainstorm for ideas as long as the figures were fair. I met with my lawyer and family insurance agent. Karl could buy me an annuity for a fraction of what the pension would be worth, which would help me plan for my own retirement.

In early September Karl wrote me the following letter. He could not bring himself to use my new married name. Nor could he use our former married name of Kreher. Instead, he chose to write Katherine Krauss, my maiden name, on the envelope.

"Katherine,

Congratulations on your recent marriage. I hope the gentleman you married is a true companion for you and can help you along the rough roads of life. I'm sorry I wasn't the man you were looking for. Yes, we have four wonderful children, and I hope by now that you have forgiven me for not wanting any more children. I just couldn't deal with the responsibilities of such a large family. Yes, we came from two different worlds.

Of course, you now have some additional responsibilities with the recent death of your mother. I loved your mother very much and I will never forget the closeness we developed at the Mayo Clinic. She was a special lady to me. I do know about settling your mother's estate and the pressures that are implied in your duties as executor of your mother's estate. I, too, have the same pressures; additionally, I must deal with my sister and her constant demands.

Throughout our years apart, Katherine, I have tried to be in touch with our children and be emotionally, as well as financially, supportive. I've done what I felt I could do under the circumstances of my financial situation. The divorce made the financial pressures very heavy for me.

I'm sure by now you have heard that I have decided to retire. The most important reason for this decision is my emotional health. My nerves are shot; the last ten years of teaching have taken their toll on my body. Our divorce, Mary's accident, and my mother's death have resulted in a much-damaged individual. Add to that the daily rigors of dealing with today's teenagers in the classroom setting. I know you can relate to these situations.

All summer I have been thinking about the deadline to retire under the district's current plan. I fooled myself into thinking that going back to the classroom would be easy, but it wasn't. I couldn't sleep at night worrying about each day's classes. The strain of lesson plans, classroom management, and meetings was too much.

When the anxieties took hold of me, my chest muscles tightened, making breathing difficult. I'm going to have another heart attack was my thinking and this time it will be my last. I chose my mental health over the money I would have received if I had stayed in teaching. I would like to see my grandchildren grow up. Craig's last phone conversation with me was the clincher; he forced me to see retirement as a necessity.

So, today, my second day in retirement, I feel a lot better and the prospects of seeing my children and grandchildren develop look good.

With a clear head not filled with anger, I'm asking for a reasonable buyout for your part of the pension. I'm not interested in any more legal hassles, just peace of mind having this pension settled once and for all.

Please think about this request for my mental health. Allow yourself some time to assess your finances and reconsider my offer.

Karl"

An Impromptu Meeting

One night in mid-September I was scheduled to meet Mike for dinner. I planned to meet him on a Thursday evening in the parking lot of Lena's condominium at about 6:00. Mike was living at Lena's temporarily so he could prepare the unit for sale. Her apartment was badly in need of paint and deep-down cleaning.

I was fifteen minutes early and parked my car next to Mike's in the lot behind the building reserved for residents. I opened the door on the driver's side for some fresh air and began to skim a woman's magazine that had just arrived in the mail that morning. I guessed Mike had gone upstairs to shower after his work day, so I decided to wait for him in the car.

Within a few moments a movement to my right caught my eye. I looked up and saw Karl carrying a bucket and some towels to his car. I hadn't recognized his car when I pulled into the lot. He glanced my way, nodded his head in greeting, and opened the trunk of his car to deposit his cleaning supplies. I walked around the back of my car and started towards him. He closed the trunk with unnecessary force and turned to face me.

I hadn't seen him since Mom's funeral in July. Dressed in jeans and a tee shirt, he looked old and thin and tired.

"Hi," I said, realizing this verbal exchange would probably be unpleasant.

"Hi," Karl replied. "What are you doing here?"

"I'm meeting Mike for dinner. Is he still up in the apartment?"

"He's taking a shower. He'll be down in a minute."

"You look tired," I said, hoping he would volunteer some information.

"Things are pretty stressful at home. I've been coming here a few afternoons each week to catch up on my rest. You've probably heard that Brenda and I haven't been getting along for quite some time. I just need to get away and find some peace."

"I'm sorry," I said. "I'm really sorry. Why do you stay?"

"Money. She'll take everything if I try to leave."

He told me again about the money he and his brother and sister had inherited, the separate bank accounts that he and Brenda kept, and how he was so worried about money that he couldn't sleep at night. Was I finally ready to accept his pension buyout offer?

The more we talked, the angrier he became. When Mike appeared in the back doorway, our conversation ended. Once again I offered to join him for counseling if he thought it would help. He took a few steps towards me, looked over at Mike, and stopped. "Thanks, but no thanks. I have all the help I need when it comes to money. Everyone wants some, including my sister, who is fighting to have me removed as executor of my mother's estate. If I kill myself, then everyone can fight over what's left. If I kill myself, then you wouldn't get anything. Maybe that's what I should do."

With jerky, awkward movements, he slid into the seat of his car, turned over the engine, and, without looking behind him, backed up and sped out of the parking lot.

My Response to Karl's Offer

I was amenable to a buyout of my share of Karl's pension provided the amount of the buyout was fair. Karl and I disagreed on what was fair.

"Dear Karl,

I apologize for taking so long to respond to your last letter. Steve and I have both been sick, and our work schedules have been very hectic.

First, congratulations on your retirement. After thirty years of putting up with teenagers, you certainly deserve to say good-bye to the school district. I wish I were in your position financially. I sometimes look back with regret on our decision for me to stay home with the children. In many ways that was a good decision, but in some ways it was not. If I had continued to teach full time, your pension would not be an issue because mine would have been equal to yours.

Second, I went back to our agreement dated December of 1993. The item we both agreed to was that you would sign a quit claim on our house if I would take less money from your pension fund. That was a good decision because we each received a benefit. I was free to sell the house and you would be able to realize a higher yearly pension amount.

Third, your request for a pension buyout is worthy of discussion because it could benefit both of us. You wouldn't have to send me money every month and, over the long haul, you would be paying me much less than what my monthly share would be. The advantage for me is that I would have some money to finish paying off my debts and put aside some funds for my own retirement.

I have talked to my lawyer and insurance agent. Let's decide on a time and place to meet; I believe we can reach a satisfactory agreement quickly.

Katherine"

The details of this agreement were within weeks of being resolved. Had it not been for Karl's mental illness, everyone's needs could have been met.

A Letter from Emily to Her Father

That fall Emily visited her father several times. She often found him sitting in his darkened kitchen wearing jeans, a white tee shirt, and badly scuffed house shoes. He sat hunched over, elbows resting on the table, his head propped up by the palms of his hands, barely acknowledging her presence. With great effort he would sometimes turn, reach for her hand, and begin to cry. "Forgive me, Emily. These are not good times for me. I am tired and I am sad, so very sad."

Frightened by her father's state of mind, she offered to take him to see a doctor. He refused. She called her brothers; they, in turn, phoned their father, offering to come for a visit. He refused their offers. Finally, frustrated by her father's unwillingness to help himself, Emily wrote this letter, not knowing, of course, that this would be the last letter from her he would ever read.

Choosing not to send the letter in the mail for fear he wouldn't receive it, she decided to deliver it in person. Emily paid a visit to her father in early October. She found him sitting listlessly in the kitchen with the blinds drawn, Brenda busily preparing her preschool charges for their afternoon naps.

Karl took Emily's hands in his and told her how much he loved her, then began to cry. He said, "How can you expect me to laugh and cry with you when I have difficulty getting out of bed in the morning?"

They talked awhile and then Emily asked him to read her letter while she was there. He hesitated, but she insisted. He read her letter three times.

"Dad,

I'm writing this letter to you for several reasons: a) I have some thoughts that I would like to share with you, b) I need to put my own thoughts into perspective, c) I would like not to have any interruptions, and d) I want you to be able to refer to this letter at any point in time because my feelings will not change.

I continually think about the letters you have written to me over the past few months. I have concluded you do not really know me. You cannot picture me, sitting in my house on my brown chair, thinking about you because you have never been where I am now. You don't know the passion and love I have found with Jack because you have not inquired. You have no concept of my volleyball goals, my expectations for higher education and a professional career after volleyball, and my desire to some day be a wonderful wife and mother.

Instead, you believe I am still a child. You continue to think that I am after some kind of financial support from you. It is obvious from your statements that you do not believe that I can take care of myself; you think I may, at some point, need your money.

Well, let me put your fears to rest. I will, at no point in my life, ask you for money again. I could care less if you ever buy me a cup of coffee. Now that we have taken care of your fears, let's talk about something much more important—our relationship.

This part of the letter may sound like a personal ad in a newspaper. But the truth is I need a father. Yes, I have needed one for the last twenty-three years of my life, but perhaps I did not realize that I needed to come forth and ask. Both of our lives are far from over, and it can not be too late for me to have a father. I need someone who wants to be an active part of my life. I need someone to laugh with me and cry with me and put his arms around me and tell me he loves me. And, from my standpoint, since I have your eyes, your athletic genes, and your competitiveness, you are the natural choice.

I don't understand your depression. Part of me wants to yell and scream at you that you have so much in front of you to live for. We make our own choices in life and dealing with problems and suffering makes us stronger people. I remember sending you a poem with that message in it after Mary passed away. I want to tell you that you have been one of the strongest people in my life and to give up now is unacceptable. But I cannot make you feel this way. It has to come from inside *your* heart, not mine.

You may be realizing that you have not done your best in your choices and/or your relationships and that you feel alone. I can only speculate because we have never talked about your feelings or fears.

I am your daughter. I am your daughter who has heard time and time again from you that you had too many children and that you have nothing to live for. I need to tell you that you are in my heart. Once again, Dad, I need you. You need to hear me. I need *you.* Not your money or your pension or your presents—I need your love and your time once in a while.

You can write about the remorse you feel over the weak bonds you have with your children until you are no longer able to write. But you can only feel sorry for yourself if you have tried one hundred percent and you did not succeed. I don't believe you or I have given one hundred percent to our relationship. You have four children who all want to make things better. You have two grandchildren who need a grandfather. More specifically, you have a daughter who loves you unconditionally. It is up to you how you respond to this letter. But don't ever tell me again that you have nothing to live for.

Love,

Emily"

Emily had composed this letter on a computer. It was found in Karl's briefcase after he died.

A Final Telephone Conversation

Karl and I talked briefly the first week in October. We set up a meeting for the following week. He called to cancel that meeting, however, because he wasn't feeling well. "I'll call you next week to reschedule," he said. But, of course, the promised phone call from Karl never came. Instead, we received a phone call from Brenda in mid-October telling us Karl was dead.

Karl's final note read:

"Dear Brenda,

I'm sorry, but I'm so tired of feeling so depressed. This is the only way I know right now.

Goodbye, Emily, Tom, Mike, and Craig. I love all of you very much, but I can't stand my mental condition like this. I'm sorry.

Karl/Dad"

Less than two weeks later, wearing large-rimmed sunglasses, a pack of tissue stuffed in the back pocket of her jeans, Emily met with our family friend and psychologist. With the tough love words of her last letter to her dad dominating her thinking, she tried to piece together the events surrounding her father's death that Saturday morning. There were so many unanswered questions: Did he have a cup of coffee first? Did he and Brenda have another disagreement? Did he give any thought to his afterlife? Did he think of *me*?

Emily wondered if her letter could have pushed him over the edge. She would often say, to no one in particular, "If he really loved all of us, he wouldn't have done this. I want to go back to the time before he died. I want to help him. If he had only let us, we could have helped him."

In less than a year, the children had faced a series of major losses. They lost their paternal grandmother. Lena had died in April of heart failure. A few weeks earlier she had tried to hurry along the process by tying a telephone cord around her neck, but her feeble attempt at suicide had failed. Although the children were not close to Lena, she represented a part of their family history.

Then I remarried without giving them a chance to adjust to a new relationship. The children worried my allegiance to them might be weakened by a husband and two stepsons.

Grandma Rose's death was a significant loss for my children. They had been closely connected to her since they were infants. During the last ten years of Mom's life, the role of grandparent and grandchild had shifted; my children had become her caretakers, and they were proud to have been partially responsible for her rehabilitation.

Then there was the issue of selling the family home and moving.

But the most devastating event of 1994 was Karl's suicide. Unable to hide their pain, the children were angry, shocked, and confused. They felt incredibly betrayed by their father's actions.

CHAPTER 51

A Legal Nightmare

When Karl wrote his final letter to the children describing the intended distribution of his assets, he could not have known that his advanced mental illness would render him so vulnerable to outside influences. The ultimate distribution of his estate in no way resembled the intent expressed in his farewell letter to the children.

Karl had made out a will. He had shown it to the children on several occasions although no one except Karl had a copy of it. Unfortunately, Karl had not filed the will, and it was not found among his belongings after his death.

The children were stunned to discover that Karl had left his entire estate—pension, real estate holdings, insurance policies, savings accounts, and his third of his mother's inheritance—to Brenda. Karl had mentioned on more than one occasion that his mother was worth close to a million dollars. Was he punishing our children for remaining with me in their childhood home?

Just weeks before his death, Karl had shared some of his financial plans with the children, stating they were beneficiaries of a $100,000 life insurance policy. Yet, after Karl's death, the policy bore the name of Brenda Kreher as sole beneficiary. Mike led a legal effort to untangle this strange turn of events, but his efforts failed to improve the situation.

Mike wrote this letter to Brenda in late December of 1994:

"Brenda,

I hope you have been able to make it through the holiday season without too much grief. I know it was a very tough one for my siblings and me. I am surprised that I haven't heard from you at all the last couple of months, but I guess everybody handles grief differently. I really would like to talk to you sometime soon about some of the issues that still need to be finalized. We need to decide on a date to get together to spread the ashes. I think the sooner we can put that behind us, the better off all of us will be.

Also, we need to determine when I can go through some of Dad's belongings that would be of interest to us (i.e., tools, golf clubs, and tennis equipment). Finally, and most importantly, I would like some input from you on some of the decisions he made with his finances in his final days. At the end of July, he wrote all of us a letter stating what monies he would like us to have in case of his unforeseen death. However, in September, after he retired and obviously before his suicide, he changed beneficiaries on a large life insurance policy. Also, there was an individual credit union account that was changed to a joint account just prior to his death.

I firmly believe that Dad wanted to do the right thing in terms of splitting his assets. We have no choice but to rely on you to carry out Dad's wishes before he succumbed to his depression and stopped thinking clearly. I really would like to know what your intentions and feelings are on this matter. Obviously, the final decision is yours, but I'm sure my Dad did not intend for us to be left with nothing.

Please let me know if you are able to meet with me in the near future. If you would feel more comfortable having your daughters present, that would be fine. However, it is very important for me to get some feedback from you on these issues.

Mike"

Brenda never answered Mike's letter. Instead, within a week the children received a letter from Brenda's lawyer listing money they owed to Karl's estate:

- Craig was supposed to return the $400 Karl had given to him the first time he, Tracey and Connor came to Illinois for a visit.

- Mike needed to repay a personal loan to his father for approximately $7,000 that he had borrowed to purchase a used car. Mike had already repaid the loan and had all of his cancelled checks as proof.

- Tom owed Karl's estate nothing because Karl had given him nothing.

- Emily was to repay a $2,500 loan against her wedding fund. Later, Emily would divide the remainder of her wedding fund money with her siblings.

The letter from Brenda's attorney also included three pages of Karl's personal inventory. Sample items included four brown plastic waste paper baskets, a yellow angular broom, three glass flower vases, two Corelle saucers, a shoe box full of pictures, assorted light bulbs, and a pick axe with a long handle.

In late March of 1995, Mike wrote a letter to the lawyer representing Karl's estate—Brenda had changed lawyers again. The letter was similar to the ones he had sent to Brenda, asking for information regarding the changes to his father's will. He asked that a list of his father's assets be sent to him and his siblings, stating that at no time were they allowed to enter the house to look at or retrieve any of their father's memorabilia.

Mike never received a response from Brenda's lawyer. The children hired their own lawyer who took their money and did nothing to investigate the case on their behalf. The children felt betrayed by their father, Brenda, and the legal system.

CHAPTER 52

The Aftermath

The days following Karl's suicide revealed more details surrounding his death. The children asked to see his bedroom, to look through his desk and briefcase for the papers he had promised they would find in his belongings. Their father had told them he and Brenda were sleeping in separate bedrooms, so this request seemed reasonable to them. But they were denied access to the house, and Brenda offered minimal information about the police investigation.

According to Brenda, she had left Karl home in bed that Saturday morning to run errands. When she returned several hours later, she noticed his farewell note on the kitchen table and the basement door closed. Frightened, Brenda called her minister; she told the children she sat on the front steps for almost an hour waiting for the pastor to arrive. She claimed she needed the emotional support and advice of her pastor before phoning the police. When the officers arrived, they pocketed the suicide note and headed downstairs.

Karl was hanging from a ceiling beam, a makeshift noose, fashioned from a length of thick, white nylon cord, around his neck. He was wearing a stained, white V-neck tee shirt and paint-spattered denim blue jeans. One dangling foot was covered with a well-worn, slip-on house shoe; the other slipper balanced precariously on its side next to a black leather swivel chair. The officers cut the rope and lowered Karl's body onto the cement floor.

Brenda did not solicit input from the children when she made the arrangements for Karl's memorial service. She did, however, ask the children to pay for the flowers and the minister's fee.

Money was a small part of the larger issue of not being valued and esteemed by their father. Karl had neglected to think about his children in terms of his personal possessions. The children had asked for the few items that characterized their father: his tennis racquets, golf clubs, a Lincoln High School sweatshirt, and a recent photograph of their father with the Lincoln tennis team. Brenda refused to relinquish these items, insisting she could produce the receipts for these artifacts. The receipts, she reasoned, entitled her to keep and/or sell the items in question. She did, however, tell the children they could have their father's oversized, ornate roll-top desk. How were they to divide a desk four ways, I wondered.

The following spring Brenda decided to have a garage sale. She called Mike on April 25 at work to let him know the dates of the sale and told him if any of the children wanted anything from their father's estate, they could come by during regular sale hours and purchase the desired items. Mike, appalled at her insensitivity, called his lawyer, who, in turn, phoned Brenda's lawyer; the garage sale idea was nixed. Instead, the children were ordered to come and pick up all of his possessions no later than Mother's Day. After that date, she planned to place his belongings in storage and bill the children for the monthly storage fee. When Mike and Tom pulled up in front of her garage with a U-Haul that Sunday morning, friends and neighbors lined the perimeter of the inside of the garage so they would not attempt to enter the house.

We were planning to move the following Friday. In addition to all of *our* boxes and paraphernalia, we now had a truck full of Karl's *stuff* in the driveway, all of which required sorting.

The strange assortment and shabby condition of the items gave us a clearer picture of Brenda's mental state. A pair of bedroom lamps with dented shades and cracked bases lay on their sides in separate cardboard boxes; a jagged shard of glass from a broken light bulb protruded from the base of an exposed socket. Several pair of torn sneakers, minus laces, lay wedged beneath a stack of soiled dress shirts and half a dozen pairs of underwear, all with stretched-out elastic waistbands. Unmatched socks with threadbare heels and ragged cuffs filled a blue, grease-streaked Rubbermaid wastebasket.

There was an odd selection of books. A thick booklet listing the itinerary for the Forty-sixth Annual State Mathematics Conference in Springfield, Illinois, made us wonder if he had planned to attend this conference. George Eliot's *Middlemarch* and a half dozen anthologies by Schiller and Goethe didn't seem to fit Karl's taste in reading material. A book by Bernie Siegel titled *Peace, Love and Healing* made more sense. The more trauma Karl had to withstand, the more he had turned to the church for healing. Yet not one passage in the book had been highlighted. Had he read through to the last chapter titled, "True Healing: Life, Love, and Immortality"?

Another book was *Anger Kills* by Redford Williams and Virginia Williams. Beneath the title on the front jacket were the words "Seventeen Strategies for Controlling the Hostility That Can Harm Your Health." Again, no highlighted passages.

On the bottom of the stack was *Fatherhood* by Bill Cosby. The first page of the book bore the name Mary Hastings, Karl's second wife. There were no notes in the margins and no highlighted passages. Had Karl read this book? If so, what could he have felt while reading it, especially the sections in which Cosby described how spanking can escalate into physical abuse and how, as children become teenagers, fathers need to relinquish absolute control and allow the children to make some of their own decisions.

Another box was filled with mementos from his second marriage: the wedding program, his and Mary's wedding rings, their wedding portrait, a shell necklace that might have been a gift from Karl to Mary, a notebook listing monetary gifts given to Karl at Mary's memorial service, several snapshots of Karl, Mary, and Mary's children, and, finally, a photograph of Mary's newly-laid grave marker, the colored autumn leaves in the background framing her date of birth and date of death.

Several boxes contained an assortment of Karl's memorabilia: several German waltz records, Karl's grade school pictures and Explorer patches and pins, assorted German coins, the college graduation booklets from Mike and Emily's college graduations, newspaper clippings from Mike's basketball career and Emily's volleyball heydays, Karl's high school diploma and two college degrees, miscellaneous tennis agendas and math lesson plans, broken trophies, a shoe box full of tacks and paperclips, a broken compass, a referee whistle, pens, pencils, flashlight bulbs, key chains, a letter from Karl's cousin describing her heart problems, an essay titled "Temper," and printouts of the children's high school report cards. There were too many memories, too many postcards, greeting cards, and letters to sort through in a single afternoon. There would be time enough later to read and to remember.

Finally, beneath the personal wreckage, lay a pair of pilled olive-green mittens. They represented my first attempts at knitting. In 1966 I had taken a knitting class at the local high school and decided to make Karl a pair of mittens as my first project. They had fit his hands perfectly. How they had lasted all these years was a mystery, but why he had saved them all these years was not a mystery.

That Mother's Day I had prepared chicken, baked potatoes, corn, salad, and rolls for dinner. We ate at the white plastic picnic table in the back yard. While I cleaned up after our evening meal, the boys decided to empty a few more boxes. I made hurried trips back and forth from the backyard to the kitchen, carrying plates, silverware, and leftover food to be wrapped, hoping to beat the shower the weatherman had predicted.

On my third trip outside, I glanced at the boys standing in front of the open garage just in time to see Mike open a black plastic bag.

"No, no, no!" he screamed. He threw the bag to the ground, sprinted around the far side of the garage, and began to retch.

Tom, labeling boxes, dropped his marker and ran to his brother's side. With one arm around his brother's shoulder, he reached for the bag with his free hand. He pulled out the white tee shirt, blue jeans, and house shoes Karl had worn the day he hanged himself. A county morgue label identified the name of the deceased, when the suicide occurred, and what the victim had been wearing at the time of the suicide. Tom held his brother close, stroking his back, unaware of the tears running down his own cheeks.

I would like to think the black plastic bag had been tossed into the mass of memorabilia unwittingly. Wrapped in the cloak of her own grief, Brenda surely intended to deposit the bag in a garbage bin. A careless, human error, that was all. Yet it was a human error that caused Mike and Tom many wakeful nights.

Brenda called Mike two days after the boys had picked up the remainder of Karl's possessions to say that Karl's ashes would be spread on Thursday. Without even consulting his brothers and sister, Mike told her they had no intentions of being present for the event.

Amid the stack of cardboard boxes, half-empty closets, and frayed nerves, we hosted a wedding ceremony in our home the Friday before we moved. It was a second marriage for a good friend and her fiancé; they had wanted a simple, quiet wedding.

The meal that followed the brief ceremony consisted of lox, bagels, and cream cheese—plus chicken and brats on the grill for their non-Jewish guests. An array of salads, relish trays, and a wedding cake rounded out the offerings.

Our tiny living room was filled with strangers as Charlie and Connie exchanged vows in our foyer. The festive celebration contrasted sharply with the solemnity surrounding Karl's final days.

The children said their good-byes repeatedly in 1995. To the only home they had ever known, an over-crowded, over-furnished, four-bedroom ranch fronting a busy highway. To the tiny bungalow their Grandma Rose called home for more than forty years. And to a beloved family member named Bear.

I have never found good-byes to be pleasant experiences; in fact, I find separation and loss incredibly painful. My heart beats against my breast bone until it aches, and held-back tears create a line of pressure from my earlobe to my shoulder. Without realizing it, I sigh deeply, over and over again.

Our family psychologist said I should write Karl a letter. "Write a letter, Katherine, to get him out of your system—to put closure on your relationship. You'll feel better when your thoughts are on paper."

I always loved writing letters, but I resented having to write this one. What would I say? Would I wax reminiscent and say that next June we would have been married thirty-one years? Would I remember our college courtship years in the letter?

Who could have known how the years would unfold for us? Who could have known that Karl would relive the anguish of his own childhood and resent the gifts and privileges our children deserved? Not even he could have known that. And who could have known that I would become so outspoken and unwilling to abandon my values? It is good we do not know what lies before us. If we knew the outcome of these critical choice points, surely we would make different decisions and spare ourselves such heartache.

It seems Karl had been running away from something for a very long time. First, from his parents. College made that flight socially acceptable. Then from his own children. Abandoning the children emotionally, and later physically, was not socially acceptable. They deserved better. Then from intimacy. I deserved better, too. Finally, he ran away from life itself. I hope I can forgive him for this weak and selfish act. Right now, though, that most holy of all acts, forgiveness, seems unattainable. I hate him for what he did to himself, our children, and me. I hate him for caring more about his own pain than the pain he must surely have known he would create for those who loved him.

Perhaps one day I can accept his decision to end his life and see it for what it was: a choice made by a man in the grips of severe depression. I will always hold him in high regard because he was the father of my children, yet how can I forgive him for hurting our children so profoundly?

One day I shall write him a letter of farewell—but not today.

CHAPTER 53

Saying Goodbye to Bear

In mid-May Steve and I moved to my Mom's home. Aunt Sophie had decided to move into a nearby retirement community close to my cousin and his family. William and I had just listed Mom's house with a local realtor; Steve and I wanted to be available to help close the sale.

The neighborhood looked the same as it had during my growing-up years. The grade school just down the block had two new wings added over the years, but the baseball field sported the same semi-withered patches of grass and concave dirt bases. Row upon row of sturdy brick bungalows and two-story look-alikes stretched from one end of town to the other. Walkers and bikers enjoyed the smell of freshly mowed lawns and newly painted garages.

Long-time neighbors of my mom, who for many years had helped my mom and aunt with routine yard work, extended their friendship to Steve and me. The only noticeable difference in this blue-collar town was the faces of the townspeople. White had given way to black.

As soon as the house sale was consummated, Steve and I would be moving to Wisconsin, a first step in our building a new life together. A new state, a new community, a new home, and new circle of friends. We savored every delicious decision: the color of paint for the walls, how to display Steve's artwork, which sets of dishes to use, how to make the entrance of the house more dramatic. It was refreshing to have good things to think about. Memories of Mom pushed into my thoughts daily, but I needed to put the sad times in my life in perspective. My happiness now was in Steve and our blended family.

In addition to selling Mom's house, there was one incident that caused my spirits to plummet during the summer of 1995—Bear's health was rapidly deteriorating.

Bear made the move with us, but the arthritis in her legs made it difficult for her to walk up and down the basement stairs. Using the laundry facilities in the basement and sorting through my mom's boxes of treasures, however, occasionally forced me to retreat to the cool dampness of the basement. Bear was as determined as ever to stay by my side. Going down the steps was easier for her than going up. Sometimes a front paw would catch on a stair as she lunged forward step by step to reach the top landing.

Within a few weeks, we noticed a marked change in Bear's health; labored breathing and continual panting became the norm. She couldn't seem to get enough air. Cranking the air conditioning didn't help. A visit to the vet and several tests confirmed she had a liver condition that might be helped by a special diet. After four weeks of private consultations and trying out three different types of pet food, her condition had worsened. I was faced with a decision every pet owner is loath to make. Should I keep her alive at all costs or should I end her suffering?

Many months after we put Bear to sleep, I wrote the following story as a tribute to her life:

> The time is 2:01 a.m. I see the numbers clearly on our clock radio. It is June 30, 1995, just days after my fifty-second birthday. I have been dreading this moment. I always knew I would know when it was "time," but I am dreading the task that lies before me.
>
> Her health, marred only by an occasional ear infection, had deteriorated quickly. During the past five months, the rapid heartbeat and a relentless hunger

for air had replaced her normal, rhythmic breathing. She had been steadily drifting away from me. Always in the same room, but positioned just out of reach.

It is 2:01 a.m., it is June 30, 1995, and it is "time."

What exactly am I supposed to do? Contact the children? I try to clear my head of emotion and formulate a plan. With the time difference, there is no point in calling Craig just yet. Mike, bogged down with work obligations, will elect not to come, but I will call him. My daughter, in training for her summer volleyball tournaments, also will not come. But I will call Emily, too.

I must talk to Tom. My youngest son had a strong connection with Bear. He prepared her meals, took her for walks and runs, invited her to sleep on his bed. Tom will come.

Then there is Steve. My husband, my soul mate, my best friend. He came into my life a scant year ago, but somehow, intuitively, understands my past sadnesses, knows why this decision is so painful for me to make. He will come, too.

Bear came into my life in March of 1983. I had gone to the local shelter one afternoon while Emily and her three brothers were in school. Muffin, our other canine family member, was dying of cancer. The children, ages 16, 15, 15, and 12, needed another dog. Maybe *I* needed another dog.

I remember kneeling in front of the cage that was home to six mixed Labs and telling them how beautiful they were. A black puppy with a raccoon face stumbled towards me on wobbly legs. She licked my fingers through the bars and wiggled her hind end in delight. This one was mine.

For twelve glorious years she was mine. A long list of depressing life events filled those years: my divorce, my mom's lung surgery and a long recovery period following a major stroke, the struggle to climb the rungs of a corporate ladder in a male-dominated environment, late nights spent studying for exams that would earn me a master's degree, the continual challenges of raising four teenagers alone, feeling isolated from my married friends, ever-pressing money worries, and too many wakeful nights spent wishing I had made different, and better, life choices.

Bear was my gift. Each evening she greeted me as if we had been separated for weeks. She followed me everywhere. Downstairs, upstairs—waited patiently outside the bathroom for the door to open. She was my faithful companion, my life-long friend. Her presence comforted me, gave my days purpose.

It is now 2:17 a.m. Her restlessness, pacing, and hiding have pushed into my consciousness. Medication has not given her relief. She is tired. And she seems so sad. I think she is telling me she is ready to die.

Unwillingly, I get out of bed, slip into my robe. She follows me into the tiny living room of my childhood home. I sit on the rough carpet with my back against the gold and black leaf-patterned couch. I tug gently on her collar, cradle her in my arms, and begin to cry.

It is now 6:30 a.m.—time to make my calls. The first one to the vet, then Tom, Mike, Emily, and, finally, Craig.

Steve comforts me, questions whether this is the right time, senses my resolve, and backs our old Chevy wagon out of the garage.

Bear and I walk around to the passenger side. I sit on the seat; she lies listlessly on the floor, too exhausted to hoist her sixty-five pounds onto my lap. I stroke her head and ears during the thirty-five minute trip. I tell her that I love her, that she's the best dog anyone could have, that I'll never forget her.

Tom is waiting for us in the parking lot of the animal clinic. His face is strained and his eyes are red.

I pick Bear up and carry her into the room assigned to us. My favorite vet, a kind and sensitive woman, is not on duty. A young man, accompanied by a helper, approaches the metal table where I have laid Bear. He asks if we would like to be alone with her for a few minutes. I nod my head. I hear myself say these words aloud: "She's ready to die, you know. We are hurting her by allowing her to live in such pain." I say these words for myself as much as for Tom and Steve. Steve is fighting back tears. Tom's face is expressionless; he cannot look at me, but he puts his hand gently over mine.

I wrap my arms around Bear's middle, press my face against her nose, kissing her again and again. Tom places his right hand on her head and the left on her rump.

Steve has the hardest job of all. Bear is looking directly at him. His hands form a cradle for her head. The young man returns. As the needle slides into Bear's left hind leg, Steve watches the life drain out of her trusting eyes. It is quick. It is final. It is gut-wrenching.

I begin to sob uncontrollably, still holding my beloved pet tight. Steve strokes my head, my shoulders, my back. It seems like a long time before I stop crying.

It is time for us to leave. We walk out to the parking lot where we hug one another and cry some more.

Tom returns to work. Steve and I drive home in silence.

Almost a year has passed since we put Bear to sleep. Twice I began to write this story and twice returned the incomplete manuscript to my writing folder.

But today I finished the story. I needed to mark the moment of her death by writing about her. I wonder if she knows how sorry I am for all the times I took her devotion for granted. She deserves to be resting peacefully wherever it is that good doggies go. I hope Bear knows how much I loved her.

With Mom gone and now Bear, I was more appreciative of Steve's presence in my life than ever before. Steve was the perfect mate for me. He loved me and told me so daily. His adoration showed in cards, notes, poems, flowers, and words of praise for my sensitivity and intelligence. I had not experienced this kind of adulation before and I hoped I would never take his love for granted.

CHAPTER 54

Jack and Emily's Wedding

The year 1995 forced us to leave the old behind and embrace the new. Craig and Tracey, still living in Las Vegas, moved into their first house, Mike purchased a three-flat in Chicago with a friend, and Tom put a deposit down on a condominium in Pinetree Knoll. Emily and her fiancé had just found a home in Woodland Hills and were busily planning their December wedding.

One of Jack and Emily's early challenges was how to communicate to their guests that, while Karl's absence would be on everyone's minds, they did not want the joy of their wedding day diminished by memories of his suicide. The elegant program cover featured a red rose, green leaves, and sprigs of white baby's breath against a light grey background. The words, "Your presence makes our joy complete," in white lettering at the top of the program encouraged guests to focus on the day.

Additionally, the last page of the program was devoted to thoughts of Karl. Both Emily and Jack wrote notes to their guests. Emily wrote a note to the guests and a short letter to her father:

"Dear Guests,

Because we would like to enjoy all of our loved ones gathered here today, Jack and I take this opportunity to remember my father in the following notes and ask that we all limit conversation of him today. Please join us while we hold him in our hearts.

Emily"

"Dad,

Through my life, both you and mom have taught me, through mostly observation, many important lessons. Mom taught me to be independent, to follow my dreams, and that only in facing the truth and reality of our experiences, can we take something valuable away with us that makes us stronger.

So, today, just like any other day, I glance back into the past at our relationship for something valuable to carry with me, to make me stronger.

And it is now that I realize I might have learned the most precious lesson from you. I've learned from you that I cannot find happiness in others unless I have happiness within myself. That I cannot truly love unless I have love for myself. Because of these lessons, I have found happiness with Jack that I never dreamed was possible.

I just wish you were here so I could thank you. I wish you were here to share this day with us.

I think of you always.

Love,

Emily"

Jack wrote this note to the guests:

"Dear Guests,

I met Karl just once, and, as a result, I will never know him as a man would normally come to know the father of his wife. I only know him through Emily, Katherine, Craig, Mike, and Tom. With these sweet and wonderful people who have taken my children and me into their loving arms, I will share more of the love and memories they hold for him when the time comes that the hurt and disappointment have gone.

Jack"

The excitement surrounding the wedding sustained us for months before and after the event. Emily and I shopped for crystal ornaments as favors for her shower, wrapped each one in Christmas paper, and ordered holiday centerpieces for the tables. Fifty guests showed up at the hotel for the luncheon, including Jack, Emily's brothers and Steve.

December 9 was a brisk, clear, sunshiny day, a perfect day for a wedding. Steve and I arrived at Jack and Emily's home early that morning even though the wedding was scheduled for 6:00 p.m. A hair stylist was busy fashioning Emily's long hair into a French twist. The bridesmaids, Jack's mom, and I each took a turn being pampered and coifed by Janna. At 11:00 a.m., dressed in a white terry cloth robe, barefoot, with every hair in place and makeup flawlessly applied, Emily disappeared into the kitchen and emerged with a tray of fruit, cheese, and hors d'oeuvres. The bride-to-be had prepared snacks for all of us because *she* was hungry.

Emily and Jack were married at the same church where Steve and I had exchanged our vows eighteen months earlier. Instead of summer floral bouquets, however, the church was decorated with red roses, fragrant greens, and silver-tinged pinecones. Plush red velvet ribbons hung from the pews and accented the dark green holiday wreaths on the altar, in stark contrast to the black sheath bridesmaids' dresses.

The wedding was a mass of bright colors, vibrant music, and woodsy smells. Jack, wearing a black tuxedo, and Emily, wearing a white lace and shantung gown, were a striking couple. Jack's mom wore a simple, but elegant, black street-length dress, and I wore a two-piece black tuxedo-style jacket and long skirt. Like Jack, Steve wore a formal black tuxedo.

But the grandchildren took center stage. Tiffany, Jack's ten-year-old daughter, walked down the aisle with perfectly measured steps, eyes fixed intently upon her father, straightfaced and somber. The two six-year-olds stood at the ready at the back of the church. Jack Jr., Jack's son, and Connor, Craig and Tracey's oldest son, hair slicked back, dressed in black knee-length tuxedos, balanced matching ring pillows, unsuccessfully trying not to giggle. Then came two-year-old Brett, clad in a white tuxedo, clutching the handle of a white wicker basket filled with red rose petals, refusing to toss them onto the white runner, a proud look-at-me grin on his face.

Just as the organ trumpets burst forth, summoning the beginning of the processional, Emily's three brothers left the groom's line at the front of the altar and positioned themselves alongside their assigned pews; each would walk his sister one-third of the way down the aisle.

Finally, my beautiful daughter, her dark hair pulled back from her narrow, heart-shaped face, moved slowly and confidently down the aisle, her face radiant with love, escorted first by Tom, then Mike, then Craig—all three sons incredibly handsome in their black tuxedos and immensely proud of their baby sister.

Feeling very humble and privileged, I delivered the wedding address, encouraging this young couple to put the demands of the marriage above all else and to be a soul mate for one another. My final words framed a familiar blessing for these two beautiful people:

"May the Lord raise you up on eagles' wings,

Bear you on the breath of dawn

Make you to shine like the sun

And hold you in the palm of His Hand."

I didn't cry much before Emily's wedding. But I did cry the day after. Where had these tears come from? Exhaustion? A longing to redo the past, reshape some of the critical events in Emily's life? Was I experiencing a sense of loss? A feeling of joy?

The wedding over, it was now time to write my farewell letter to Karl.

CHAPTER 55

Christmas Day

Christmas Day, 1995

"Dear Karl,

Today is Christmas Day. You have been gone for fifteen months and you have missed so much. You have missed fifteen months in the lives of your children and grandchildren.

Last year Thanksgiving and Christmas were especially hard for the children. They shed tears of anger and disappointment and blamed themselves for not being able to help you face and overcome your illness. That was me ten years ago. I blamed myself for not being able to help you. I didn't know how to make you happy. I didn't know what to do to help you.

I hope you have finally made peace with yourself for all you have done and for all you have left undone. We all must make peace with ourselves. I struggle to make peace with your decision to take your life; there are times when anger engulfs me and forgiveness seems unattainable. Today forgiveness seems possible—remote and just out of reach—but possible. I trust that time will heal our wounds.

We held you in our hearts earlier this month when Emily married Jack. Emily was beautiful, Karl.

Carlos made her dress—Venetian lace and silk shantung in a sheath style so becoming on her tall, slender body. She was stunning—you would have been proud of her.

We tried our best to cover for you. Our sons walked Emily down the aisle. Tom began the processional with her at the entrance to the sanctuary. When he had walked a third of the way with Emily, he handed her off to Mike, stepping behind them. Then Mike took her arm and walked another third of the way, handing her off to Craig, who completed the walk and turned her over to Jack. But the ceremony wasn't quite right without you; we needed you there with us.

I gave the wedding address, encouraging Jack and Emily to put their marriage above all else and to be soul mates for one another. I know you struggled with that word, Karl, yet life can be so much easier when you are with someone who truly understands you. I told the story "The Gift of the Magi" by O. Henry. Stella and Jim, the main characters, sold their most prized possessions to buy Christmas gifts for one another. That's what married life should be: two persons giving their most prized possessions for the sake of the other.

Emily didn't forget you on her special day, Karl. She wrote a letter to the guests and a letter to you; they were printed on the back of the church program. Jack also wrote a note for their guests to read. He expressed regret that he would never know the father of his wife.

One of the best outcomes of our Christmas dinner today is the decision to get together often to see where each of us is in the grief process, to see how we can help one another. But we realize that helping one another will only come after we have helped ourselves. Your children are now seeing that very clearly. You saw that, too, Karl, but you saw it too late. I'm sorry for you.

Today has been a very emotional day for all of us. You need to know we all miss you. Your untreated illness and suicide have created pain for all of us, yet we still love you and miss you.

I wish you peace on this beautiful Christmas Day.

Katherine"

CHAPTER 56

Epilogue

I still can't believe he did it. Killed himself, I mean. It has been five years since my children received the phone call from Brenda telling them of Karl's death. The pain and sadness—it all seems so pointless now. There were so many people who could have helped Karl, but he couldn't bring himself to ask. There are times when I still believe *I* could have helped him.

What finally pushed Karl over the edge? No one will ever know for sure, but in those final moments he must have felt abandoned and powerless. Heritage was a critical factor: parents devoid of emotion coupled with Germanic *stolz* (pride). He had experienced the ravages of war and poverty and was forced to adapt to a new culture that his parents never accepted as their own. The arrogance and need to win may well have been a cover for an inferiority complex. The emotional and physical signs of untreated depression, panic attacks and heart trouble may have fueled his fear of not being able to control the world around him.

Then there was a string of personal losses: our divorce, his estrangement from our children, Mary's death, the decline of his third marriage, his mother's death, my marriage to Steve, my mother's death, and his inability to continue teaching.

His letters tell us he had occasional periods of clear thinking. How difficult it must have been for him to realize his complicity in our divorce and see how he once had the power to change the course of events. The money issue, while it was one of the final issues we had to deal with, could have been easily resolved in everyone's favor, had he not felt his entire world was spinning out of control.

While those closest to him will never know just what he was thinking that October morning in 1994, one thing is sure. He left a legacy for his children that will never be forgotten: a legacy of pain, anger, and sadness.

Craig

I can still hear the disappointment in Craig's voice when he talks about his father. After his father's suicide, Craig became more cynical, less trusting. His brothers and sister say that at the age of thirty-three, he demonstrates some of his father's traits. His arrogance, stubbornness, and the unexplained and unexpected bursts of anger directed towards his wife and sons are so like his father.

For Craig, holidays and birthdays are still tarnished by sad memories and unresolved anger. This past October, I unknowingly sent Craig a birthday card exactly like the one his father had sent to him the year before. Craig became angry at me for choosing that card, yet how could I have known?

What drives Craig's anger? About a year ago I offered Craig the names of two professionals skilled at dealing with depression. Craig scoffed at my suggestion that he seek help. An odd reaction for a man who has chosen nursing as his life work. He is so willing to help others, yet refuses help for himself.

I wish he would work as hard for his peace of mind as he does for worldly goods. I am incredibly proud of Craig's perseverance in the face of adversity. I love him for his wit and sense of humor and desperately want him to be all that he can be.

Mike

Mike maintains less of a distance from Steve and me than he did when we were first married. At thirty-two, he is a new father and is re-establishing his priorities. Mike, like me, has an overdeveloped sense of responsibility. He wants to carry the emotional load for the rest of us, but sometimes hurts himself in the process. During the past five years Mike has been reluctant to talk about his father; he is uncomfortable talking about death in general. He tends to create unnecessary stress in his life to see if he's up to the challenge of coping with it.

A few years ago Mike had a mild seizure; the doctors thought he might have lupus anticoagulant, a medical condition, which, if untreated, can be life threatening. The results of tests taken at two different hospitals were contradictory. One test offered conclusive evidence of his illness; the other did not. It is difficult for Mike to accept a lifetime of medication, hardly palatable for the son of a self-made man who told his sons, "Only women go to doctors; real men tough it out." Mike struggles with the question, "How can I reconcile a macho image with sensitivity to the needs of others?" I love this child with all my heart. The world is a better place for his existence, but my heart aches for the sadness in his life.

Tom

Tom continues his search for love, for attention, for acceptance by his twin brother, and for a sense of family. Tom received more emotional bruises at the hands of his father than his siblings. Like Craig, he has an unresolved anger that surfaces at odd moments. He wants to create a distinct identity for himself, but, in doing so, camouflages the real Tom—the caring, feeling Tom.

Like his twin brother Mike, a lack of self-esteem prevents Tom from forming healthy intimate relationships. Up until recently he has invariably chosen women who are far less interested in him than he is in them. Their rejection feeds his low self-esteem and fuels his anger. During his growing-up years, Tom vowed he would never marry; now he is driven to marry. *Whom* he marries appears to be secondary to achieving the goal of getting married and starting a family. Is he trying to prove he can be a better parent than his father was? At thirty-two does he fear being alone? I love Tom so much—he is kind, gentle, bright, and loving. I pray he will find the right partner.

Emily

Then there is Emily. Emily was in junior high when her father and I were divorced. Her small, secure world was shattered. So many questions must have gone through her mind. Where should her allegiances lie? Would she still be living with her brothers? Would she have to move away from the safety of her childhood home? Would there be enough money for her to go to college? She wants the world to know she is strong, competent, and liberated, but I sense that underneath she is scared. She is beautiful, wise, spirited. I long to hold her in my arms, as I did when she was a child, and tell her how much I love her.

Four years ago Emily married a man sixteen years her senior. Was she looking for the stability of a ready-made home? Was she drawn to the restlessness and competitive spirit Jack and her father share? Jack has been a welcome addition to our family. He consistently demonstrates his genuine love for his two children and for Emily. I hope my three sons can learn from his example.

Choices

I left Karl in 1985 to show my children we are not victims of our heritage. We can, indeed, create our own future. I made choices and then lived with the choices I made. So must we all. There is no turning back.

I learned these lessons through my choices:

- Love does not conquer all. The love I felt for Karl did not soften the emotional and physical blows he inflicted on the children. In the end, it was a matter of survival. I was always the stronger one, more open to self-discovery. Yet having survived, even knowing I *deserved* to survive, I wrestle with guilt because he did not.

- We must stay true to our values. The importance of family, personal growth, the joy of achievement—all of these values are worth defending.

- The worth of a parent is just as important as the worth of a child. Children need to learn that parents deserve to have fulfilling and meaningful lives.

- We need to spend time with our children. Hold them, love them, sing to them, make them laugh, be close to them at all times. Ask them what they're thinking and tell them it's okay to challenge our thinking as long as they do it in a respectful manner.

- We must question traditional social mores. I grew up believing divorce was bad. I now realize, in some cases, divorce is necessary for survival and growth.

- We must accept the fact that we cannot control the actions of the people around us; we can only control our own actions and reactions to circumstances. We can suggest, model, and encourage, but we cannot mandate the actions of others.

- We need to learn to ask for help when we need it, to turn to our family and friends in our vulnerability. Asking for help makes us strong, not weak.

- We can choose to absorb the best traits of our parents and grandparents and discard the worst.

- It is critical to forgive ourselves for poor choices we have made. I continue to work on forgiving myself and forgiving Karl. I must be patient with the process.

I think of Karl and the final days of his life less often now. But when the memories push into my consciousness, I am sad. We would have celebrated thirty-five years of marriage together. We built a history together and then destroyed its very foundation.

Karl wrote in one of his letters, "In time, perhaps your anger will subside and forgiveness will follow. I know that you love me as much as I love you." Indeed, my love for him was as great as his love for me.

Some day I will be free from the specter of doubt and guilt. Some day June will come and I will not think of our anniversary. Some day September will come and I will not think of Karl's birthday. Some day October will come and I will not think of his suicide. Some day I will be free.

About the Author

Katherine Rose Kreher is an independent business owner who teaches business communications skills to corporate employees. She is an instructional designer, trainer, speaker, and coach.

Katherine's first career was teaching English and speech to high school students at a high school in the Chicago suburbs. After having four children, she opted to be a stay-at-home mom for thirteen years. Katherine counts raising her children as her second career.

When her three sons became teenagers, Katherine knew there was a possibility she would have three young adults in college at the same time. Unable to secure full-time employment in secondary education because of a reduction in force, Katherine transferred her communications skills to the business world—thus began her third career.

After working for a manufacturing company for seven years, Katherine felt limited by the "glass ceiling" and decided to strike out on her own as a small business owner. Life circumstances propelled her back into Corporate America for a short time. Several years ago, however, she resumed her role as an independent business owner and is content with her current career.

Although Katherine has created many facilitator and participant guides for companies, written numerous case studies and articles for organizations, and designed a writing skills training manual for use in her writing workshops, *A House Divided: A Story of Survival* is Katherine's first full-length book.

VISIT

WWW.KREHERBOOKS.COM

TO ORDER ADDITIONAL COPIES OF

A HOUSE DIVIDED: A STORY OF SURVIVAL